Religion and the
New Immigrants

Religion and the New Immigrants

How Faith Communities Form
Our Newest Citizens

MICHAEL W. FOLEY *and*

DEAN R. HOGE

OXFORD
UNIVERSITY PRESS

2007

OXFORD
UNIVERSITY PRESS

Oxford University Press, Inc., publishes works that further
Oxford University's objective of excellence
in research, scholarship, and education.

Oxford   New York
Auckland   Cape Town   Dar es Salaam   Hong Kong   Karachi
Kuala Lumpur   Madrid   Melbourne   Mexico City   Nairobi
New Delhi   Shanghai   Taipei   Toronto

With offices in
Argentina   Austria   Brazil   Chile   Czech Republic   France   Greece
Guatemala   Hungary   Italy   Japan   Poland   Portugal   Singapore
South Korea   Switzerland   Thailand   Turkey   Ukraine   Vietnam

Copyright © 2007 by Oxford University Press, Inc.

Published by Oxford University Press, Inc.
198 Madison Avenue, New York, New York 10016

www.oup.com

Oxford is a registered trademark of Oxford University Press

Library of Congress Cataloging-in-Publication Data
Foley, Michael W., 1945–
Religion and the new immigrants : how faith communities
form our newest citizens / Michael W. Foley and Dean R. Hoge.
   p. cm.
Includes bibliographical references and index.
ISBN-13 978-0-19-518870-7
ISBN 0-19-518870-5
1. Church work with immigrants—United States.   I. Hoge, Dean R., 1937–
II. Title.
BV639.I4F65 2006
200.86'91209753—dc22   2006013245

9 8 7 6 5 4 3 2 1

Printed in the United States of America
on acid-free paper

Acknowledgments

This book originated in a three-year study of worship communities serving immigrants in the Washington, D.C., area. That project, which we codirected, was one of several similar projects funded by The Pew Charitable Trusts as part of its Gateway Cities Project. Researchers in each of the seven "gateway cities"—Chicago, Houston, Los Angeles, Miami, New York City, San Francisco, and Washington, D.C.—met on two occasions and exchanged notes and results. All shared a common focus on the role of religion in the civic and social incorporation of the new immigrants; but each project was developed independently by a team of scholars from the urban area in question. We extend our thanks to The Pew Charitable Trusts for its support and to Dr. Kimon Sargeant, our program officer at the Trusts, for his unfailing helpfulness throughout the process. The opinions expressed in this volume are those of the authors and do not necessarily reflect the views of The Pew Charitable Trusts.

The research for this book was carried out under the auspices of the Life Cycle Institute at the Catholic University of America. We thank the staff of the Institute—Woinishet Negash, Mary Anne Eley, and Ann Kasprzyk—for all their efforts on our behalf throughout the duration of the research and writing of this book. Our colleague Jim Youniss provided wise counsel and encouragement throughout the project. Other colleagues, including the late Che Fu Lee, Paul Sullins, and Lene Jensen, contributed to the research effort in a variety of ways. Dr. Lee's and Dr. Jensen's contributions are acknowledged in the notes. Paul Sullins was our web master.

In designing the study, we had the help of an advisory panel of scholars with proven track records in the study of immigrant religion. We would like to thank Yvonne Haddad, Donald Miller, Milagros Peña, Alex Stepick, and Manuel Vásquez for sharing their time and thoughts with us. Fenggang Yang, whose doctoral work on Chinese immigrant religion under Dr. Hoge predated our study, provided invaluable advice on researching the Chinese community in the Washington, D.C., area. Helen Rose Ebaugh, Donald Miller, and Mark Chaves were also generous with their time at various stages of the research project.

As we began the project, we sought the advice of religious leaders and specialists in the area in identifying worship communities that serve a high proportion of immigrants. Andrea Johnson undertook the initial survey of worship communities to identify those serving significant immigrant populations, compiled the results and set up our database, prepared preliminary reports, and provided enormous assistance in conducting three forums with religious leaders as we explored some of the results of the research. She also returned late in the project to oversee organization of a forum on immigrant worship communities and social service delivery.

The research reported here would have been impossible without the efforts of a number of younger scholars who took on major portions of the ethnographic and survey work. Okyun Kwon came to us as a postdoctoral scholar to devote two years full-time to researching the Korean communities. His deep knowledge of Korean worship communities in the United States, along with his indefatigable energy for research, gave us in-depth studies of three Korean communities and 90 interviews with as many Korean pastors in the area. Maria Eugenia Verdaguer mastered the anthropological database we used for assembling field notes and devoted the final six months of the project to systematically sorting through the ethnographies. Jessica Falcone picked up the fieldwork with Hindu and Sikh communities after our first researcher left us to go to law school and broadened our knowledge of these communities immensely. She also spent days with members of the Sikh communities in the immediate aftermath of the events of September 11, 2001, as they attempted to forge a response. Maha Alkhateeb provided important insights into the Muslim communities as researcher and an active participant observer. Other field researchers included Victor Amadi, Shanya Purushothoman, and Stephen Zhang. Jackie Wenger helped in training our researchers in ethnographic methods.

The survey of pastors described in the introduction engaged the efforts of our field researchers but also required additional staff. Gwen Lewis was indispensable for completing the effort to survey African pastors. Ronald Luna completed the survey of pastors of Salvadoran churches, drawing on his own ties in the evangelical community to give us access to many of these churches. Kounian Ding carried out the survey of Chinese pastors and subsequently helped enter and code our data, along with Ismail Demirezen.

As we extended our research to look into the relationship between immigrant worship communities and local social service agencies, we had the help of Zeenie Latif, Susan Stephens, and Jo Anne Schneider. Jo Anne, in particular, saw to the analysis of our quantitative data on cosponsorship of social service and community organizing efforts, carried out in-depth interviews with representatives of social service agencies, and applied her own sophisticated understanding of social welfare provision in the United States to the project. Thanks to Jo Anne's efforts, we staged a conference that brought together religious leaders and representatives of social service agencies to examine our findings and dialogue among themselves.

In writing this book, we had the benefit of a number of critical readers. Eric Hanson read the first version of the book and gave us invaluable advice on how to restructure the content and recast the argument. Lene Jensen, Okyun Kwon, Maria Eugenia Verdaguer, and Jim Youniss read and commented on individual chapters. We thank all of these individuals and two anonymous readers for Oxford University Press for their comments and suggestions, with the usual qualification that whatever faults remain can be attributed to the authors alone.

This was a truly collaborative project. Foley oversaw the ethnographic research and directed the research team, with Hoge participating actively in all of the team's meetings and deliberations. Hoge directed the construction of the survey instrument and statistical analysis with Foley's active collaboration. When it came time to begin writing this book, both authors participated in drafting and revising chapters. The final product reflects the work of many researchers, some of it captured in conference papers presented along the way or in unpublished field reports, on which we have drawn freely as we attempted to tell our story. It also reflects our joint efforts to make sense of the rich ethnographic and statistical data that the project produced. Though we have had to leave out much that was of interest in the course of our study, we hope the book does justice to the work of all those who took part in the project.

Contents

Religion and the
New Immigrants

Introduction

The wave of immigration that swept over the United States in the last quarter of the twentieth century and that continues unabated today has provoked enormous controversy. Some 10.4 percent of the population at the time of the 2000 census was foreign-born, still below the peak achieved in 1910, when the figure reached almost 15 percent. But the overall number of immigrants, at 28.4 million (twice the earlier peak) and their geographic spread throughout the nation have reawakened concerns reminiscent of nineteenth-century controversies. Are the new immigrant altering American culture and undermining our ability to maintain national unity? Are their efforts to maintain their native cultures and languages, the emergence of ethnic enclaves and institutions, and their continuing transnational ties fragmenting America and challenging the claims of the American political system on its citizens? Will the new immigrants be assimilated like the immigrants of the nineteenth century, or does continuing immigration threaten to perpetuate cultural differences that evade easy reconciliation?

These are not new questions, though they are sometimes posed as such. Reacting in part to the revival of ethnic identities and claims in the wake of the civil rights movement and in part to the new immigration, intellectuals as diverse as the liberal historian Arthur Schlesinger Jr. and the conservative pundit William Bennett have worried that the growing "multiculturalism" of American society threatens national unity (Schlesinger 1993; Bennett 1992).

Many scholars have responded by pointing to the diversity of the new immigration, with its high proportion of professionals and entrepreneurs, rapid rates of English acquisition among the young, and overall economic success; but others have worried that the poorest immigrants are being assimilated into relatively dysfunctional American subcultures, creating an immigrant "underclass" that will not enjoy the opportunities traditionally associated with immigration (Portes and Rumbaut 1996; López and Stanton-Salazar 2001). And the growing visibility of religious bodies outside the "Judeo-Christian tradition" poses the question, as Diana Eck, director of Harvard University's Pluralism Project, puts it, of how the United States might forge a healthy religious pluralism in the face of the immense diversity of religious expression the new immigration has brought (Eck 1996).

This book addresses these concerns both directly and more obliquely by looking at the role of one set of institutions—local worship communities—in the lives of the new immigrants. Such communities are important in the lives of many, though not all, immigrants. As institutions designed to serve some of the most profound human needs, they often play an important role in the lives of immigrants, who face all the challenges and anxieties of life in a new and foreign culture. As institutions that express deeply held cultural convictions and ways of doing things, local worship communities are central to many immigrants' efforts to maintain and adapt their culture to the new situation. As organizations embedded in American civil society, worship communities provide special avenues for incorporating newcomers into the fabric of American life. And as communities in many cases created by and for immigrants, they reflect particularly well the multiple ways that recent immigrants and their children struggle with adaptation to American society.

Among students of American religion and historians of immigration, it has become virtually a truism that religion plays an important role in the lives of immigrants to this country. If ethnic and immigration studies have otherwise lagged behind, both disciplines are catching up, but questions abound. What is the character and extent of this role for the new immigrants? How do religious institutions serve newcomers to the United States? What do they do for immigrants and their offspring, and how do they help shape their experience of life in the United States? Do they promote their incorporation into American life and civic affairs, or hinder that process? And how do they shape the ethnic and religious identities of immigrants?

This book attempts to answer these questions. It reports the results of a three-year study of worship communities serving immigrants in the Washington, D.C., area, sponsored by The Pew Charitable Trusts. The core of the book is an analysis of our survey of some 200 local worship communities—

Catholic and Protestant churches, Buddhist and Hindu temples, Muslim prayer centers and mosques, and Sikh congregations—in Washington and its Maryland and Virginia suburbs. In addition, we draw on ethnographies of 20 of the same communities, as well as similar studies of immigrant groups elsewhere across the country.

What we find, not surprisingly, is enormous diversity. Just as the new immigration is more diverse than that of the nineteenth century, the sorts of religious institutions that serve the new immigrants and the ways they affect their lives vary greatly across religious traditions and from worship community to worship community. There are certainly patterns, however, and we find that these are shaped not so much by ethnicity or culture as by the peculiar circumstances of immigration and reception of each group, their religious tradition, and the organizational culture of their worship community. We find that immigrant churches, mosques, temples, and local worship communities of all sorts assist immigrants in a variety of ways, some of them directly contributing to their incorporation into the new society: they provide psychological and cultural "refuge" for newcomers that entails new, and sometimes enduring, social networks and social capital; as institutions in America's civil society, they participate directly in community affairs to one degree or another and give their members opportunities to do so as well; they provide social services and contacts for immigrant members, in some cases promoting their incorporation into the American political system through naturalization classes, voter registration, and get-out-the-vote efforts; and they help shape immigrants' images of themselves, not only morally and spiritually but as members of our society and polity. Some worship communities do one or more of these things better than others. In the chapters that follow, we look more carefully at each of these dimensions of service to their members and to the larger society. Here, though, we want to set the stage by considering more closely the sorts of concerns that have been raised about the new immigrants, the state of the literature, and the contribution that a study of worship communities might make to the ongoing debate.

The Question of Assimilation and the New Immigrants

Political scientist Samuel Huntington maintains that the old questions are more troubling today than in the past because of the changed circumstances of immigration. In Huntington's view, Hispanic immigrants, and Mexicans in particular, pose a special challenge because of the massive number of people speaking one immigrant language (threatening the dominance of English as the national language), the proximity of borders with Latin America (promising continuing immigration, no matter what the legal regime), the cultural assertiveness of Hispanic immigrants (who insist that their cultural values are in many ways superior to many "American" values), and the persistence of many Latin Americans' political ties to their homelands (Huntington 2004). Huntington's worries have been well answered elsewhere, but similar concerns about the new immigration are widespread, exacerbated by the events of September 11, 2001, and the fears generated by suicide bombings in London in July 2005, carried out by second-generation young Muslim men.[1] "Assimilation" is widely seen as the answer to such concerns, reflecting the unexamined notion that the assimilation of previous waves of immigrants was relatively straightforward and untroubled.

The assumption that "assimilation" in the past was either a straightforward process or inevitable has come under considerable fire since the 1950s. The revival of "white ethnicity" in the 1960s and 1970s, in part as a reaction to the Civil Rights movement, in part in response to the marginalization of urban, working-class descendants of the last wave of immigration in the city politics of Philadelphia and other deindustrializing cities, called attention to the persistence of ethnicity and raised questions about the viability of the assimilation hypothesis. Some, like sociologist Herbert Gans (1979), saw the vestiges of immigrant culture as manifestations of a "symbolic ethnicity" that would ultimately disappear. Others, like Nathan Glazer and Daniel Moynihan (1970), interpreted ethnicity as a primarily political recourse, useful for mobilizing populations around issues of perceived social, economic or political marginalization. Others have argued that ethnicity for those groups that enjoy a societal identification as "whites" has largely become a matter of choice, while for blacks, many Hispanics, and persons of Asian descent, ethnicity and race have become much more a matter of social ascription (Waters 1990, 1996).

Despite the differences among these positions, most scholars today have adopted a constructivist notion of ethnicity that recognizes the changing character of ethnic identification, the active roles of both insiders and outsiders in shaping ethnicity, and the prevalence of ethnic identification in "becoming American" (as Gerber, Morawska, and Pozzetta put it, "ethnicization is Americanization," 1992, 60, as cited in Yang 1999, 20). This means, among other things, that immigrants may well succeed in being integrated into American life in the education system, on the job, socially, and politically (what Milton Gordon [1964] termed "structural assimilation") while retaining significant elements of their cultural identity at home and in selected venues, bypassing "cultural assimilation" to one degree or another. At the same time, cultural identity can be an important ingredient in the political presence of a group. Such identity, however, is often "invented" out of disparate cultural materials, as people from diverse backgrounds in a home country become "Italian" or "Irish" or "Vietnamese" for social and political purposes in this country (Conzen et al. 1992; Sollors 1989). The overall picture of "bumpy-line assimilation" (Gans 1992) seems to capture well the history of the last great wave of immigration but is helpful, as well, in thinking about the trajectory of the new immigrants (Jacoby 2004).

Ethnicity has been an integral part of American pluralism since the mid–nineteenth century, as Conzen and her colleagues (1992) have shown. They argue that its "invention" corresponded on the one hand to increasing concern that cultural cohesion was necessary to the success of the democratic experiment and on the other to immigrants' efforts to assert their peculiar contributions to American life and protect their place within it. Thus, middle-class Germans (among whom the notion of the "melting pot" first gained currency) argued that German culture had important contributions to make to American society and that German Americans had a duty, accordingly, to promote and protect their cultural heritage. Irish immigrants promoted the celebration of St. Patrick's Day in the 1840s and 1850s as a largely secular holiday for promoting an agenda of Irish nationalism and republicanism, defense of the American Catholic church, and the advancement of the Irish in America. "The artfulness of this synthesis was that Irish leadership could argue that nothing more proved the loyalty of the Irish to their new homeland than their republican aspiration to participate in the tasks of self-government" and their devotion to promoting similar self-government in their homeland (20–21). Transnational loyalties and full citizenship in the United States, even in the 1840s, were treated as inseparable ingredients of the immigrant experience. The Cuban American experience of the late twentieth century was another example of this combination, which we shall find embodied in some of the more activist immigrant worship communities of our study.

Just what are the dimensions of contemporary immigrant "assimilation" that worry contemporary critics? If American-ness is defined in terms of consumer values, then the evidence seems clear that most immigrants have assimilated. While many cling to the foods of their native lands (to the extent that they can acquire them), most have eagerly adopted American eating habits to one degree or another, certainly by the second generation, with all the deleterious health consequences that entails.[2] Any stroll through a Wal-Mart or Target can confirm that immigrants contribute their share to the growing national appetite for the appliances and appurtenances that fill the American household (Menzel 1994; Shor 2004). In terms of employment, important segments of the new immigrants have been integrated into professional and technical positions, particularly in the new information technology economy—a sharp contrast with the overwhelmingly working-class first-generation immigrants of a hundred years ago. The majority, whether professionals, self-employed, or working-class, have sought out and found employment niches that are vital to the growing U.S. economy, as have immigrants throughout our history (Waldinger, Aldrich, and Ward 1990; Waldinger and Der-Martirosian 2001).

The economic integration of the new immigrants, then, does not seem to be in question, whether we look at the question from the point of view of consumer habits or employment. Nor should cultural integration present significant concerns, given what we know about both previous immigrant experience and the current second generation. Indeed, there is compelling evidence that even in Hispanic enclaves like Miami, immigrant youth and the second generation in general achieve English fluency faster than was the case in the past, thanks perhaps to the pervasive influence of American television both here and abroad (Portes and Schauffler 1996; Rumbaut and Portes 2001). Huntington (2004) has raised the question of the identification of recent immigrants with American values, without noting that the "values" to which immigrant parents frequently object are materialism, selfishness, disrespect for elders, and laziness. Huntington and others have also pressed concerns about identification with American society and polity more broadly, given widespread transnational ties (see, for example, Levitt 2001). Here, too, prevailing evidence does not appear to support the critics' concerns. Douglas Massey and his colleagues have shown that most Mexican immigrants come without the intention of staying in the United States; but they also demonstrate that over time, the determination to return home fades, and Mexican immigrants increasingly regard the United States as "home" (Massey et al. 1987). It is doubtful, moreover, that the same dynamic applies to other immigrant groups, even to Central Americans, separated by large distances from their homelands, though it is worth reminding ourselves that as many as half the Italian immigrants of the nineteenth century eventually returned home. Transnational ambiguities are not new to the most recent wave of immigration. Numerous studies, moreover, attest to the commitment of immigrant and second-generation youth to this country; indeed, their assimilation is a source of great concern to their parents. In a study connected to our own research project, Lene Jensen found that the second-generation youth saw themselves as "American" in significant and inescapable ways, and even their parents note that the immigrant experience has "Americanized" them to an important degree (see chapter 6).

The question, by and large, is not whether immigrants will be incorporated into American society (they are every day) but the terms of incorporation and how such incorporation takes place. In contrast to the literature on the economic, social, and cultural assimilation of recent immigrants, however, very little work has been done on their civic incorporation. Here the concerns of the critics have some basis in the little we know. Americans in general have abysmal rates of political participation. Scarcely 50 percent vote in presidential elections, and the number drops precipitously for congressional, state, and local races that do not happen to coincide with a presidential election. Cynicism about our political system, moreover, is growing. Civic participation generally is higher, but scholars have raised concerns about apparently falling rates of civic engagement among the American public, as well (Putnam 2000). Among immigrants, rates of naturalization and citizenship are considered low by historical standards, and somewhat lower among Latin Americans than other immigrant populations, even considering the effects of length of residence on rates of naturalization (U.S. Census Bureau 1999, 20). Over a third of all immigrants are currently naturalized citizens (Lollock 2001). But even among naturalized citizens, rates of voting are low, though not uniformly so (DeSipio 1996). And the little evidence we have suggests that immigrants are less likely to be members of formal associations, perform community service, be politically involved apart from voting, or participate in other ways in community affairs—with the important exception of school affairs. Though these results undoubtedly change with the second generation, we have very little data on which to base such a judgment. The one organization in civil society to which immigrants tend to belong with greater frequency than the larger population is the local worship community (Jasso et al. 2000). It behooves us to ask, accordingly, what these organizations do to assist in the incorporation of immigrants and their children into American society. And given a growing body of literature that points to local worship communities as important sources of civic skills and civic engagement in American society (Rosenstone and Hansen 1993; Verba, Schlozman, and Brady 1995), we will want to pay attention to the contributions of such organizations to the civic incorporation of immigrants.

Immigrant Institutions as Problem or Solution

Before we do so, however, it seems important to address one more aspect of the current controversy over immigrant incorporation into American society. Just as what can only be called the new nativism has assumed a dubious notion of assimilation as the norm, it also echoes questionable understandings of the role that immigrant residential enclaves and institutions play in American life. Though residential enclaves are fast fading as the distinctive setting for immigrant life in the United States (see, for example, Singer et al. 2001), the immigrant worship communities we will encounter here arguably form part of a "virtual immigrant enclave," even where the immigrant group in question is geographically dispersed. Here in the worship community, members of an ethnic group can come together around cultural symbols and practices that resonate with them. They can reinforce ties among themselves and between themselves and the culture and people they have left behind. Proponents of assimilation often worry that such ties, and the enclave institutions that perpetuate them, have the effect of isolating immigrants and their children from the larger society, threatening national unity in the eyes of some, or imperiling the immigrants' own chances for economic and social betterment according to others. John Arthur's conclusions to his study of Ghanaians in Atlanta, Georgia, are typical of such judgments:

> Within their ethnic affiliations, the immigrants are able to create
> enclaves whose relationships with the outside community are defined
> solely in economic terms. Even when African immigrants form sec-
> ondary associations outside of their immigrant enclave groups, these
> relationships are usually not as close-knit as those that are formed
> along ethnic lines. In general, these secondary groups confer little or
> no status on the immigrants; neither are they important in facilitat-
> ing immigrants' integration in American society. Moreover, the
> strong intra-ethnic ties that immigrants forge among themselves
> serve to impede social integration, leading to further isolation and
> disengagement from wider social discourse. (2000, 88)

Alejandro Portes suggests another possibility. Immigrant enclaves, enclave institutions and intraethnic ties provide a rich context for learning and advancement for otherwise disadvantaged minorities, provided that they enjoy sufficient material, moral, and human resources. In a community rich in intertwining ethnic ties, members gain access to moral, psychological, and financial resources that may well be lacking for more isolated (and "integrated") immigrants. They will also be out of reach in uniformly poor communities (Fuligni 1998; Portes and Rumbaut 1996, 250; Portes and Zhou 1993). Particularly for the second generation, a diversified immigrant community can provide the guidance and encouragement of a multitude of adults, opportunities for employment and advancement, and a moral compass that may be lacking in school and peer groups (Fuligni 1998; Portes 1995; Portes et al. 1993; Zhou and Bankston 1998).

Crucial to this argument is the character of the resources that ethnic enclaves and enclave institutions, such as worship communities, make available.
Where ethnic communities are diverse and interactions across class lines are
fluid, such communities and the institutions in which they are embodied can
provide the sort of "leg up" to new immigrants and to the second generation
that Portes, Zhou, and others have suggested. Where communities are generally poor, their institutions may nevertheless provide participants with a richer
array of contacts and opportunities than the larger environment—or they may
not. Much depends upon the character and orientation of the institution itself.
As we shall see in the chapters that follow, immigrant worship communities
differ significantly in the ways in which they help their members connect with
and adapt to American society. All serve, to one degree or another, as a place
of refuge, a "haven in a heartless world," to use Christopher Lasch's formula, where immigrants and their offspring can find cultural as well as spiritual sustenance. They nourish difference; and the assertion of difference, as
R. Laurence Moore (1986) has argued, has always been central to becoming
American. At the same time, many of these communities are decidedly "of" the
society in which they are set: they belong to wider coalitions and associations of
religious organizations, many of them ecumenical in character; they provide
volunteers and donations to local charities; they maintain contacts with local
authorities; they participate in community affairs. One of the most striking
findings of our study, already alluded to, is that those worship communities
most committed to the problems of their immigrant members and the countries from which they came are the most thoroughly integrated into American
life and politics. This should come as no surprise, since home-country activism
has been a hallmark of immigrant involvement in American political life since
the early nineteenth century, as we have already seen; but it stands in sharp
contrast to the worries of observers like Samuel Huntington about the effects of
"transnationalism" on American national identity. Nevertheless, other communities are only marginally connected to the larger society and rarely serve to
help integrate their members into American life. Understanding how worship
communities differ in these respects and why will be an important part of our
undertaking in the pages that follow.

Explaining Variation

In chapter 1 we develop a theoretically informed portrait of the dimensions
of civic incorporation that churches, mosques, temples, and other sorts of
worship communities might help promote among immigrants and their

offspring. We also offer a framework for understanding the enormous variation among worship communities in these respects. Briefly, we look to three
sets of factors to explain the differing contributions of worship communities
to immigrant incorporation. First are the differing circumstances of the immigrant communities themselves. Some come as refugees, with or without
the sanction and support of the federal government, others as undocumented
workers; others have permanent legal status or easy access to permanent residency. Some are confined to low-wage, largely dead-end jobs in the service
sector; others have been brought here by the promise of professional employment and rapid upward mobility. Some face considerable prejudice and
the prospect of assimilation into an "underclass" in American society; others
are treated as members of "model minorities," and see the prospects for themselves and their children as bright.

Second, immigrant worship communities have their own distinctive "organizational culture," largely drawn from the distinctive religious tradition they
represent, but also subject to the efforts of religious and lay leaders sharing a
vision of the purposes and character of the community.[3] Some are largely
"houses of worship," where worship services featuring little lay participation
are the main focus of attention, accompanied, perhaps, by efforts at religious
education. Individuals and families, apart from a small core of active members,
typically come to worship services with little interaction with others in the
community. Other worship communities, typically with many fewer members,
have a "family"-style organizational culture, characterized by close ties among
members and a focus on fellowship alongside worship and religious education.
Such worship communities rarely have the resources to mount social service
programs or maintain extensive ties outside their walls, but they tend to the
needs of their members through informal exchanges. A third type is a "community"-style organization, where efforts are made to "build community"
among a larger membership through a variety of activities and subgroups,
answering members' interests and concerns. A fourth is the "civic leader"
worship community. Much rarer than the other three types, this is a worship
community that takes as an important part of its mission a role in community
affairs, through participation on civic committees and task forces, frequent
institutional presence at civic events, active participation in the political process
and current events, and widespread ties to other worship communities and to
civic and political organizations in its city or region.

Finally, religious tradition helps shape organizational culture, but it also
plays a role in forming religious leaders' and lay members' notions of obligation toward the larger community; gives leaders and laity distinctive terms
with which to frame responses to issues of the day; and provides alternative

interpretations on which activist clergy or laity may draw in shaping the profile of a particular community.

Together, we find, these three dimensions of difference explain most of the variation among worship communities that might otherwise be attributed to cultural or ethnic differences. This is not to say that cultural values and practices do not shape the life of worship communities. Vietnamese Catholic churches are clearly different in important respects from Salvadoran ones. But such differences have less impact on the ways Catholic churches in general attend to their immigrant members than do the differences in circumstances of Vietnamese and Salvadoran immigration and the distinctive styles of "church" that individual pastors impose upon their parishes. Salvadoran Catholic and Protestant churches, for example, are more like Chinese Catholic and Korean Protestant churches, respectively, than they are like one another. And such differences extend not just to style of worship but also the degree to which each is connected to social service and civic organizations, the sorts of services and activities available to members, and the ways each helps prepare its members for citizenship. Because pastors have a certain leeway, in the Catholic Church to impose one or another organizational culture on their parish, differences between Catholic and Protestant churches are not absolute; but to say this is only to underline, once again, that cultural differences have less to do with our story than might be expected.

Our explanatory framework does not render easy distinctions or judgments. Religious tradition, organizational culture, and the demographic characteristics of the immigrant group, we find, interact in complex ways to shape the contribution of local worship communities to the incorporation of recent immigrants. Where poorer immigrants are concentrated in worship communities that themselves lack resources, individuals and families may find community and spiritual and material support in their religious lives but little opportunity or incentive to become involved in the wider society. This is mainly a phenomenon of relatively small, evangelical Protestant congregations and the smaller mosques serving a largely single-ethnic population. By contrast, Catholic parishes with high concentrations of relatively poor Hispanic immigrants tend to provide a wider range of contacts with the larger community, more community services, and greater incentives to participate in American society, thanks to the richer stocks of social capital their pastors typically enjoy. This is particularly true where parish leadership sees promoting such connections as an essential part of its mission. The large, multicultural mosques in our study area played similar roles for a generally more affluent population. Hindu temples, on the other hand, are structured as "houses of worship," with relatively few opportunities for wider interaction, even among worshipers; but the professional status and affluence of many members of the Hindu community ensures their ready integration into American society through work, school, and community life outside the temple. Class, the character of the worship community, and leadership interact in these examples and others throughout the study to produce distinctive sorts of experiences in and through the local worship community.

An Institutional Focus

Ours is a primarily institutional focus. We look at churches, mosques, and temples of various kinds and ask how they are structured and run, who participates in them in what ways, and what sorts of programs they offer their members. Religious organizations are often crucial in individuals' lives. They provide social ties, they channel opportunities and motivations, and they teach values and worldviews about how to live. By focusing on religious organizations and what they do and set out to do, we can get a sense for the ways immigrants are incorporated into one important institution in civil society, the sorts of social capital made available to them in and through their worship communities, the kinds of services and learning opportunities they might gain in these contexts, and the sorts of identities and obligations that are urged upon them in this often influential setting.

As we shall see, the answers to these questions differ significantly across religious and ethnic groups. How each group answers them, moreover, will shape in important ways their encounter with the United States. The extent to which this is the case, we assume, depends upon how extensively worship communities occupy the time and energy of participants. However powerful the hold of religion on people's consciousness, the impact of a local worship community on their lives will be minor if immersion in the community occupies no more than an hour or two on a Sunday morning. At this level of involvement, other institutions—family, workplace, school, even the soccer club—may have far greater impact. Nevertheless, even at this level of involvement, religious institutions can promote attitudes and behaviors and provide opportunities that help shape the immigrant experience. Local worship communities that demand more intense sorts of involvement will have proportionately greater impact.

Religion matters in people's lives. It matters especially for people with strong religious commitment and strong church involvement. How important is religion in the lives of the new immigrants? Unfortunately, little reliable social science data exists to answer this question.[4] What scattered data we do have tells us that immigrants to the United States from most parts of the world tend to be more actively religious after immigration than they were in the home countries before coming. Korean immigrants, for example, are significantly more likely to be Christians upon coming to the United States than the population at home, both because greater numbers of Christians migrate to this country and because of conversion once here (Min 1992). As much as 70 percent of the Korean population in the United States is associated with a church. But researchers studying other immigrant groups have reported increased religious practice among immigrants as well (Fenton 1988; Smith 1999; Williams 1988; Yang 1999). If this is indeed the case, then, at least in this respect, the new immigration is much like the old, which was also, in the words of historian Timothy Smith, a "theologizing experience" for many (Smith 1978).[5]

In addition, recent immigrants are more actively religious than other Americans. The pilot portion of the New Immigrant Survey found that 41 percent of those surveyed reported attending religious services weekly or more often, compared with 29 percent in the nonimmigrant population surveyed by the General Social Survey in 1994 (Jasso et al. 2000, 74–76).[6] In chapter 2, we present rough estimates of the proportions of immigrants from various parts of the world who attend predominantly "immigrant" worship communities in the Washington, D.C., area. And we draw on our ethnographic studies throughout to get some sense of the impact of the religious institutions we study in the lives of participants. First and foremost, however, we are concerned with what local worship communities do for immigrants and their offspring.

Not only individuals but also religious organizations are influenced by the immigrant experience in America. Mosques in the United States are unlike mosques in Egypt or Pakistan. Hindu temples in the United States are unlike temples in India in important respects. Catholic and Lutheran churches are different here from those in Central America or Africa. Some have argued that both American legal norms and the force of the Protestant example pushes religious institutions of diverse origins to change in the direction of the Protestant "congregation." And, indeed, many immigrant religious institutions have adopted elected boards of trustees, fundraising efforts, and social programs (Warner and Wittner 1998; Yang and Ebaugh 2001). But at the same time that the American experience is transforming immigrant religious institutions, those institutions are transforming the religious landscape in the United States, literally and figuratively (Eck 1996). We will take up both these questions in the conclusion.

The Religion and the New Immigration Project

Our project was one of seven "gateway cities" projects funded by The Pew Charitable Trusts to investigate the role of religion in the lives of the new immigrants. Our goal was to explore the role of those worship communities that served a significant number of immigrants in promoting their social and civic incorporation into American life. To permit greater possibilities for generalization, we chose to compare a wide range of groups across a range of religious traditions. We also wanted to combine the depth of ethnographic study with the quantifiable data that survey research could provide. In the end, the research team that we assembled produced ethnographic studies of some 20 worship communities; our survey sampled 200 of the 552 worship communities we identified as serving the groups we were interested in.

Choosing immigrant groups for study proved more difficult than we thought. A straightforward attempt to study the largest national-origin groups in the Washington, D.C., area would have left aside both religious and ethnic groups of some interest. We chose instead a mixed strategy. We wanted to study a broad array of religious traditions, including Muslims, who are increasingly visible and active civically in the area but none of whom, with the exception of Indian Muslims, come from the top 10 sending countries in the region. At the same time, we wanted to study the most important immigrant groups in the area, including the diverse array of African immigrants, who make up a notable subset of the immigrant community here. African immigrants have grown in numbers and visibility in the Washington area over the last two decades, though they remain a minor presence in most other gateway cities. They face the special situation of visual identification by the white majority with the African American community, though their relations with the latter are often rocky. Both because Washington is a relatively important site of African immigration and because of the special issues this presents, we decided to study churches serving this group. Many Africans are Muslims. African Christians, however, appear to be the more numerous among the immigrant population, and the number of churches serving Africans is quite large. Therefore, we focused our attention on Protestant, Catholic, and independent African churches serving this population.

The remaining groups in our study were chosen on the basis of the relative size of the immigrant population coming from a given country or cultural area. Salvadorans make up the largest single Latin American population in the area and the largest immigrant population from any country. They also are here under peculiarly unfavorable circumstances, not shared as widely with any other large immigrant group in the Washington area. Though many came as refugees from a cruel civil war, U.S. foreign policy at the time dictated a prolonged refusal to grant Salvadorans refugee status, leaving the majority without documents. A temporary accommodation persists to this day, but many Salvadoran are here without documents, and even many of those with temporary work permits remain uncertain as to how long they will be permitted to stay in the country. On the whole, Salvadorans are poorer than most other immigrants in the area, more likely to work at menial jobs, and less likely to have attained permanent residency or citizenship. A number of Catholic churches and a wide variety of Protestant churches serve the Salvadoran community.

Koreans are much more likely to be employed as small business people or to work for fellow Koreans in small businesses.[7] Our evidence, like that of other researchers in the field, suggests that they are also more likely than most immigrants to participate actively in a local worship community. They are overwhelmingly Protestants—though not all were Christians when they left Korea—and there are a few Catholics and Korean Buddhists among them. They tend to live dispersed in suburban communities throughout the Washington, D.C., area but generally in the more affluent areas, and most belong to small churches.

Chinese immigrants have a longer presence in the area than most other immigrants—there is a small, old "Chinatown" in downtown Washington— but their numbers grew rapidly in the 1980s and 1990s. Traditionally, the community has been dominated by ethnic Chinese from Taiwan and Canton, but increasing numbers of Chinese from Vietnam, Hong Kong, and mainland China have complicated the picture. Most of the worship communities serving the Chinese population are Protestant, but there are a number of Catholic churches and Buddhist temples.

Indian immigrants belong to all the traditional religions of India. The Hindu, Jain, Sikh, Buddhist, and Indian Christian communities all have centers of worship in the area. Indian Muslims also participate in area mosques, though no mosque is exclusively, or even predominantly, Indian. We chose to focus our attention on the two largest of these religious groups, the Hindus and the Sikhs. The area has seen a ferment of temple building over the last several years, with two major new temples dedicated in 2002 alone. The smaller Sikh community, meanwhile, has also built a number of gurdwaras, or congregations, reflecting both the growth of the community and ongoing political and personal divisions within it.

We ended up with the following set of target groups: Salvadoran Catholics and Protestants; Korean and Chinese Protestants, Catholics, and Buddhists (though Protestant churches predominate among both groups);[8] Hindu and

Sikh Indians;[9] West African Protestants and Catholics; and Muslims from all parts of the world. Because most of the local mosques are multiethnic, they presented the opportunity to look at worship communities where religious identity seemed to trump ethnic identity.[10] Similarly, the contrasts between Protestant and Catholic Salvadorans; between mainline Protestant, Catholic, and independent African churches; and between Hindu and Sikh worship communities offered insights into the power of religious tradition to shape immigrant institutions and experiences while holding ethnicity and national origin constant. Finally, the diverse ethnic and national origins of West Africans and the varied settings—some multicultural, some monoethnic—in which they worship allowed us to look more closely at the ethnic dimension of worship community formation and evolution.

At the beginning of the project in the summer of 2000, we compiled a list of all the churches, mosques, and temples serving our target groups in the Washington, D.C., area, based on directories, interviews with religious leaders, and word-of-mouth contacts. We carried out a preliminary survey on the basis of this list, attempting to identify those worship communities that served a significant proportion of immigrants in our target groups. Our field workers visited a number of these worship communities and chose field sites, where they carried out ethnographic studies over the next two years. Researchers worked from detailed guidelines drawn up by the principal investigators. We met monthly throughout the research phase, dealing with difficulties, reviewing findings, and trying out interpretations. Researchers produced field notes, which were entered into a field note database utilizing the N-vivo program, which permits coding on the go, complex categorization and retrieval, and the matching of quantitative and qualitative data. They also wrote final reports detailing their observations in each of their research sites. We have drawn on both these sources in the account that follows.

This book is based on these sources plus the results of a survey conducted over the first half of 2002. Most research on religion and immigration to date has relied on case studies as a primary source of data. This is true even of recent large-scale endeavors (Ebaugh and Saltzman Chavetz 2000; Warner and Wittner 1998). It seemed important, accordingly, to attempt a more systematic sampling of worship communities, even if these were drawn from just one region of the country. Our focus is on worship communities as institutions. We have been fortunate to be able to draw on the recent National Congregations Survey (NCS), which shares a similar focus, for inspiration and specific question items.[11] Though we have had to modify some questions to suit the peculiarities of worship communities serving immigrants and added others, we have been able to compare our results on many measures with the national representative sample utilized in the NCS.[12]

Outline of the Book

The book proceeds as follows. Chapter 1 lays out what we mean by "civic incorporation" and what we think local worship communities can contribute to immigrants' civic incorporation. We outline four ways in which religious organizations might enhance the incorporation of immigrants into the wider society and polity: through (1) the social capital embodied in the worship community itself; (2) their participation in an institution that is itself a participant in civil society; (3) the civic skills fostered within the worship community and the opportunities for volunteering and civic involvement it provides; and (4) the ethnic and religious identities that inform the terms on which immigrants and their offspring see themselves incorporated into the larger society. We also develop an explanatory framework to understand the considerable differences in the degree to which and ways in which local worship communities contribute to immigrant incorporation.

In chapter 2, we lay out some of the characteristics of the new immigration, including existing evidence on their degree of civic incorporation and political participation and the place of religion in their lives. After a brief look at the history of immigration to the Washington, D.C., area and the current distribution of immigrants throughout the area, we look at each of the immigrant groups who are the subject of our study, discussing both what we know about the demographics of this new population and the history of the religious institutions that have grown up to serve it.

Chapter 3 explores the sorts of social capital that these worship communities provide for their members and attempts to explain differences across ethnic groups and religious traditions in terms of the size and diversity of the worship community and its organizational culture. We find that some Catholic and mainline Protestant congregations, many mosques, and some Sikh gurdwaras provide significant social, economic and political linkages for immigrants, while most of the small, conservative Protestant churches serving Salvadorans, Koreans, and Chinese might provide valuable social ties but little in the way of "bridging social capital." Catholic parishes and Hindu temples that maintain a primarily "house of worship" style of organization nourish few social ties of any sort outside the small circle of lay people who may be involved in the maintenance and governance of these worship communities.

More uniformly poor communities are limited in the sorts of resources that might make whatever social capital they nourish "rich," but worship communities that themselves maintain wider ties to social service agencies, civic organizations, and government make up to some extent for these deficiencies. Organizational culture accounts for much of the difference among worship communities in these respects, but it is the theological orientation of religious and lay leaders that tends to shape organizational culture.

In chapter 4, we turn to the civic presence the worship community maintains. Is it actively integrated into community life, a "civic leader" sort of organization? Or is it turned in on itself and on the needs and concerns of its own members? Does it maintain rich ties to social service agencies, community organizations, government offices, and the political world? Is it connected to other worship communities across racial, ethnic, and theological lines? Or are its ties confined to its own sister communities? The answers to these questions will shape not only the social capital that members experience in participation in a worship community but also the style of civic engagement that is modeled for them and often actively promoted from the pulpit and in the everyday life of the community. Again, we find that some Catholic churches, many mosques, and most mainline Protestant churches are more likely to enjoy multiple ties to the larger society, provide a rich array of social services and volunteer opportunities, and encourage a more active participation in society than the smaller, evangelical churches and the big "house of worship"–type churches and temples. Civic activism is rare, but it often involves active commitment to "homeland" causes and the defense of the immigrant community itself.

Chapter 5 explores the ways worship communities contribute to the development of civic skills, as well as their efforts to mobilize members for civic engagement. Some worship communities provide ample opportunities for lay involvement in worship services, community life, and governance, thereby training members in skills potentially useful in civic life. The smaller, conservative Protestant churches, Hindu ashrams, and Sikh congregations are especially good examples. Others—more focused on worship or more hierarchically organized—provide few such opportunities. Many Catholic parishes, Hindu temples, and mosques are examples of this pattern. Even where such training in civic skills is abundant, though, an emphasis on serving the worship community, rather than participating actively in the larger society, may mean that the religious body does little to promote civic participation.

Chapter 6 takes up the question of the role of local worship communities in shaping, forging, or reinforcing ethnic and religious identities. Worship communities promote a sense of self among members that is also a sense of difference, as R. Laurence Moore points out (1986). The emphasis may be on religious differences that define people's moral and spiritual stance vis-à-vis the larger culture or elements of it; or it may be on ethnic differences. In many cases, both sorts of identity are important, and they help shape the civic and political stance of members. Homeland causes or the plight of an immigrant group in this country may become rallying points for the assertion of ethnic or religious identity; but only some organizational cultures and religious traditions promote civic engagement around such issues. Some Salvadoran Catholics have mobilized around immigration issues, but Salvadoran Protestants generally have avoided political involvement. Sikh congregations responded quickly to attacks on Sikhs following September 11, 2001, but attacks on Hindus did not elicit a similar response in those communities. At the same time, most people seem capable of claiming multiple identities, invoking one or another according to circumstance. Worship communities help crystallize versions of immigrant identity, but they may also be arenas of struggle over the meaning of a religious or ethnic identity. Studies of second-generation youth, including work tied to our own project, suggest that youth enmeshed in religious communities are at once appreciative of the moral and cultural heritage of their parents and engaged in becoming Americans on their own terms.

The concluding chapter attempts to draw these threads together, laying out the diversity we encountered at every step, the most important reasons behind it, and the significance of our findings for contemporary concerns about immigrant incorporation. In general, we argue, immigrant worship communities, however diverse, provide important resources for members' adaptation to the difficult circumstances of immigration. They are psychological, moral, and cultural refuges, but also important sources of social capital for many immigrants. Worship communities are also one important manifestation of the immigrant presence in American civil society. To one degree or another, all of them must interact with the agencies of government, neighbors, and other civil society organizations. They may maintain themselves in relative isolation, of course, but they nevertheless symbolize the pluralism Americans value. Many immigrant communities are well connected to other organizations, agencies, and groups. A few are actively involved in American civic and political life. Whether isolated or deeply involved, moreover, most worship communities contribute to some degree to the development of skills relevant to civic life, at least among their most active members. Many encourage volunteer service to the larger community. A few avidly promote active citizenship. An enhanced sense of identity, even where it portends an assertion of difference from other Americans, as it invariably does, does not detract from civic incorporation but shapes the terms on which immigrants and their children will work out their engagement in American society. Churches, mosques, temples, and other sorts of worship communities are schools for living, where immigrants and others address many of the issues of living in a strange new land and acquire tools and resources, moral and spiritual, as well as social or economic, for making their way in our society.

I

Becoming American

How does religion affect the immigrant experience in a new society? What impact does religious faith and participation in a religious community have on immigrants and their children? Does it contribute to integration into the larger society, or simply provide immigrants with a "haven in a heartless world" where they can garner comfort and renew their energies in their struggles to adapt? Does the immigrant church or mosque or temple "hold people back," keeping their attention focused on "the old country," as one Arab American activist told us heatedly? Or do such institutions play an active role in preparing people for life in the larger society, orienting their gaze to American politics and civic life, perhaps, at the same time that they promote country-of-origin causes? The answers are not easy to discern, as we shall see. Nor are they the same for all immigrant groups, religious traditions, and worship communities. Nevertheless, seeking answers is important both for understanding the role of religion in the immigrant experience and for theorizing more generally about the role of religion, and religious institutions in particular, in the civic life of the United States.

In this chapter, we develop an approach to answering these questions that centers on three broad accounts of civic incorporation. Churches, mosques, temples, and other worship communities can contribute to immigrants' incorporation as sources of "social capital"; as civic actors in their own right; and by training members in "civic skills," cultivating a sense of identity to guide civic participation, and mobilizing individuals to act civically. We also identify what we consider to be the most important set of variables that are relevant to explaining how local worship communities differ in each of these respects. Characteristics of the immigrant groups in question—most important, circumstances of immigration and the context of reception that immigrants meet—play a crucial role here. But so, too, do the peculiar "organizational cultures" of the various worship communities. Following the work of Penny Edgell Becker (1999), we identify four such cultures: the "house of worship," the family-style worship community, the community-style congregation, and the civic-leader worship community. Religious tradition is a third and final factor. It may shape the organizational culture of a worship community. But it also influences the role of lay people in the community, the character of the obligation they are taught to feel toward the larger community, and the resources for alternative interpretations of the tradition that might affect these impacts. The degree to which immigrants continue to enjoy "transnational ties," we argue, is ambiguous: in some cases, such ties tend to deflect attention away from civic engagement here in the United States; in others, such ties feed on and encourage civic involvement here as well as abroad. The chapter thus develops a model to describe the variety of ways in which religious institutions—and particularly those serving immigrant communities—may contribute to civic incorporation and participation and predict whether and to what extent individual worship communities will play an important role in their members' lives in this respect.

Thinking about the Civic and Social Incorporation of Immigrants

The question of the role of religion in the incorporation of immigrants is often approached as a psychological one. How do religious beliefs and practices help people adjust to the circumstances of immigration? Do they contribute to successful adaptation and integration into the new society? Or do they tend to hold people back, attaching them to the old country and old culture and blocking processes of acculturation that might enable them to better adapt to their new surroundings? We approach the question in a different way, drawing on a growing body of thinking about the role of associational life in modern democracies. We ask: How might participation in churches, mosques, temples, or other worship communities contribute to people's incorporation into the larger society? What sorts of resources and opportunities might such institutions provide? How might they shape immigrants' abilities to relate to the larger society? What could they contribute to their social and civic education? How might they mold immigrants' understanding of themselves as citizens and members of this society?

Our approach stems in part from the critical reappraisal that the notion of "assimilation" has undergone over the last quarter century, in part from a new appreciation of the role of institutions in shaping citizenship for all members of modern societies. Throughout the twentieth century, scholarly and popular thinking about the incorporation of immigrants into American society was dominated by the notion of assimilation. In the seminal work of Robert Park and its elaboration by Milton Gordon, the prevailing view of immigrant assimilation was that of a unidirectional process that ended in the immigrant population's loss of most of the distinctiveness that set them off from Anglo-Americans (Gordon 1964; Park and Burgess 1924). According to Gordon's version of the model, assimilation starts with acculturation, the acquiring of the distinctive "cultural patterns" of the host society. It ends in "identificational assimilation," when individuals no longer think of themselves as members of this or that immigrant or minority group but assume, instead, an exclusively American national identity. Along the way, processes of "structural assimilation"—that is, integration of a "minority group into the social cliques, clubs, and institutions of the core society at the primary group level" (Gordon 1964, 80–81)—facilitated the passage to full-blown identificational assimilation. The beginning and end of the process, in the classical view, were clearly psychological in nature, requiring individuals to shed their family and historical heritages as they acquired the tastes, attitudes, beliefs, and allegiances of the host society.

Critics of the assimilation theory, including Gordon himself, pointed to the seemingly irreducible quality of certain differences, including race and religion, among many immigrant groups. The resurgence of "white ethnicity" in the 1970s seemed to confirm the view that whatever became of the manifold heritages of immigration, the result was not a homogeneous "American" mass society (Alba 1990). Ethnic pluralism was recognized as a constitutive feature of American life, even if some intellectuals and members of the general public have continued to worry about a dilution of public life and common purpose as a result. Nor was it clear that individuals benefited in surrendering their cultural distinctiveness. Persistent evidence seemed to show that in certain respects "assimilation is bad for your children's health," as one scholarly synthesis put it (Rumbaut 1997).

Though some have argued that a revised assimilation model remains the best description of the long-term consequences of immigration for many individuals (Barkan 1995; Morawska 1994), there is little agreement on just how immigrants assimilate. The notion of acculturation suggests that it is a matter of unlearning habits, attitudes, and behaviors acquired in one's homeland and learning new ones; but how does one go about doing this? It seems clear that the children of immigrants assimilate in this sense rather rapidly, but there is little consensus on the most important means by which this is accomplished. Is it beneficial for children to be plunged into an English-only environment? Or do they need the anchor of their own language? (A growing consensus suggests that children learning more than one language do better in school. See Portes and Rumbaut 1996, 199–207.) Is exposure to mass media the key, or are integrated neighborhoods and schools the best route to assimilation? And what are the children of the new immigrants being assimilated to? Alejandro Portes, Rubén Rumbaut, and others have recently argued that the different trajectories of immigrant groups and their children can be traced to differences in the American subculture they have to deal with in neighborhood, workplace, and school environments; and they have adopted the term "segmented assimilation" to capture those differences (Portes 1995; Rumbaut and Portes 2001; Zhou et al. 1998). Eva Morawska suggests that one of the most important variables in assimilation is a lack of ethnic networks and institutions, a situation usually associated with small numbers of immigrants from the same group in a given community and a lack of significant ties beyond the community (Morawska 1994, 79–81). But this is a condition notable for its absence among most immigrants, particularly in urban settings; yet most acculturate rapidly, if only partially, in the workplace, schools, and other institutions of daily life, whatever the immediate circumstances of residence and ethnic community.

Such difficulties suggest a need for caution in dealing with the notion of assimilation. We have chosen, rather, to adopt the more neutral term "incorporation" to describe the effects we are interested in. Like assimilation, incorporation implies some movement on the part of the host society (Gordon's "structural assimilation"). And that, in turn, implies that immigrants have acquired skills and working knowledge that would facilitate their participation in this or that aspect of the larger community's life. But incorporation does not imply that immigrants necessarily shed their distinctive customs or beliefs. Nor does it posit that they assume indiscriminately the norms and behaviors of a supposedly monolithic host society. Incorporation means playing a part in a larger society and polity, but that part may equally well be built on distinctiveness as on commonality. Its opposite is not only keeping oneself and one's own apart but also passivity. It is hard to imagine any immigrant who is not incorporated in some sense. The question, then, has to do with the extent and quality of incorporation.

We focus here on the "civic" incorporation of immigrants, but that implies a broader "social" incorporation. When we refer to "social incorporation," we are thinking about the degree to which immigrants have contact with those outside their immediate families and ethnic or religious circles, the sorts of opportunities they have for economic advancement, and their ability to make their way in the school system and with relevant agencies and institutions of American life. "Civic incorporation" concerns the degree to which immigrants, and the organizations to which they belong, are active in neighborhood and community efforts, their interest in civic affairs, and their participation in the political process. Social incorporation may or may not lead to civic incorporation. But social incorporation may pave the way for greater civic engagement, and civic incorporation suggests growing social incorporation as well.

How might local worship communities further the civic and social incorporation of immigrants? In developing our answer, we draw on various strands of recent thinking about the meaning of associational life for modern democracies. Starting with Peter L. Berger and Richard John Neuhaus's *To Empower People* (1996 [1977]), American social scientists and political pundits began to revive earlier notions about the importance of what Berger and Neuhaus called "mediating structures" in sustaining community life and furthering public purposes. This line of argument soon merged with a new enthusiasm for the power of "civil society" for positive political change, stemming from struggles against authoritarianism in Eastern Europe and Latin America.[1] By the time Robert Putnam published his *Making Democracy Work* (1993), there was a receptive audience for the argument that participation in the diverse associations of civil society contributed to a "virtuous circle" of commitment to norms of reciprocity and civic engagement, social trust, and networks of mutual affection and cooperation, with positive effects for social and political collaboration. Summing up such positive mechanisms of sociality under the heading of "social capital," Putnam (2000) gained wide credence for the notion that associational life and the "social trust" it bred could be prime movers in promoting civic engagement and "making democracy work."

These arguments were not without their critics (see, for example, Foley and Edwards 1997; Portes and Landolt 1996). But they stimulated fresh thinking and research into the ways participation in the institutions of civil society might contribute to civic engagement. While much of the research did not fully support the optimistic formulations of Putnam and his imitators, it has pointed to a variety of ways associational life might shape people's relations with the larger society. At the same time, the notion of civil society was enlisted to think about the contributions of nonprofit organizations and voluntary associations to the functioning of modern democracies.

Theorists have offered increasingly nuanced appraisals of the role of voluntary associations in modern democracies. Nancy Rosenblum (1998) has argued, for example, that freedom of association and the values of pluralism in American society mean that all sorts of groups may proliferate, not all of them conducive to the development of democratic or liberal political norms. Such groups may be important in people's lives, nevertheless, and may play an important role in assuring diversity and pluralism in our society. In *Democracy and Association* (2001), Mark E. Warren elaborates a framework for understanding the differing impacts on democratic practice that different kinds of associations might have. Some sorts of groups may be better at developing the capacities of democratic citizens; others may be best at stimulating public opinion and debate; and still others may be adapted to represent political interest, exert pressure on authorities, and help organize the political process. The most effective sorts of advocacy groups, to take one example, rarely involve their membership in democratic decision-making. Bridge clubs and neighborhood groups may be governed formally or informally in a democratic fashion but have little interest in the larger political system. Associational life thus has myriad effects on democratic practice and values, not all of them congruent (Rosenblum 1998; Warren 2001).

Empirical studies have also underlined differences among kinds of organizations in the sorts of effects they have on individuals' attitudes and behaviors. Dietland Stolle and Thomas Rochon, for example, analyzed data on the membership of a wide variety of associations in the United States and Europe and showed that members of political associations were the most politically active but less likely to show high levels of social trust, trust in institutions, or tolerance. Members of community associations and clubs, by contrast, registered high levels of social trust and norms of reciprocity (Stolle and Rochon 2001). Carla Eastes's careful comparison of two choral groups (2001) demonstrates the subtle ways that organizational differences and leadership style may affect participants' norms and the development of social and civic skills.

Theories of Civic and Social Incorporation

The debate on civil society in the United States thus has pointed to multiple ways that the associations people belong to might have an impact on their participation in the larger society and polity. While many, following Putnam, have focused on social capital (variously understood), others have taken up earlier lines of argument about the importance of civil society in providing formal and informal social services to people. Others have argued that civil society is effectively a forum in which public issues can be developed and debated, so that membership in at least certain sorts of associations promotes civic engagement through dialogue and debate. Still others have noted, along lines also broached by Putnam, that associations may play a role in helping people develop skills and encounter the opportunities necessary for managing other aspects of life, including civic participation. Some point to the expressive role of associations and their role as vehicles for the development of personal and collective identities. Finally, there are those who dwell on the representative functions of civil society organizations as actors in their own right, echoing the work of interest group researchers.

In the analysis that follows, we distinguish three broad lines of argument about the ways participation in churches, mosques, temples and other worship communities might have an impact on the civic incorporation of immigrants. The "social capital argument" holds that a key determinant of civic engagement is the extent to which individuals are immersed in networks characterized by trust, norms of reciprocity, and mutual respect. Citing the observations of Alexis de Tocqueville about the role of associations in American life, exponents of this approach argue that associations nurture civic virtues and encourage civic engagement. They also link individuals and their communities to others, providing both solidarity and resources beyond the immediate confines of the family and integrating people into a larger whole. The "civil society argument" focuses on the role of associations themselves in the larger society. They may provide members with institutional linkages (also a form of social capital) via their own engagement as social service providers or civic actors. Their involvement in the larger society may also provide both incentives and opportunities for community service or political involvement.

The "civic participation model," finally, focuses attention on the role of associational life in training people in skills crucial to political involvement and mobilizing them through face-to-face contact in concrete acts of civic participation. Some sorts of associational involvement appear to be more important than others, proponents of the model argue, by training people in such skills as running meetings, organizing events, public speaking, and contacting public officials. Similarly, some sites may be more likely to put people into contact with civic activists who can recruit them for campaigns or events. And they may self-consciously or un-self-consciously encourage members to think of themselves as a certain kind of person or citizen, with important implications for their involvement in civic or political action.

Each of these approaches has considerable merit. Each illuminates different, sometimes overlapping, ways associations promote civic engagement among Americans, both native-born and immigrant. In the next few pages, we elaborate in more detail on each of these approaches specifically as they apply to immigrants and to worship communities. In each case, we will formulate broad propositions derived from these bodies of theory to guide our own exploration of the evidence. These propositions are not hypotheses but theoretically grounded possibilities describing how worship communities might contribute to the civic and social incorporation of immigrants. As we shall see, in practice, worship communities, like the larger civil society of which they are a part, differ significantly among themselves in the degree to which they have assumed the possible roles the theorists have laid out for them. In the final section, we will develop an account of the variables most likely to explain such differences and offer some hypotheses to be tested as we explore the data.

The Social Capital Argument

While the notion of social capital has gained considerable cachet, there is little agreement over precisely what the term refers to. For some researchers, social capital includes any feature of social life that might facilitate common action, from institutions and networks to habits of cooperation and reciprocity to trust (Coleman 1988). Robert Putnam and others have emphasized the socially constructive features of social capital in this sense (Putnam 2000). Others point out that cooperation and reciprocity may be turned to socially destructive as well as good purposes (Portes and Landolt 1996). Some researchers and theorists argue, moreover, that this widely accepted notion of social capital is a grab bag of phenomena that are not tightly related to one another. Newton, for example, shows that social trust bears little relationship to outcomes generally associated with social capital (1999).

For the sake of conceptual clarity, we adopt the narrower definition of social capital first proposed by Pierre Bourdieu, who defined it as the actual and potential resources available to individuals by virtue of their participation in social networks (Bourdieu 1986, 248–49; see also Foley, Edwards, and Diani 2001; Lin 2001). The central proposition of the social capital argument for our purposes may be summarized as follows: *Local worship communities can furnish valuable opportunities for immigrants to broaden their circle of acquaintance, providing resources of support, mutual aid, and access to jobs and other benefits. Such "social capital" embedded in local worship communities contributes primarily to social incorporation, but it may also have political implications.*

How might local worship communities provide social capital in this sense for their members? First, membership in local worship communities often stems from already existing ties based on family, friendship, and local community. Worship communities may embody and strengthen these ties. Second, the community itself may develop social networks over and above those that members bring with them. Formal and informal social gatherings, more formalized study and prayer groups, work teams, and governance structures all provide people with new avenues to forge ties and take advantage of the moral and material support that others in the community can offer. Third, local worship communities are sometimes actively linked to other, similar communities, both within their own religious tradition and beyond it. Religious events, rallies, conventions, and summer camps provide opportunities for members of different communities to get to know one another and establish ties. In some instances, such contacts enable members to reach beyond their own neighborhood, class, ethnic or racial group to others with whom they share common religious beliefs and commitments. Finally, local worship communities often maintain ties to second-order religious organizations such as denominations and associations of churches. They may also have connections with local social service agencies and local and national advocacy organizations. These sorts of connections permit at least some members of the community access to a wider world of service, work, and outlook.

The last three sorts of ties are what some researchers in the social capital literature refer to as "bridging social capital." "Bridging" social capital links people of diverse backgrounds, communities, and institutions and thus provides them with resources and opportunities they might not have had within the confines of their own narrow circles. "Bonding" social capital, on the other hand, is characteristic of tightly knit communities, where members know one another well and can provide moral and material supports drawn from their own resources (Saegert, Thompson, and Warren 2001). But the notion of social "capital" implies that we might assign values to the different sorts of social ties (and the resources they give people access to) that people enjoy in a given social setting. One line of research on social networks suggests that social ties are more valuable the more varied and dispersed they are (Burt 1992; Granovetter 1974). All things being equal, individuals with ties to people from a variety of social classes, professions, ethnic groups, and so on will enjoy more opportunities than those whose ties are narrowly confined to people of their own race, class, religion, and gender. Alejandro Portes, on the other hand, argues that the stronger and denser the ties among members of immigrant communities, the greater the ability of their children to resist what he calls "downward assimilation," the pressure to conform to peer cultures that might disparage success in school and work, and the greater the likelihood that they will succeed in the larger society (1995, 256–62).

The possible contradiction might be resolved if we consider the distinction between the two sorts of social capital, each important in its own way. In poor communities—including poor worship communities—bonding social capital may give individuals little in the way of material support or direct opportunity for advancement; it might nevertheless provide the guidance and motivation young people need to take advantage of the slim opportunities available and thus move ahead in American society, as Portes argues. But, Portes points out, ethnic communities are often not uniformly poor. Ethnic entrepreneurs and well-educated professionals may mix freely in some communities with day laborers with only a primary education. Sharing common national or ethnic origins, language, and sometimes religion, individuals of various social strata may establish ties across class and educational divides that would be much more significant in the larger society. Here "bonding" facilitates "bridging."

We would expect local worship communities to be relatively rich sources of bonding social capital, especially those where social ties are enriched and reinforced through regular interaction in a multitude of activities. What sorts of resources such social capital represents, of course, will depend upon the composition of the community. A community that is diverse in income levels and occupational niches would provide greater potential resources to members than a uniformly poor community. This is the essence of Portes's arguments for the superior economic and social benefits of an "ethnic enclave economy" and a strong ethnic community (Portes 1995; Portes and Rumbaut 1996). A community with a preponderance of high-income members will be still richer in social capital, if the social networks genuinely give all members access to one another. What is true for financial resources, of course, applies as well to others sorts of resources. In recent research on social networks, the most commonly cited other sort of resource is job opportunities. But social ties developed within a worship community may also enable immigrants to resolve legal problems, help their children find their way through the school system, or find outlets for their own civic energies.

Worship communities that enjoy ties to the larger society, moreover, are likely to provide additional links and resources to their members, and often to their neighbors as well, through social services and advocacy activities. In this case, bridging social capital often extends beyond the ethnic and religious community to other groups and organizations in society. Some worship communities, for example, maintain regular relations with certain social service agencies, referring members and others to these agencies for specialized services. Worship communities that enjoy this sort of bridging social capital, accordingly, could be expected to help their members deal with legal problems, achieve citizenship, learn English, acquire job skills, cope with school systems, do their taxes, or handle any one of the dozens of tasks and responsibilities that come with life in a new society.

Social services are more than just support for survival in a new land. They also help integrate immigrants into society. Achieving proper documentation or citizenship is an important step in social and civic incorporation. So is learning English, gaining skills for advancement, and learning how to deal with the various institutions of American society. Even gaining access to basic necessities like food, clothing, and medical care arguably contributes to the process of incorporation. Cecilia Menjívar, for example, notes (2000) that the Salvadoran women in her study enjoyed richer contacts with the wider community than the men, thanks to their contacts with social service agencies. As intermediaries for such contacts, worship communities can be important sources of bridging social capital for immigrants and agents, in this respect, of their social and civic incorporation.

Not all worship communities enjoy the diversity, the richness of ties to other organizations, or the range of social services that these examples suggest, just as some provide relatively little in the way of bonding social capital. In fact, we encountered significant and systematic variation among the worship communities we studied in these respects. Later in this chapter, we develop a set of explanatory variables that can help us account for such variation.

We should note the incompleteness of the social capital argument. Though the sorts of social ties that worship communities may provide can facilitate social and civic incorporation, the notion of social capital gives us little purchase on the specifics of incorporation. Civic incorporation, in particular, appears to be only an accidental by-product of the sorts of variables considered in the social capital argument. We need to specify more carefully, then, the ways the social capital encountered in worship communities might contribute to civic incorporation. Such communities might link members to others outside the community through joint worship services and participation in ecumenical events and organizations. It might provide them with contact with community organizations, civic associations, and public officials. And it might encourage volunteering and social service in venues and with groups not directly affiliated with the community. Such possibilities, however, are better theorized in the "civil society argument"—to which we now turn.

The Civil Society Argument

The last two or three decades have seen the revival of the notion of "civil society" first developed as a way of describing the increasingly complex societies of eighteenth-century Europe. Though the term has assumed many meanings in recent debates, we focus here on one central argument, namely, that voluntary associations of all sorts contribute to the vitality of modern democracies as civic actors, through their own contributions to society and their direct participation in civic affairs. Immigrants who take part in such associations, we would argue, benefit from the incorporating effects not just of the social capital they find embodied there, the civic skills they acquire, and the mobilizing work of individuals within those organizations—they are incorporated, as well, as members of an organization that plays a significant role in the larger community. Applied to worship communities, the central proposition of the civil society argument is this: *Local worship communities may themselves play an important role in local, national, or international efforts, representing immigrants in civil society, carrying out public works on their behalf, and advocating for them or their causes. In doing so, they provide significant opportunities for members of those communities to become active in local civic life, and they contribute to their identities as civic actors.*

Worship communities occupy roles in the larger society in a number of ways. Some host child care centers, scouts, clinics, twelve-step groups, athletic clubs, and other community and social service groups and organizations. Even if hosted organizations pay a modest rent, the local worship community is playing an important role in providing "free spaces" for community activities (Evans and Boyte 1986). Worship communities may also partner with agencies performing social services for the needy in other parts of their region, the nation, or abroad. Besides missionary activities of all sorts, local worship communities may provide funds, in-kind donations and volunteers to homeless shelters, soup kitchens, housing programs, substance abuse programs, and other services to the needy. They may contribute to local or national-level organizations and campaigns to address pressing social problems of all sorts. They may join as "sister parishes" with needy worship communities in other countries or contribute to programs to aid refugees, feed the hungry, or promote development abroad. This sort of civic and charitable activity involves lay people directly as civic actors and provides some of the training in civic skills and mobilization stressed by the civic participation model (discussed later). Even where the worship community facilitates continued immersion in the affairs of the home country, such transnational ties can ultimately contribute to greater participation in this country on behalf of homeland causes (Basch, Schiller, and Blanc 1994; Levitt 2001, 143–51).

Worship communities may also assume civic roles through direct participation in the public sphere. Pastors and other religious leaders frequently assume leading roles in community affairs, with or without the active coparticipation of the broader membership of the worship community.[2] In some cases, they become prominent spokespersons for their immigrant or ethnic causes. Pastors and lay people may play roles as representatives of the worship community in interfaith coalitions and on civic boards and task forces, intervene with government officials on issues of concern, and interact with the media. Some worship communities are politically active, inviting local and national officials to speak, sponsoring candidate forums, or welcoming favored candidates to the pulpit, even taking stands in elections. Others eschew electoral activism but play an active civic role. They may officially sponsor or cosponsor public events, social service initiatives, community organizing campaigns, marches or demonstrations, and a host of other efforts. Prominent members may play important roles in founding and directing community associations and social service agencies. The worship community may support such efforts through financial contributions and volunteer efforts, or it may provide volunteers and donations on a regular basis to faith-based organizations outside their immediate purview. In these ways, the worship community contributes to the larger society, incorporating its members directly and indirectly into American civil society through its own institutional presence as a civic actor and by giving members opportunities to assume roles in the activities it supports.

Some such efforts are often strategic: religious and lay leaders sometimes decide that the best course for the acceptance of their people by the larger society is through their own positive collaboration in civic affairs. In other cases, the choice is a personal one on the part of a pastor or lay leader, often grounded in an interpretation of religious doctrine that stresses community service or social justice. In either case, the effect on individuals within the worship community will be indirect, except to the degree that such participation becomes a matter of community consciousness and choice or personal involvement. But worship communities that participate in significant ways in social service delivery, care for the needy, or civic affairs can shape members' conceptions of themselves as civic actors. This impact, however, is captured better by our third approach, the civic participation model.

The Civic Participation Model

In their study of the bases of civic participation in American life, Sidney Verba, Kay Lehman Schlozman, and Henry E. Brady (1995) note that membership in a local congregation provides citizens with opportunities to develop such "civic skills" as public speaking, leadership, organizing meetings, and writing letters. For instance, 32 percent of their respondents who were church members reported attending a meeting where decisions were made, 17 percent said they had planned such a meeting, and 18 percent said they had made a speech or a presentation. Verba, Schlozman, and Brady go on to show that religious participation is especially important for poor and minority citizens, since they are about as likely to be church members as their better-off counterparts but are substantially less likely to learn civic skills through higher education, on the job, or in other voluntary associational settings. Thus, they conclude, local worship communities play the role of the "great equalizers" in preparing citizens for civic involvement. These observations provide the basis for the first proposition of what we call the civic participation model, an expanded version of Verba, Schlozman, and Brady's own model: *Local worship communities help build civic skills. They provide direct and indirect training in such basic skills of citizenship as organizing and leading a meeting, raising funds for specific causes, writing letters to public officials, and representing others in a meeting or public assembly.*

The Verba, Schlozman, and Brady model of civic participation goes beyond many studies of political participation in paying attention to a broad array of ways in which citizens play a role in the political life of the country:

> working in and contributing to electoral campaigns and organizations; contacting government officials; attending protests, marches or demonstrations; working informally with others to solve some community problem; serving without pay on local elected or appointed boards; being active politically through the intermediation of voluntary associations; and contributing money to political causes in response to mail solicitations (1995, 42)

are some of the political acts they cite. They point in particular to the role of specific sorts of organizational venues—churches, unions, and the workplace—in teaching civic skills; encouraging volunteering; and introducing participants to networks through which they may be recruited to overt political acts, from voting to joining a demonstration. Only a minority of local worship communities, of course, actively promote political involvement. But even the most apolitical may provide ample opportunities for acquiring leadership, public speaking, organizational, and other skills relevant to civic involvement. Unions and the workplace may provide more such opportunities, but local worship communities do so more reliably for a more varied number of Americans.

Mark E. Warren carries this line of analysis further. He argues that de Tocqueville's emphasis on the importance of associations for training citizens in the skills and dispositions of citizenship, while generally well founded, is too broad to be true in all cases, for all associations. Instead, he develops a list of five sorts of "democratic effects" that different sorts of associations might have on participants: efficacy; information; political skills; civic virtues; and critical thinking (2001, 70–77). "Efficacy" is the term often used to describe an individual's sense that he or she is capable of making a difference. It can be developed, presumably, by experiences that instill confidence, assertiveness, and active participation—especially where those experiences do, in fact, lead to success. Citizens need to be informed in order to act, as well as having a sense that they can make a difference. Some associational venues are better than others at providing participants with the basic information of citizenship, keeping them up on public affairs, or filling them in on specific issues of public interest. Warren's list of political skills, moreover, goes further than that of Verba, Schlozman, and Brady to include "speaking and self-presentation, negotiation and bargaining, developing coalitions and creating new solutions to problems, learning when and how to compromise, as well as recognizing when one is being manipulated, pressured, or threatened" (72). Associations that deal regularly with problems of collective action—of mobilizing people to work together at the local level—are more likely to develop such skills, Warren reasons, than those focused on influencing distant centers of power or organized hierarchically around a charismatic leader who is reluctant to delegate or negotiate power.

The list of civic virtues that has been proposed over the centuries is long and controverted. Nevertheless, it can help guide our look at the role of worship communities in civic incorporation. Warren focuses on specifically moral and attitudinal effects that might contribute to support for norms of democratic process and equity. This may be too narrow a restriction, since not all of civic life is democratic, and much of it involves group action on behalf of narrowly conceived group interests. But we might agree that such effects of associational life as trust and norms of reciprocity (promoting cooperative action), tolerance and its reciprocal, self-respect, and a willingness to work with others beyond one's narrow group are all important building blocks of civic virtue. Finally, Warren notes: "One can feel effective, have information, possess political skills, relate to others with reciprocity and trust, and *still* fail to reflect on one's own interests and commitments and their relationship to those of others" (2001, 75). Critical skills, Warren argues, are central to democratic citizenship. Again, this largely normative position may be too narrow for our purposes, since much that goes into everyday politics, even in democratic systems, relies more on the mobilization of unquestioning supporters and bargaining among narrow interests than on deliberation based in critical thinking. Nevertheless, civic incorporation beyond unquestioning participation requires a degree of critical thinking to arouse an individual's interest in civic questions and guide judgment on alternative solutions.

In the development of both civic skills and critical thinking, associations— and worship communities—can be expected to differ substantially among themselves. Those that promote member involvement in the daily life of the organization, engage a broad number of people in governance, and sustain democratic practices in at least part of their organizational life will contribute more than those governed by a single, charismatic leader or a permanent, board-selected staff whose daily practice requires little member involvement. As we shall see, specific forms of governance differ markedly among religious traditions, but actual practice may differ from official polity as well. The degree of lay involvement in the day-to-day life of a worship community and in its worship services also differs markedly across traditions and from community to community within a single religious tradition. Some worship communities thus fit the civic participation model of Verba and colleagues better than others. Again, we will come back to the question of how such variation might best be explained below.

Worship communities are also frequently sites for reflecting on the social and political realities of the day. Warren observes that associations whose operations stand at a distance from politics and markets are most likely to be venues where participants encounter information on public matters not compromised by power or money interests (2001, 78). Such organizations are more likely to inform a diverse public debate and to motivate members to critically evaluate political claims. Worship communities clearly meet Warren's basic criteria. Notice that critical thinking may arise from a sense of distance from the larger society; it need not be cultivated within the community for use against the basic premises of the community. Indeed, critical reflection on the larger society is often accompanied by astonishing confidence about one's own in-group. But dissent and critical reflection are quintessential components of the American system in our official and quasi-official self-portrait. As Laurence Moore observes, religious and ethnic difference have frequently been the distinctive ways in which diverse people have become Americans (1986). And, Huntington's polemics notwithstanding, recent scholars of ethnicity have generally sided with Andrew Greeley in arguing that ethnic feeling is "not a way of withdrawing from the rest of society so much as an institution for dealing oneself into it" (1977, 21). Worship communities that nurture and encourage a sense of religious or ethnic difference create the basis for critical distance, even if the thinking that accompanies it embodies what Moore calls "a sense of antagonistic culture" (xi).

We might formulate these observations as a second broad proposition: *Local worship communities help immigrants deal with questions of ethnic or religious identity. They may help forge or reinforce such identities, or they may encourage their subordination in pursuit of some ideal of confraternity. They may strengthen them or modulate them. In either case, the sense of identity developed in and through common worship may encourage immigrant participation in the larger polity.* Worship communities can play a pivotal role in the formation of communally based ethnicity, because they provide what many immigrant groups today lack—a venue where members of the group come together on a regular basis, where their native language is the norm, and where institutional structures provide opportunities for members of the group to play a role and even assume leadership. At the same time, religion makes its own identity claims. Religious beliefs and practices define the boundaries of a religious community much more rigorously, Richard Alba notes, than can be the case for most ethnic communities in contemporary America: "Who can say what beliefs or practices constitute being Irish or Polish?" (1990, 305). The universalism of religious claims, on the other hand, contrasts sharply with the exclusivity of national and ethnic ones, and the two are often in tension.

Worship communities may thus assume part of the burden of shaping and reinforcing ethnic identities as immigrants confront the experience of adapting to a new world, but they also shape that identity in accordance with their own needs and logic. The identities that immigrants assume upon coming to the United States are products of both home country experience and reception (Waters 1996). Guatemalan Indians in the United States, for example, may not speak Spanish and may not in any case feel comfortable as part of a larger Guatemalan, Central American, or Latin American community, though they are treated as "Hispanics" on all sides. Because of their small numbers, and despite linguistic differences among migrants from diverse indigenous communities, they may find it useful to adopt the recent fiction of a "Mayan" identity hammered out in the context of civil war in their country of origin (Warren 1998; Wellmeier 1998).

Religious identities are similarly constructed and arguably more voluntary in character than ethnic ones. Nevertheless, members of immigrant communities may find their religious choices severely constrained by the ways fellow immigrants interpret the type of religious expression most representative of their common ethnic identity. Mexican Protestants can experience considerable isolation among those who feel that veneration of the Virgin of Guadalupe is essential to being "Mexican." Local venerations and practices can come to dominate a given parish even among Catholics, defining narrowly what it means to be a "Filipino" or "Vietnamese" or "Hispanic" Catholic.

Collective identities, both religious and ethnic, have political salience to the degree they shape people's perceptions of their relations and obligations to the larger society. The orientation that collective identities provide may stress the distinctiveness of the collectivity or emphasize its commonality with others outside the circle of the group. It may encourage engagement under

certain circumstances, or be utilized as a protective measure, closing off involvement with a world apprised as dangerous. Religious and ethnic identities
may provide a basis of in-group solidarity on which to build multireligious
and multiethnic coalitions; or they may block such cooperation.[3]

In some cases, homeland causes become the basis for greater involvement in local affairs and U.S. national politics, as immigrant groups mobilize
through their worship communities to support causes back home or to influence U.S. policy toward the homeland. Recent immigrants are no different
in this respect from immigrants in the past, many of whom gained a distinctive
sense of ethnic identity, and a distinctive place in American politics, through
mobilization on behalf of their country of origin (Conzen et al. 1992). Ethnic
identity in the American context thus cannot be equated in any straightforward
way with separateness, even where it depends upon separate institutions like
ethnic religious communities or associations. As Fenggang Yang remarks, "for
many contemporary immigrants becoming American and retaining ethnic
identity are simultaneous and cohesive processes" (Yang 1999, 17). Separate
institutions set immigrants apart from others, but they may also provide a
springboard for incorporation as civic actors.

One mechanism by which they do so is by giving immigrants a sense that
they are members of a collectivity whose voice can count. Recent studies have
emphasized that low levels of immigrant political participation are frequently
overcome where immigrant groups enjoy sufficient numbers to hope to play a
political role in their communities and where there has been explicit mobilization of immigrants to achieve citizenship and exercise their voting rights
(DeSipio 1996; Leighley 2001). Local, ethnically identified worship communities can further a sense of immigrant political potential, quite apart from any
explicit attempt to address political issues, insofar as they help immigrants see
themselves as part of a significant element in American society, distinguished
by immigrant, religious, ethnic, or racial status. A few local worship communities will encourage and build upon such a sense of empowerment and actively
promote citizenship, voting, and direct political action on behalf of this or that
cause. More common are those worship communities that provide immigrants
with citizenship preparation classes or encourage them to become engaged in
their communities through volunteering and civic activism, without actively
promoting one or another political position. While both stances are relatively
rare, they are not uncommon, and where they occur they can be important
contributions to the civic incorporation of immigrants.

Whether and to what extent an immigrant's sense of difference becomes
mobilized civically and politically, of course, depends on diverse circumstances,
including, most immediately, the character of religious and lay leadership

within the community. A final proposition of the civic participation model holds that *local worship communities may promote civic incorporation by actively mobilizing their members for service to the community, participation in public meetings and demonstrations, or voting.* Churches, mosques, temples, and other worship communities frequently provide opportunities for volunteering, often encourage volunteer service to the larger community, and sometimes promote the political involvement of their members. This "mobilizational" role is an important one, according to Verba and his colleagues (see also Rosenstone and Hansen 1993), because most civic participation comes about thanks to a personal contact who encourages or cajoles a friend, family member, or acquaintance to take some action. The local worship community is one important setting where this may take place. This is especially the case where members enjoy relatively rich social ties, thanks to Sunday morning social hours, small group organizations where members meet face-to-face on a regular basis, or any of a host of other activities frequently found in worship communities. Social networks can thus become important networks for mobilization. But civic and political motivation also responds to the religious commitments of the community and its leadership. As we shall see, some religious traditions focus exclusively on the religious life of their adherents and the worship they owe the deity. Others have a more decided place for community service, civic engagement, and even political action in their ethical canon. Leadership may play a decisive role in shaping a community's character in this respect, and some of the variation we will encounter has to be attributed to the efforts of dedicated leaders. But we will need a more systematic account of the sources of variation in order to explain the differences among worship communities in their role in the civic and social incorporation of immigrants. We take up that task in the remaining part of this chapter and, as we do so, give some taste of the findings that follow in more detail in later chapters.

Explaining Variation

Not all worship communities are rich in social capital. Some provide few opportunities for participants to acquire civic skills or be mobilized as volunteers or politically active members of society. Few churches, mosques, or temples play leading roles in civic affairs, and fewer still are politically engaged. How do we propose to account for the considerable diversity we will encounter? How salient are differences in national origin or religious tradition? To what degree does leadership and the theological and strategic proclivity of individual leaders explain the differences that interest us?

In looking for explanations, we shall certainly have recourse to idiosyncratic features such as individual leadership style or inclination. But we also think we can discern in the often systematic variation among worship communities more general sources of explanation. In the following pages we develop three major sets of variables. First, following recent work on immigrant adaptation, we stress the *circumstances of migration and reception* experienced by particular immigrant groups. Second, we look to differences in *organizational culture* among worship communities. Finally, we consider the character of the *religious tradition*, particularly as it influences organizational culture and the choices leaders make in shaping their communities. Over against these more general explanatory variables, we will find, national origins and culture play relatively little role. Other variables such as size of the worship community or access to resources turn out to be closely correlated with organizational culture, religious tradition, and circumstances of reception and will play a role in the context of those more theoretically grounded variables.

Circumstances of Migration and Reception

Scholars of immigration have increasingly adopted an "interactive model" to account for aspects of immigrant adaptation in the United States. In their work on ethnic entrepreneurs, Waldinger, Aldrich, and Ward (1990) first used this term to characterize an approach that took into consideration the interaction between the structure of opportunities immigrants faced and characteristics of the group itself. Alejandro Portes and his colleagues have generalized this approach to account for a wider range of outcomes. These scholars point out that some immigrant groups are distinguished by the socioeconomic characteristics of the group itself. Some immigrant populations, most notably Mexicans and Central Americans, are overwhelmingly drawn from the poorer strata of their home societies, with low levels of education and job skills the prevailing pattern among them. Other groups are dominated by highly trained professionals, recruited by firms that guarantee them easy entry into middle-class and upper-middle-class status once in the United States. Indian migrants exemplify this profile, but so do Chinese immigrants from Taiwan and Hong Kong. Still other groups, such as Koreans and many Africans and Chinese, typically bring with them the wherewithal and the skills to start life in the United States as entrepreneurs and small proprietors. Differences in experience, attitude, and human capital have profound implications for the adaptation of immigrant communities in the United States.

At the same time, Portes points out, the context of reception can have a profound impact on chances for success in the United States. Portes and

Rumbaut identify three such contexts: the policies of the government, labor market conditions, and characteristics of the immigrant ethnic communities that newcomers are joining (1996, 83–93). Government has attempted to regulate immigration with increasing rigor over the last several decades, but this has been accompanied by the opening of a variety of channels for legal immigration for migrants from around the world. Where the basic conditions for legal immigration are fulfilled, government policy can be considered neutral. In the case of refugees approved by federal authorities, the government has actively facilitated immigration and resettlement, expending considerable resources in providing for newcomers and integrating them into American society. In other cases, notably that of most of the Central American refugees in the 1980s, the government refused recognition of refugee status and treated newcomers from the region with the same hostility as other undocumented immigrants. Lack of documentation adds to the precariousness of life for many immigrants from Mexico and Central America, who already face labor market discrimination and limited prospects in the low-wage jobs to which they have access.

Labor market conditions vary enormously among immigrant groups, in part thanks to the differences in human capital already alluded to, in part due to the privileges accorded certain professional categories of workers in immigration law. But the character of local labor markets also must be taken into account. In some regions, jobs may still be available in unionized or unionizable manufacturing and processing operations, with the potential for significant wage gains. Others areas, including the Washington, D.C., area, have lost their industrial base or never had one and are currently characterized by dual labor markets, with a high-wage technology-based sector on the one side and a low-wage service sector on the other, each drawing on different populations for the bulk of their workers. Entrepreneurial opportunities also vary from region to region, affecting possibilities for immigrant entrepreneurs (Light and Gold 2000, 12). Labor markets may also be skewed by patterns of discrimination and channeling that open some opportunities to certain immigrant groups while closing others. Discrimination may mean that certain groups are confined to low-wage menial labor, while members of other groups are readily promoted and given managerial responsibilities. Channeling occurs when immigrants of one nationality gain a foothold in a particular job category or workplace and bring along others as openings occur. The phenomenon is so common that it has been closely identified with "chain migration" to selected communities and labor markets in the United States. As a result, widespread notions about certain nationalities occupying distinctive economic niches are well founded in fact (Waldinger and Der-Martirosian 2001).

Finally, Portes and Rumbaut argue, the character of the ethnic community where immigrants settle may have a profound impact on their adaptation. In some cases, immigrants settle where no such coethnic community exists. Where discrimination is not an issue, they may integrate as readily and rapidly as they are able. Where discrimination is an issue, they may create their own niche as small business owners or find themselves merged with other oppressed minorities. In other cases, an ethnic community exists but provides access mainly to the sort of low-wage jobs already occupied by members of the community. The community itself may provide moral and cultural support but little in the way of resources or opportunities for advancement. Without institutions and enterprises of its own, it may not be able to counter the downward pull of equally poor neighbors on the second generation (Portes 1995). A more diverse ethnic community, on the other hand, can provide opportunities for economic advancement to adults and moral support and sanction for youth, reinforcing ethnic ties while promoting the sorts of attitudes and behaviors necessary for achievement in school and the workplace (Portes 1995; Zhou and Bankston 1998).

How might these factors apply to our questions? First, Portes's work underlines the importance of the economic condition of immigrant groups in trying to understand the ways their worship communities differ in their contributions to civic incorporation. Poorer groups are simply less likely to enjoy the level of social capital and the diversity of contacts and resources of better-off immigrant populations. On the other hand, being more needy, they are more likely to participate in worship communities that seek informal and formal means to address those needs. Such worship communities are less likely to play a role as civic actors in ministering to the needs of people outside their own members and neighborhoods, but they may be more involved in advocacy on behalf of the immigrant population they serve and are more likely to forge relationship with social service agencies and advocacy groups also serving that population. More privileged immigrant groups and those with a significant mixture of poor and well-off, well-educated and less well educated are likely to worship in communities that are themselves diverse, thus richer in social capital and in resources generally. These worship communities are also more likely to play a role in the larger society, primarily through contributions to social services for the needy elsewhere. They may also play advocacy roles, particularly where they see themselves as victims of discrimination or where they hope to influence U.S. policy toward their homelands.

The character of the ethnic community can also be expected to have an influence on characteristics of worship communities. Where ethnic communities are small and scattered, immigrants from those backgrounds are likely to seek communion with others outside their own ethnic group. Other forms of identity, such as religion, race, or regional origin will tend to define these worship communities. Thus Muslims from countries that have sent few immigrants to the United States and who thus find few coethnics in their new surroundings can be expected to worship together with other Muslims from around the world. Hispanics from Honduras and Peru and Argentina will seek out fellow Hispanics, even if that means they are minorities in Salvadoran or Mexican-dominated churches, or they may integrate themselves into Anglo-dominant worship communities if they command enough English to feel comfortable doing so. Africans whose ethnic or national group is poorly represented in an area will worship with African Americans or become part of multicultural worship communities alongside immigrants from other parts of Africa and the Caribbean. Where an immigrant group enjoys a sufficiently large community of coethnics, on the other hand, we can expect to find ethnic worship communities to emerge as part of that community.

In diverse and integrated ethnic communities, we can expect, following Portes, that ethnic worship communities will usually include both long-settled immigrants and newcomers, as well as growing numbers of the second generation. These more settled communities can be expected to enjoy more resources and a greater diversity of ties outside the community. Poorer, but still large, ethnic groups may find that worship communities are important vehicles for solidarity and social support; but unless these worship communities can draw on richer sources of social capital outside the immediate ethnic group, they are likely to remain poor themselves, with few material benefits to offer their members. Whether uniformly poor or more diverse, however, ethnic groups may be religiously divided. This may mean that one or another religious group remains isolated from the larger ethnic community, with insular ties to coreligionists but few of the sorts of connections to the larger society we would expect with older and better integrated ethnic communities. Or both communities may have such ties, but quite isolated from one another.

This last observation, however, suggests that religion sometimes trumps ethnicity and national origin, even among relatively large immigrant groups, so that newcomers' conception of themselves as immigrants or as Americans may be first in religious terms and second in ethnic ones. Such expressions as "Irish Catholic" or "Korean Buddhist" capture this phenomenon perfectly. Social and civic identity, then, may depend crucially on religious tradition. But this, too, is partly a matter of the context of reception. Most Koreans, whether or not they were Christians in their homeland, now find themselves in an overwhelmingly Protestant ethnic group. Most immigrants from Latin America, though raised Catholic, reside in dioceses that are struggling to provide enough

Spanish masses and Spanish-speaking priests to serve the community. They also encounter eager evangelizers ready and willing to incorporate them into evangelical, Pentecostal, Mormon, Jehovah's Witnesses, or Seventh-Day Adventist congregations. Koreans convert and join churches in astounding numbers. Hispanics are increasingly divided. Both contexts are self-reinforcing. And both help shape the character of the worship communities that emerge and their relations with coethnics of other religions.

Organizational Culture

Local worship communities differ tremendously in the way they are organized and governed, the character of lay participation in both worship and the everyday life of the community, and the sorts of activities they carry on. One way of grasping these differences, and of explaining their systematic character, is through the typology of "congregational models" developed by Penny Edgell Becker to characterize the disparate "organizational cultures" of local worship communities (Becker 1998, 1999). Some worship communities, Becker found—through in-depth ethnographic research on 23 Protestant, Catholic, and Jewish worship communities—are largely "houses of worship" whose primary focus is on worship and religious education and where individuals or families come and go with little or no interaction with others. Others see themselves as a "family" for their members, a source of intimate connections, stressing commonality among them, with little stress on outreach. Such "family"-style worship communities tend to be small, and they put their energies into worship, religious education, and sociability within the local religious "family." Those that strive to create "community" for their members are generally larger, more diverse in interests, and more committed to providing niches for the expression of particular interests among their members. Creating community is a self-conscious effort, in part because of the larger size of the worship community, but in part because of the groups' emphasis on responding to the diverse needs and interests of members. Despite the lack of intimacy at the level of the larger worship community, members tend to find personal satisfaction in committee work or smaller faith groups within the congregation. Finally, there are worship communities that carve out a place for themselves as moral or civic leaders in their city or county or even state. We will call these "civic leader" worship communities. Here the pastor often assumes the key role in taking stands on social and political issues; but the worship community as a whole backs such activism, sending representatives to public meetings, organizing forums and opportunities for public figures to speak, and so on.

Becker bases her classification largely on self-description, but she finds that certain features go together in each of her categories and that the categories predict distinctive sorts of conflict and patterns of conflict resolution among worship communities. "Family" congregations, for example, "focus on three core tasks: worship, religious education, and providing a close and family-like place for members. These three things are the only ones mentioned consistently in bulletins, newsletter, and promotional materials. They also are the only three things that people identify as things the congregation does well" (1999, 89). In keeping with their family-like ethos, they tend to "suppress disagreement and avoid debate on political or social issues" or even doctrinal controversies (86). Conflict tends to revolve around "control of things that have become valued in their own right by lay members who have great feelings of ownership of the congregations" and result in often acrimonious interpersonal divisions, sometimes splitting the congregation (93–94). "Community" congregations actively engage in "community-building" efforts among the membership. In Becker's words, "at the heart of the community model is the commitment to balance caring for each member's needs with exploring what stands to take on potentially divisive moral, social, and political issues" (103). Conflict is frequent, but centers on issues, not personalities, and is often resolved through long processes of consensus-seeking. Such congregations take on a wide variety of tasks, with significant lay involvement at all levels, but the emphasis is on the life of the worship community and personal involvement, not civic activism. That sort of orientation is reserved for the "leader congregation."

We encountered Becker's discussion too late to incorporate a search for similar self-descriptions in our ethnographic studies or survey questions, but indicators of Becker's typology can be read off our data. In some respects, Becker's typology is simply a way to classify many of the differences we are attempting to explain. But to the extent that it helps us explain persistent patterns, "organizational culture" is an important variable. As a way of organizing a worship community with sticking power over time, it is clearly an independent variable for our purposes. At the same time, it would be worthwhile to be able to explain how this or that organizational culture came to dominate in a particular worship community. Becker finds that official measures of "church polity," that is, the constitutional arrangements that determine how worship communities are organized and governed, do not correlate well with organizational culture. As we shall see, Catholic parishes, which are officially structured as hierarchical organizations with a primary mission of worship (administering the sacraments) and religious education, may sometimes look more like Becker's "community" model than a "house of worship." They may even fit the profile of a "civic leader" worship community. This means that religious tradition, including preferred forms of organization, might explain general tendencies among worship communities in a given tradition but cannot account for significant variations. As we will see, religious and lay leadership choices often shape organizational cultures in unexpected ways, and our explanatory frame will have to remain open to the role of such agents; but, we argue later, in many cases leaders draw on alternative interpretations and practices embedded in the religious tradition to justify innovation.

Each of these models of organizational culture has implications for the role of worship communities in contributing to civic incorporation. In regard to social capital, a "family"-style worship community is much more likely to provide intimate ties and supports for its members than a "house of worship" or even a "civic leader" congregation. Ties may be looser but richer in terms of diversity of resources within a "community"-style worship community than in the more homogeneous social setting of the family-style community. The civic leader congregation might be expected to provide greater and richer bridging social capital, thanks to its efforts to engage with the larger community.

The civic leader worship community, by definition, is one that plays a role in the larger society as a civic actor, but community-style congregations can also be expected to cultivate linkages outside the worship community itself and may engage the larger society through representation in civic action efforts, on the boards of interfaith organizations and social service agencies, and in relatively long-term relations with a variety of other civic actors and community agencies. Both sorts of worship communities may take up ethnic or home country causes in local and national forums and initiatives. Family-style worship communities are less likely to play these sorts of roles, not only because of their smaller size but also because of their focus on the religious and social life of their own members. The house of worship community's overwhelming focus on worship and religious education, coupled with the relatively loose ties among members and infrequent opportunities for joint action, mean that this sort of worship community, too, is unlikely to play a civic actor role.

Civic leader, community-style, and family-style worship communities may all contribute to the development of civic skills among their members, though with differing scope and implication in each case. Civic leader worship communities may involve the membership only peripherally, particularly where a charismatic leader dominates the community's presence on the public stage. But they may also provide important opportunities for at least some members of the community to participate in civic affairs and may develop a sense of civic engagement and empowerment even on the part of members who are relatively inactive. Where they also sponsor a broad range of programs on their own or in conjunction with others and draw upon volunteers from the community to do so, they may train members in a wide range of skills important to civic life. They can also be important vehicles for mobilizing people, both as representatives of the community and on behalf of the programs, causes, or candidates they espouse.

Community-style groups characteristically sponsor a range of activities with heavy participation from members. The emphasis on community also spills over into worship services, where lay people may be quite involved. Leadership development, organizing, negotiating, and bargaining may all be constant parts of the worship community's regular life. Such communities also typically mobilize members for volunteer work, both within the community and in activities hosted, sponsored, or supported by the community. They may also be important arenas for political mobilization around causes or candidates of particular interest to members.

Family-style congregations are likely to depend heavily on lay participation for their daily functioning. Lay participation in the worship service may instill confidence, nurture public speaking skills, and build leadership. Members may gain skills in organizing events, administering a budget, and self-governance. But both because of the small size of such communities and because of their intense inward focus, they are less likely to involve members in activities outside their own walls, less likely to mobilize them as volunteers or political actors, and more likely to occupy whatever time members have to spare in activities related to their own community life. Family-style worship communities develop deep reservoirs of personal trust and norms of reciprocity, but unless they are explicitly oriented toward civic action, these qualities are likely to contribute to an inbred organizational culture that can even stand in the way of institutional growth and rejuvenation (Olson 1989). To the degree that lay participation, volunteerism, and lay governance are focused exclusively on the inner life of the community, all of these potentially "civic" effects are likely to have little impact on civic incorporation, at least in the short run. As Robert Wuthnow observes of evangelical churches' rather poor showing in promoting volunteering and community involvement, it is not that these churches don't promote civic engagement (and civic skills), it is because they enjoy such intense community lives in themselves that members simply have no time left over for wider involvement (1999, 343).

Similarly, we can expect family-style worship communities to be ethnically homogeneous precisely because of their stress on intimacy, but ethnic identity is less likely here than in other settings to be a cause for political or civic mobilization. On the contrary, it is likely to be closely tied to religious identity, and together ethnic and religious identity serve as markers guaranteeing the shared background on which intimacy can be built. At the most, ethnic identity may provide the basis for identification with other, similar worship communities and for directing what charitable activities these small worship communities are able to engage in. Ethnicity is more likely to be a motivation for civic engagement in a community-style or civic leader worship community, where these are dominated by members of one ethnicity or national origin. In more diverse worship communities of this type, religious identity and ideals are more likely to provide the basis for civic engagement. The house of worship, similarly, may stress religious identity where the population served is ethnically diverse; but it may equally well see itself as a reservoir of culturally specific religious practices, if it serves primarily one ethnic group. In either case, political mobilization and encouraging civic engagement are unlikely to be seen as part of its mission.

Religious Tradition

Differences in religious tradition, we already noted, may account for broad tendencies toward one or another organizational culture. Catholic, Hindu, and Muslim worship communities are more likely to be formally structured around the house of worship pattern than Protestant or Sikh congregations, thanks to distinctive conceptions in each case about what worship and the worship community are all about. At the same time, certain traditions include reservoirs of theological and ethical thinking or alternative practice that can reshape the way worship communities act and see themselves. The Catholic social justice tradition and the "social gospel" in mainline Protestantism are examples. The social teaching of the popes and the innovations of Vatican II have often pushed Catholic communities to reach beyond Catholic liturgical focus on the sacraments and to challenge the hierarchical organization of the parish to include community building and lay leadership as key components of worship and parish life. The social gospel expands the scope of many mainline Protestant congregations, even small ones, from the more family-style congregational model to a community-style or civic leader stance. In Hinduism, an ashram under the direction of a guru, or inspired teacher, provides an important alternative to the typical Hindu temple, which epitomizes the house of worship. In many ashrams, lay people and monks in training often play important roles in the life of the community, which has much more the feel of a congregation or "family" than Hindu temples, with their almost exclusive focus on worship.

Religious tradition thus helps account for some of the chief features of institutional culture outlined here. At the same time, it may have its own, more direct implications for the sort of social capital that individual worship communities enjoy, the kind of lay involvement (and thus training in civic skills) that is permitted or encouraged, and the attitude of clergy and lay people toward civic engagement. Traditions that put overwhelming emphasis on worship and spirituality may take for granted certain ethical norms, including commitment to the larger society, without stressing them in teaching and practice. More powerfully, traditions such as evangelical and Pentecostal Christianity, which emphasize salvation via participation in a close-knit "community of saints," may confine outside linkages for most purposes to like-minded communities of believers. Such traditions sometimes paint active participation in the public sphere as dangerously "worldly" and discourage the devout from civic engagement. Religious traditions that identify sacral priesthoods as crucial intermediaries with the deity may restrict lay participation, particularly in worship and governance, providing fewer opportunities for the development of civic skills than more egalitarian traditions. Other traditions provide plenty of roles for lay people in their standard governance structures and worship practices. Religious traditions, of course, are famously open to reinterpretation, and our cases will show how religious and lay leaders draw on alternative traditions or arguments from necessity to reframe traditions and restructure worship communities away from the norm. The spectacular rise of the "religious right" among evangelicals is a case in point (Green, Rozell, and Wilcox 2003). But religious tradition can be expected to exert significant influences on how and to what degree worship communities promote the civic incorporation of immigrants.

In sum, characteristics of the immigrant group itself, including the context of reception; the institutional culture of particular worship communities; and religious tradition may all help to account for significant differences in how and to what extent worship communities serving the new immigrants contribute to their civic incorporation. These factors interact, and the degree to which one or another plays a role may depend crucially on lay or religious leadership. Evangelical churches, for example, might be thought to excel in the development of "civic skills," providing multiple opportunities for lay people to grow in leadership and other abilities that might be transferred to the civic realm. Yet they typically do little to mobilize individuals for community service or political participation, claiming much more time and resources from their members for the affairs of the church and for evangelization. Their organizational culture and theological tradition puts great stress on providing the intimacy of an extended family for their members and utilizing the relationships created in this way to promote the moral and spiritual development of their members and of the worship community as a whole. Though such efforts often help people cope with poverty or discrimination or the loneliness of the immigrant condition, they do little directly to integrate participants into the larger society. Where such churches serve an overwhelmingly poor community, facing a hostile reception in the United States, they may become "havens in a heartless world" and important sources of psychological and moral support, but provide little in the way of material resources, social services, or social ties to the wider society and a richer range of opportunities. Where they serve a more affluent community, they may reinforce both ethnic ties and the sense of ethnic isolation that the immigrant community experiences.

Worship communities that stress religious devotion (the "house of worship") may likewise do little to promote active citizenship or help immigrants adjust to the institutions of American life. They may reinforce ethnic identities through their everyday practices and occasionally take up homeland causes as part of their understanding of their religious mission, but their civic activism will depend upon lay leadership outside the normal bounds of everyday practice. More hierarchically organized worship communities of all sorts may do relatively little to promote the growth of civic skills through involvement in worship activities or meaningful lay participation in governance, but wherever the organizational culture of the particular worship community is oriented toward building community, promoting their members' development, and playing a role in the larger society, they may actively encourage civic activism and provide multiple opportunities for volunteering or political action. The factors that affect civic incorporation are thus multiple and interacting, but they are not random, and we shall see systematic patterns as our story unfolds. No simple lessons about the role of religion in civic incorporation emerge from this study, but we will gain a richer understanding of a complex and often contradictory process by looking more closely at the contributions of local worship communities to the incorporation of new immigrants.

Conclusion

Local worship communities may contribute to civic incorporation in a variety of ways: as reservoirs and builders of social capital, as civic actors, and as promoters of civic participation. Three sets of variables help us account for significant variation in how and to what degree worship communities contribute to civic incorporation: the circumstances of reception of the immigrant group; the organizational culture of the worship community; and the religious tradition to which immigrants and worship community belong. These three factors, separately and interactively, shape the role of worship communities in the civic and social incorporation of immigrants.

Worship communities often provide participants with social capital— social ties or networks that give people access to significant material and social resources. The tightly knit social group that characterizes many worship communities provides multiple social ties for participants, and some of those ties may link them to significant resources, including opportunities for immersion in the larger society economically, socially, and civically. The worship community may also provide a variety of opportunities to develop valuable connections outside its confines. Such bridging social capital can provide access to jobs, educational and training opportunities, and community and political involvement. The value of the bonding social capital available in the community depends crucially on the economic and social status of the members of the community themselves and, more generally, on that of the immigrant community represented here. The extent of social capital, both bonding and bridging, depends on the organizational culture that characterizes the worship community, and this, in turn, depends upon both religious tradition and the ways local leadership has shaped the community.

Worship communities are actors in civil society by definition, but some may remain relatively isolated and passive, while others may choose from a variety of active roles. Some will provide social services to members, drawing on formal and informal linkages with other organizations and agencies. Others will focus on one or a few charitable efforts to share their resources with the needy in their area or overseas. A few will set out to play a role as leaders in civil society, participating actively in civic affairs, sending representatives to meetings, promoting specific causes, and sponsoring and cosponsoring events of interest to a wider public. Religious tradition and organizational culture explain much of this variation, but so do the circumstances of reception of the immigrant group(s) represented in a given worship community. More needy groups will tend to be associated with worship communities that provide a wealth of services to their members and neighbors, though whether they do so also depends on their religious tradition and organizational culture. More affluent groups will be more likely to sponsor charitable outreach elsewhere. Some of these may emerge as civic leaders, but only if religious tradition and organizational culture have been shaped to permit such a role.

Finally, worship communities may shape members' civic participation— by training them in skills that are relevant to civic life, mobilizing them to participate more actively in their community, and helping to shape their sense of themselves as a certain kind of American and citizen. Lay participation in worship services and the everyday life of the community may provide opportunities to hone public speaking skills, learn how to organize meetings and events, acquire skills at negotiation and coalition building, learn to manage budgets, and practice democracy. Worship communities may provide extensive opportunities and incentives to do volunteer work within the community and in service to the larger society. They may mobilize people to march, demonstrate, write letters to public officials, acquire citizenship, and vote. They may sharpen participants' sense of difference as members of an ethnic minority or as representatives of a specific moral and religious tradition. And they may mobilize members politically around such identities. Whether and to what extent a worship community helps develop "civic skills" depends on the religious tradition to which it belongs and the ways that tradition's governance structures and expectations about lay involvement are implemented. It also depends upon the organizational culture of the community, which may do little to encourage lay involvement or, alternatively, treat such involvement as central to the life of the community. Civic mobilization likewise hinges on both religious tradition and organizational culture, while the circumstances of reception may be crucial in determining the likelihood that a given community will have a majority of one ethnic group, the availability of an ethnic "cause" around which to rally, and the sort of leadership that might be available for such mobilization.

The chapters that follow examine each of the mechanisms of civic incorporation sketched here and lay out our findings on the ways local worship communities in the Washington, D.C., area serve to incorporate the new immigrants. As the model developed here predicts, we find considerable variation across immigrant groups. But as we examine the factors that account for this diversity, we will find that very little can be attributed to specifically ethnic or national origin, that is, to cultural differences among immigrants. Rather, organizational culture, religious tradition, and the circumstances of immigration—which in some cases will be quite different in other parts of the country for the same immigrant group—will account for the differences we have observed. Ethnic and national origin groups certainly differ among themselves in all sorts of ways, but characteristic differences among them in the economic niches they occupy, the residential patterns they establish, and the sorts of roles they come to play locally and nationally depend as much or more on local and national circumstances of reception as on the cultural dispositions they may bring with them, as Portes and others have shown. Similarly, a closer look at the religious institutions that serve the new immigrants and the ways they differ among themselves will make it abundantly clear that institutional context, more than cultural disposition, has profound implications for how immigrants see themselves as religious people and members of American society.

2

Profiles in Diversity

Immigration to the Washington, D.C., metropolitan area reflects both the continuities with the past and the genuine novelty of the new immigration. At the same time, Washington is distinctive among immigrant destination cities in a number of ways. We start with an overview of the new immigration, nationwide and in the Washington, D.C., area, and then turn to a brief profile of the worship communities serving major immigrant communities in the region.

The United States has been a nation of immigrants since its birth, but the largest wave of immigration before the late twentieth century began in the 1870s and peaked in 1910. It dropped off drastically in the wake of the restrictive laws of the 1920s, the Great Depression, and World War II. Immigrants from Europe were still welcome under the quota system established by the Immigration Act of 1924, but thousands of aspirants from Africa, Asia, Latin America, and the Middle East were shut out by the severe limits on the quotas for those regions.

All of this changed with the Immigration Reform Act of 1965, which drastically liberalized the quota system. Under the new rules, Europeans were no longer uniquely favored, while Africans, Asians, and Latin Americans enjoyed greatly enlarged opportunities to enter. In addition, family reunification provisions were liberalized, and new measures were put in place to enable employers to seek skilled foreign workers for professional and technical positions. The result was dramatic change. A second wave of immigration began and has continued unabated until today, so that by 2000, the foreign-born population was approaching the record levels set in 1910, when 14.7 percent of the U.S. population was foreign-born. The 2000 census found that 11 percent of the population was foreign-born, with 43 percent of these having arrived since 1990 (U.S. Census Bureau 2000).

After 1965, the immigrants' countries-of-origin changed, with most coming from Latin America and Asia. In the 1960s, the hospital industry sought trained nurses from the Philippines and India. Starting in the mid-1970s, the end of the war in Vietnam led to a wave of Vietnamese refugees, then another at the end of the decade, as tens of thousands of "boat people" left Vietnam in search of refuge in the United States. In the 1980s, the emerging information technology industry recruited skilled engineers from Taiwan, Hong Kong, and India. Political turmoil and an economic downturn in the 1980s brought millions of Koreans to the United States as well. The end of the "bracero" program that had brought Mexican workers to the fields of the West Coast and the Southwest from 1942 to 1964 spurred increasing illegal immigration from that country (Massey et al. 1987). Civil wars in Central America and economic hardship throughout Latin America in the 1980s brought millions of Latin American immigrants, both legal and illegal, seeking refuge and work. But immigration from Africa and the Middle East also increased in response to the new quota system and growing opportunities, particularly for professionals.

Like earlier immigrants, most of those in the new wave settled in a few "gateway cities." But now the gateways were not just eastern and midwestern cities such as Boston, New York, Philadelphia, and Chicago. Miami, Houston, and Los Angeles were new gateways, reflecting the shift in country of origin of many of the new immigrants. Washington, D.C., which had experienced little immigration before the 1970s, also became a major gateway and today ranks fifth among cities receiving immigrants.

The new wave of immigrants is more diverse in education and income than was the last great wave a century earlier. Many more are professionals or highly trained engineers and scientists. This is largely a result of the new immigration laws, which provide special opportunities for highly skilled potential immigrants. Since 1985, the average level of education among immigrants, except for that of Hispanics, has equalled or exceeded the average level of education of native-born Americans—something new in the history of American immigration. At the same time, large numbers of unskilled workers occupy the bottom rungs of the employment scale, as immigrants did throughout the nineteenth century, and some observers fear that the majority may remain there in a new, bifurcated economy (Sassen 2001; Waldinger et al. 2001).

The New Immigrants in the Washington, D.C., Area

Immigration to the Washington, D.C., area is relatively recent, compared with that to other gateway cities such as New York or Los Angeles. Washington has no history of old immigrant neighborhoods, and in this way it is poles apart from cities like Baltimore, Philadelphia, or Brooklyn. With the exception of a small early Chinatown, the Washington area has had no urban ethnic enclaves. In the 1970s, 1980s, and 1990s, many immigrants settled in the new suburbs, with no strong concentrations in any one locality, presaging a pattern now found more widely throughout the United States. Salvadorans, Vietnamese, and Africans remain in the District of Columbia in large numbers, but these groups, too, are also dispersed in the suburbs, both in distinctive immigrant clusters and scattered among the wider population (Singer 2003; Singer et al. 2001).

While the general patterns of immigration to the Washington area are similar to those across the country, both the overall pattern of immigration to this area and the profiles of the individual immigrant groups are distinctive. The largest single sending country has been El Salvador. With 104,960 foreign-born residents of Salvadoran origin in 2000, the Washington area is second only to Los Angeles in the number of Salvadorans who have settled there. But Salvadorans make up just 12.6 percent of the immigrant population, with immigrants from the rest of Latin America and the Caribbean making up another 26 percent. Mexicans account for a growing proportion of that number. By contrast, Latin American immigrants are over half the immigrant population nationwide, with Mexicans making up the overwhelming majority in such gateway cities as Los Angeles and Houston. Asian immigrants account for 36 percent of the total foreign-born population in the Washington area (as compared to 25 percent nationwide); the primary sending Asian nations are India (45,835), Korea (45,610), and China (including the mainland, Hong Kong, and Taiwan, at 42,151). But Washington also has received many immigrants from the predominantly Islamic countries of the Middle East, North Africa, and South and Southeast Asia—roughly 18 percent of the foreign-born population come from these countries (Lee and Wang 2000).[1] Finally, the area has long been a magnet for immigrants from sub-Saharan Africa and the English-speaking Caribbean. Jamaica and Trinidad and Tobago alone account for 27,958 foreign-born residents; and at least 61,500 immigrants from sub-Saharan Africa have settled in the region, with Ethiopia, Nigeria, and Ghana contributing roughly 20 percent each to that total.

Washington thus has no one predominant immigrant group, and we find concentrations of immigrant populations here that are not well represented in most other areas in the United States. Though immigrants from Latin American and the Caribbean make up 51 percent of the immigrant population nationwide, they are less than 40 percent of those in the Washington, D.C., area. Asian immigrants make up 25 percent of the immigrant population nationally, but 36 percent locally. And African immigrants, grouped together with miscellaneous "others" as 8 percent of the immigrant population in recent census reports (Lollock 2001), make up over 11 percent of Washington area immigrants. In the lack of a single preponderant national origin group and the relative diversity of national origins, the Washington area resembles New York City more than some of the other new gateways such as Los Angeles or Houston (Singer 2003).

Profiles in Diversity

Immigrants to the Washington area display the same diversity in circumstances of immigration and socioeconomic characteristics that we see nationally. The bulk of Salvadoran and Vietnamese immigration to the area was driven initially by the flight of refugees from those countries, but in very different circumstances. Whereas the Vietnamese had largely been granted legal refugee status by the time they reached Washington, and enjoyed the government sponsorship and support that comes with that status, Salvadorans have fought a long battle in the courts for such recognition and have rarely been granted it. Instead, those who arrived before 1991 were granted Temporary Protected Status (TPS) in an important court settlement, allowing them to work legally in this country but subject to periodic crises of renewal and the ever-present threat that they will be returned to El Salvador with the next change in policy. The majority of Salvadorans in this country, moreover, do not enjoy the protection of TPS, and many of them came here illegally. Most come with limited job skills; over half have less than a high school education. Though a rising middle class of Salvadorans is gaining stature in the Washington area in business, government, and politics, most Salvadoran immigrants depend on low-wage jobs in cleaning, landscaping, the restaurant business, and construction.

Overall, just 10.6 percent of the Washington area's immigrants were living in poverty at the time of the 2000 census, half the rate of New York, Los Angeles, and Houston, roughly two-thirds the national average for all immigrants, and close to the nonimmigrant average of 11.1 percent (Singer 2003;

Lollock 2001). But this figure conceals a bifurcation between poorer immigrants from El Salvador and Mexico and the large numbers of relatively affluent immigrants from other parts of the world. Among Indians, Koreans, Chinese, and many Muslim immigrants, for example, levels of education, job skills, and professional experience are relatively high. Nationally, over 70 percent of Indian men have completed college, and 40 percent have had at least some postgraduate education. Over 50 percent of Indian women have a college degree. Many Indians in the Washington area work in well-paid information technology positions. Roughly half of all Indian immigrants nationwide work in professional or executive/managerial positions. Large numbers of Chinese, Korean, Middle Eastern, and African immigrants also enjoy relatively high levels of education and professional attainment, though a significant proportion of each group also lack a high school degree, and a middle strata of small business owners among all these groups sometimes struggles to make ends meet. In terms of income, many immigrants from India, China, Korea, and the predominantly Muslim countries of South Asia, the Middle East, and North Africa fare quite well. Of immigrants from these areas, 20 to 30 percent earned more than $50,000 annually in 1997. Immigrants from sub-Saharan Africa, however, were not as likely to do so well, despite similar levels of educational and professional attainment, bespeaking the continuing impact of racism directed at blacks in America.[2]

The New Immigrants and Civic Incorporation

Differing levels of education and job placement have obvious implications for the civic incorporation of immigrants, as do such important variables as language training. We will look at the impact of worship communities on civic incorporation in the following chapters. Here, we consider briefly the evidence on differences among immigrant groups in rates of participation in civic affairs and politics. As we shall see, such differences are tied more to variations in education and language achievement than to specific cultural or country-of-origin factors. The data cited here are drawn from the National Household Education Survey (National Center for Educational Statistics 1996). In this survey, a national sample of adults 18 years of age and above were selected for interviews on their civic involvement. Since interviews were conducted in English, we can expect bias toward those who handle English fluently. Among immigrants, those who have lived here longer, or came to this country with some English, are likely to be better represented than newer immigrants from countries where fewer opportunities presented themselves to learn English.

Although foreign-born subjects were not asked for their specific countries of origin, they were broken down by self-ascribed racial/ethnic identification: non-Hispanic whites and non-Hispanic blacks for the native-born, and Asian immigrants, immigrants of African descent, and "Other" immigrants (including those from both Latin America and Europe) for the foreign-born. Because the survey records just 144 foreign-born respondents out of a total sample of 1,753, we must take care about putting too much weight on these findings.

The National Household Education Survey (NHES) included a number of questions on activities relevant to civic incorporation, from newspaper reading to membership in groups to attending public meetings and voting. Because up to two-thirds of the foreign-born in the United States today are not naturalized citizens, voting rates are low, though among those eligible to vote, Asian and African immigrants tend to be more likely to vote than Hispanics. Over 28 percent of immigrants of African descent say they have voted in the last five years, as do 32.4 percent of Asian immigrants; the figure falls to 12.8 percent for immigrants in the "Other" category, which includes those from Latin America and Europe. These figures are congruent with those available from pooled data of the General Social Survey (GSS).

Though native white Americans have the highest percentage who say they read a newspaper daily (62 percent), immigrants of African descent and those from Asian countries are very much the same as native black Americans (above 50 percent), while other immigrants (undoubtedly represented mostly by Latin Americans) had the lowest percentage (27 percent). Over 90 percent of African immigrants and over 70 percent of Asian immigrants watch or listen to national news daily; almost 69 percent of other immigrants do so. Immigrants in all categories are thus as likely or more likely than the native-born to be attending to national news. Asian and African immigrants are also as likely as native whites to have read a book in the last month. Other immigrants, again, had the lowest percentage reading books. Facility with the English language and differences in educational attainment undoubtedly lie behind this pattern. Among respondents to the NHES, more than 70 percent of African immigrants claimed to speak English as their first language. Around 50 percent of immigrants from Asian countries spoke mainly English at home. By contrast, almost 80 percent of immigrants in the "Other" category spoke a non-English language at home.

Similar patterns appear in regard to indicators of civic incorporation not so obviously tied to literacy and command of the English language. Among respondents to the NHES survey, over half of both African and Asian immigrants report belonging to at least one organization (including unions, professional organizations, churches, and community groups), while just un-der 40 percent of those in the "Other" category do so. In all cases, immigrants are less likely to belong to organizations than the native-born, over 60 percent of whom report membership in at least one organization. In regard to par-ticipation in religious services, however, Asian immigrants follow closely be-hind native African Americans (50 percent attend church regularly), while immigrants of African descent are the least likely to do so.

As in the case of organizational membership, participation in community activities of all kinds is overall lower for immigrants than for the native-born. Thus, while 40 percent of native-born whites and 49 percent of native blacks report doing community service (including both volunteering and working with a church or neighborhood association), only 24 percent of African im-migrants, 38 percent of Asian immigrants, and 27 percent of other immigrants engage in such activities. The disparities are even greater for expressly politi-cal activities, in part, presumably, because many respondents are not citizens. Thus, just 14 percent of Africans, 5 percent of Asians, and 7 percent of others report having given money to a political cause, as compared with an average of 18 percent among the native-born. While an average of 37 percent of native-born respondents have contacted a public official about an issue, just 12.5 percent of immigrants have done so. While 31 percent of the native-born report having attended a public meeting, just over 17 percent of immigrants say they have done so.

The Latino National Political Survey (LNPS), based on a larger sample of immigrant and nonimmigrant Hispanics nationwide, gives somewhat higher figures for Hispanics. While just 23 percent of noncitizen Mexican immigrants and 17 percent of noncitizen Cubans report having participated in community affairs, the figures rise to 41.5 percent and 37.2 percent, respectively, for Mex-ican and Cuban naturalized citizens. But these figures are markedly lower than the 57 percent reported by non-Hispanic whites (DeSipio 1996, 138). If par-ticipation in school affairs is included, Hispanic respondents of all sorts more or less match their non-Hispanic white counterparts. Again, however, language ability and socioeconomic status seem to account for the patterns observed here better than ethnicity or culture-specific factors. Language ability contributes to the lower rate of naturalization among Hispanic immigrants in general, but other factors play a role as well. Louis DeSipio's careful analysis of the results of the National Latino Immigrant Survey (NLIS) and the LNPS show that com-mand of the English language, age, income, and age at entry to the United States are consistent predictors of naturalization, whether the dependent variable is actual citizenship or application for citizenship. The NLIS and LNPS data also allows us to sort out the factors that most probably make for greater or lesser involvement, including legal status, length of stay in this country, proficiency in English, and level of education. As it turns out, community involvement of all sorts is closely correlated with the same sets of factors that affect naturalization and voting (DeSipio 1996, 202).

Religion and the New Immigrants

Throughout American history, religion has been important to immigrants, in many cases even more than it was prior to their coming (Dolan 1975; Gleason 1992; Stark 1997; Tomasi 1972). Timothy Smith (1978) put it succinctly: immigration to this country, he writes, was often a "theologizing experience." Nevertheless, the religious practices of different groups have always varied a great deal, particularly in the significance accorded regular worship with a local worship community.[3] If participation in local worship communities is an important source of civic engagement for many, we need to know the extent to which recent immigrants take part in such communities. Unfortunately, we have little data at our disposal. The U.S. census has not polled on religious preference since 1920, and few national-level surveys have been undertaken with sufficient scope to include a reasonable number of the foreign-born in the population sample. One recent development has altered this picture somewhat. Results of the pilot version of the New Immigrant Survey (NIS), which includes two questions on religion, have been published. The NIS was designed to remedy our lack of knowledge about immigrants to this country. In cooperation with the Immigration and Naturalization Service (INS), researchers polled a stratified, random sample of all those admitted to legal permanent residence in the United States in the months of July and August 1996 (Jasso 2000). The survey thus gives us the first reliable data on recent immigrants, regardless of English language proficiency. But its sample is severely restricted to some of the most recent immigrants and to those who have attained legal permanent resident status. The questions on religion, moreover, are restricted to one question on religious preference and another on attendance at religious services. We draw on this limited data, nevertheless, supplemented by the authors' own comparison with 1994 GSS responses from the small sample of foreign-born individuals that survey reached. This source, too, is limited, in that the GSS is conducted solely in English, effectively screening out many immigrants from non-English speaking countries who have less education or shorter length of residence in the United States.

The NIS data do not appear to support the common contention that immigrants are more religious, on average, than the native-born population; but comparison with the GSS data on the foreign-born suggests that they become so over time. Thus, 83 percent of immigrants reported a religious preference, while 90.6 percent of the native-born population does so. At the other end of the spectrum, almost 15 percent of immigrants but just 9 percent of the native-born declare that they have "no religion." When we turn to the GSS data for 1994, of the 214 foreign-born respondents, almost 93 percent express a religious preference, and only 9.1 percent say they have "no religion" (Jasso 2000). Since this population includes a mix of newcomers and immigrants who have been in the country for some time, with a probable skew toward the former, we can be fairly safe in assuming that the longer immigrants remain in this country, the more closely they approach the norm in declaring a religious preference.

The story is quite different when we consider attendance at religious services. In general, those recent immigrants who claim religious affiliation are more likely to attend services on a regular basis than others, both the native-born and the broader immigrant community. Whereas just 29.3 percent of the nonimmigrant population surveyed in the 1994 GSS reported attending services weekly or more frequently, the figure for the immigrants interviewed in the NIS Pilot was 41 percent.[4] This is higher than that for the foreign-born surveyed by the GSS, 34.2 percent of whom reported at least weekly attendance. Thus, the newer immigrants who do claim a religious affiliation are more likely than either the larger native-born or foreign-born population to actually attend services on a regular basis. This is true across faith traditions, with new immigrant Catholics, Protestants, Jews, and adherents of other traditions all substantially more likely to participate in religious services than native-born residents and than the immigrant population as a whole. Similarly, the proportion of NIS respondents who never attend services is smaller than among the native-born population.

These figures are suggestive only. They confirm the widespread impression that religious institutions, local congregations in particular, are important to recent immigrants and that immigrants tend to be more religious than the general population. They indicate that this is true across immigrant populations. The data suggest, at the very least, that religious institutions may be important vehicles for reaching immigrants and that they may play a significant role in their adjustment and their civic engagement in the United States.

Evidence from the Washington, D.C., Area

A comparison of census data with our survey of worship communities serving Protestant and Catholic immigrants from El Salvador, Korea, China, and West

Africa and Hindu and Sikh organizations serving the Indian community provides a bit more evidence on the religious participation of these immigrants. In 2000, we attempted a complete census of worship communities serving these groups in our study area. Our requirement was that the regular participants in any worship community had to include at least 20 percent from one of the immigrant groups we were focusing on. Of the 275 worship communities that we were able to reach and that fit our criteria, 45 percent were 100 percent from one or another of these immigrant groups, while the rest were ethnically mixed. Table 2.1 compares the estimated number of participants in these worship communities with the overall immigrant population for each national or regional grouping.

Consonant with other studies, we found that some 70 percent of Koreans in the area participate regularly in a Christian (mainly Protestant) worship community (Hurh and Kim 1990). On the other hand, just 41 percent of Salvadorans in the area regularly attend immigrant worship communities, Catholic or Protestant. There are two possibilities: most Salvadorans may not regularly attend church (a result that would confirm other studies of Hispanic groups in the United States), or large numbers of them attend church in mainly nonimmigrant congregations. The figures for Chinese and African immigrants must be read with considerable caution. Though some surveys have suggested that as many as a third of Chinese immigrants belong to a Christian church, some 19 percent of Chinese Americans are Buddhists, according to the Pilot National Asian American Political Survey.[5] A significant, but unknown, proportion of sub-Saharan Africans in the United States are Muslim. Moreover, anecdotal evidence suggests that a good many African Christians attend churches not characterized by high immigrant memberships. Indeed, most of

TABLE 2.1. Religious Organizations Serving Six Immigrant Groups in the Study Area

	African	Chinese	Indian	Korean	Salvadoran
Number of immigrants	61,540	42,151	45,610	45,835	104,960
Estimated number of worship communities	75	21	17[a]	192	103
Estimated number of immigrant regular participants	9,000	5,000	10,000	32,000	43,000

[a]Includes only Hindu and Sikh worship communities. Three Indian Christian churches and a Jain community in the study area are not included here.

Source: Line 1: Census (U.S. Census Bureau 2000) for the Washington Primary Metropolitan Statistical Area (PMSA). The PMSA also includes outlying counties, but our study area accounts for 90 percent of all foreign-born people in the area. Lines 2 and 3: authors' telephone survey, summer 2000.

the African immigrant congregations included in our study are distinctly multicultural, with a majority from either the native white or African American population.

Similar cautions are in order for the Indian immigrant results. About 22 percent of Indians "regularly attend" a Hindu temple or Sikh gurdwara. A small percentage of the Indian population in the area attend Indian Christian churches, multicultural Seventh-Day Adventist congregations, or other Christian churches. But roughly 12 percent of the population of India is Muslim, and area mosques include an unknown number of Indian Muslims. The low figure for "regular participants," however, is also accounted for by the fact that, for many Hindus, temple worship is often only occasional. In the more detailed survey conducted later in our research, leaders of temples reported relatively small numbers of regular attendees, but quite high numbers of people attending over the course of the year.

We have left the Muslim communities out of our reckoning because we have no very good way to estimate the Muslim immigrant population. Nevertheless, patterns of Muslim worship and answers to the same set of questions on our survey of mosques suggest that the situation is very much the same for the mosques as for the Hindu temples—relatively small numbers of regular attendees versus large numbers at particular times of the year. Differences in the place of collective worship in the religious life render estimates of "religiosity" based on some notion of regular attendance difficult to compare across religious traditions. Nevertheless, if we are interested in regular attendance as an indicator of the possible effects of participation on the civic and social incorporation of immigrants into American life, we would have to conclude that temples and mosques are likely to play a smaller role in these communities than do churches among Korean immigrants.

Immigrant Worship Communities in the Washington, D.C., Area

The churches, mosques, temples, and other places of worship that serve the new immigrants today vary widely in size, organizational form, program, and philosophical orientation. Their impact on the social and civic incorporation of immigrants and their children can be expected to vary every bit as much. How can we get a handle on this diversity? We start by mapping it as best we can and trying to explain some of the variation. We also compare the local worship communities of our sample with those surveyed in the National Congregation Study (NCS) to see how worship communities serving immigrants differ from a representative sample of all congregations in the United States.[6] Then we look at three major types of local worship communities: those that stand alone and are predominantly immigrant in composition; those that are part of larger worship communities but have separate worship services for the immigrant community; and those that incorporate a large number of immigrants into an integrated worship community. Finally, brief profiles of the immigrant groups and their worship communities will provide important background for the detailed treatment that follows.

WHO SERVES THE NEW IMMIGRANTS? The worship communities we surveyed ranged from small Baptist congregations serving two or three dozen people to huge Catholic parishes with several thousand members, from close-knit Sikh gurdwaras of a few dozen families to mosques drawing 12,000 people to major festivals. Both our survey and the ethnographic studies focused on worship communities serving at least 20 percent immigrants. In the vast majority of cases, such "immigrant" worship communities were overwhelmingly composed of persons born outside the United States (see tables 2.2 and 2.3). Thus 87 percent worship communities serving Salvadorans and 86 percent of those serving Koreans were three-quarters or more immigrant in composition. Those serving Africans and Chinese, on the other hand, tended to have smaller percentages of immigrants. Many of these African communities were "multicultural" congregations, with a majority white or African-American population. The Chinese congregations, by contrast, while almost exclusively Chinese in ethnicity (and language of worship), are older worship communities, serving an older ethnic community. Another important difference lies in the percentage of recent immigrants (arrived within the last five years) in these communities. Only in the Salvadoran worship communities do we encounter a high percentage with sizable numbers of recent immigrants. Just 24 percent of African congregations reported that more than 30 percent of their members were recently arrived to this country, while just one of the Chinese communities and none of the Indian ones had this high a percentage of recent immigrants. As we

TABLE 2.2. Immigrant Composition of Worship Communities by Ethnicity

	African	Chinese	Indian	Korean	Salvadoran
Number of cases	37	15	13	63	53
Worship communities with more than 76% adults born outside the United States (percent)	30	47	59	86	87
Worship communities with more than 31% adults immigrated within the last 5 years (percent)	24	7	0	13	43

TABLE 2.3. Profile of "Typical" Immigrant Congregation versus National Average

	"Typical" Immigrant Congregation	National Average (NCS Data)[a]
Date of founding worship community	1985	1927
Number of regular participants	409	169
Percent female members	57	59
Percent without high school diploma	27	16
Percent with college degree	39	24
Percent over 60 years	16	29
Percent under 35 years	38	30
Percent household income under $25,000	26	37
Percent household income over $100,000	8	4

[a] The NCS data included just 34 non-Christian worship communities out of a total sample of 1,200. We have excluded these from our profile here. In addition, because of the sampling techniques, the NCS data overrepresents Catholic parishes. We have adopted the weighting proposed by Chaves (1999) to correct for this effect.

will see, those communities with higher percentages of nonimmigrants and older arrivals tend to have more resources and are better able to sponsor programs for their members.

The immigrant worship communities we surveyed thus represent a wide spectrum on a variety of measures. The "average" place of worship is scarcely meaningful across such a spectrum, but a comparison of such an average with NCS data on a nationally representative sample of worship communities can help us discern the distinctiveness of immigrant worship communities (see table 2.3). The average immigrant worship community claims a little over 400 people in regular attendance. But it touches well over 1,000 people in the course of a year. It was founded in 1985. It has more women in attendance than men, and over 25 percent of its members do not have a high school diploma, while almost 40 percent have college degrees. Just 16 percent of the members are over 60; another 38 percent are under 35 years of age. Some 26 percent of its members earn under $25,000 a year, while just over 8 percent earn over $100,000. Almost 80 percent of its members are foreign born.

By comparison, the average congregation in the United States is much older. It also tends to be smaller, with just 169 people in regular attendance, as opposed to the 409 in the typical immigrant congregation. Nationwide, worship communities average a high proportion of female members (59 percent), but this proportion is only marginally higher than that of our average immigrant congregation. Almost 29 percent of the typical congregation's members are over 60, while 30 percent are under 35, making their membership older, on average, than that of the immigrant worship communities in our sample. They have fewer members lacking a high school degree than we found in the typical immigrant congregation, but also fewer with a college degree. And they are notably poorer than our average immigrant worship community, with some 37 percent of their regular participants living in households earning less than $25,000 and just 4 percent in households with over $100,000 a year in earnings.

Such comparisons do not take us very far, given the enormous diversity among these worship communities. We might start by looking at the socio-economic characteristics of the immigrant populations served. For simplicity's sake, we start by focusing on differences across ethnic and regional ("African") groups, then look at the same data across religious traditions. Because we have no very reliable way of estimating the Muslim population in the area by ethnic origins, we will get a clearer idea of their socioeconomic profile when we turn to comparisons among worship communities of differing religious traditions.

The most striking differences come out in the demographics of these congregations: almost half of Salvadorans, in the average Salvadoran congregation, have no high school diploma, as opposed to 30 percent of Koreans, 10 percent of Africans, 7 percent of Chinese, and just 4 percent of Indians. Conversely, large percentages of Indians, Chinese, Africans, and Koreans have a college degree or higher, versus just 8 percent of Salvadorans. Salvadorans also tend to be much younger, with just over 8 percent over 60 years of age and nearly 50 percent under 35. They are also much poorer. Forty-four percent of Salvadorans in the average congregation live in households that earn less than $25,000 a year. In the last respect alone, the profile of the typical Salvadoran congregation approaches the national average reported in the NCS. The average Chinese congregation, by contrast, counts among its members as many as 14 percent with household incomes over $100,000 a year, as do an astounding 28 percent of members of Indian (Hindu and Sikh) worship communities.

TABLE 2.4. Profile of Immigrant Worship Communities by Country/Region of Origin

	African	Chinese	Indian	Korean	Salvadoran
Date of founding of worship community	1973	1985	1979	1986	1990
Number of regular participants	361	228	633	339	397
Percent of female members	63	53	53	59	55
Percent without high school diploma	10	7	4	30	48
Percent with college degree	51	68	72	40	8
Percent over 60 years	18	20	13	20	8
Percent under 35 years	36	42	24	30	50
Percent household income under $25,000	28	12	3	18	44
Percent household income over $100,000	8	15	28	7	2

TABLE 2.5. Profile of Immigrant Worship Communities by Religious Tradition

	Catholic	Protestant	Muslim	Hindu	Sikh
Date of founding of worship community	1979	1985	1987	1982	1974
Number of regular participants	1,140	239	903	737	411
Percent of female members	54	58	42	53	53
Percent without high school diploma	45	27	22	3	6
Percent with college degree	23	36	60	80	56
Percent over 60 years	20	15	17	14	11
Percent under 35 years	42	39	39	23	27
Percent household income under $25,000	36	27	23	3	3
Percent household income over $100,000	7	6	14	31	20

Similar differences appear when we break down our results according to religious tradition (see table 2.5). Not surprisingly, more men than women participate in Muslim worship communities, but Hindu and Sikh communities look more like their Christian counterparts in this respect. Members of Muslim, Hindu, and Sikh worship communities are much more likely to have college degrees than their Christian counterparts, and much less likely to lack a high school diploma (though this is true for 22 percent of Muslims). Hindu and Sikh communities also have smaller proportions of both older and younger members than do others, perhaps reflecting the recent migration of Indian professionals to this country. And, as we have already seen, these communities tend to be much wealthier than other immigrant communities.

Most of these differences reflect familiar differences in the populations served. Salvadorans are generally younger, poorer, and less well educated than the other immigrant groups in our study; their large numbers among the Catholics represented here contribute to a similar profile among Catholics. Indians, whether Hindu, Sikh, Muslim, or of other faith, tend to be professionally trained and well-off financially. This is also true of Chinese immigrants, though their immigration is older. Koreans and Africans who have managed to come to this country often have the means to establish themselves professionally or in a small business (Light and Gold 2000). The demographics of their worship communities roughly mirror the demographics of the general population. Such factors can affect the ways religious institutions serve immigrants. The relative wealth of Muslim, Hindu, and Sikh immigrants has enabled them to build sometimes elaborate centers of worship of their own. High proportions of these communities, we found, own their building, and many of these were established quite early in the immigration history of these groups.

The size of the immigrant group, however, can also be an important factor in explaining differences in characteristics of their worship communities. The African survey results offer a case in point. Their congregations are much more likely to be part of a larger parish or church than any of the other groups. They are also significantly more likely to worship together with others outside their ethnic group. These characteristics are undoubtedly a matter of the size of the immigrant population. Where Africans from particular national or ethnic groups are present in sufficient numbers, we encounter separate congregations. Nigerians represent the largest single national community among Africans in the Washington area. Of 16 worship communities identified with significant Nigerian populations, 12 were self-standing congregations (including one mosque), and two others had separate worship services for Igbo members. Several of these communities were identified with the Igbo ethnic group, and one with the Yoruba, though none maintained exclusive boundaries. The Nigerian case seems to confirm that, as immigrant groups grow sufficiently large, they will tend find ways to worship together and apart from others. This finding confirms one of the oldest findings in the sociology of religion, namely that like tends to worship with like.

Other differences among worship communities, however, reflect the religious traditions that have come to serve particular immigrant groups and their peculiar styles of organization. Table 2.4 displays some of the basic characteristics of local worship communities across religious traditions. Not surprisingly, Catholic churches tend to have been founded earlier and to enroll decidedly more members than Protestant ones. Thus, though our sample included 40 Protestant churches serving Salvadorans but just 14 Catholic ones, the latter claimed to have some 15,600 regular participants among them, while the Protestant churches accounted for just 5,800. But the Catholic parishes are almost matched in size by Hindu and Muslim worship communities, which tend to accommodate large numbers because they are organized, first and foremost, as "houses of worship," to use Penny Becker's terminology (1999). Sikh worship communities, organized in principle on recognizably "congregational" lines, tend to be smaller, though still not as small as the Protestant churches.

Among Protestants, Korean congregations are much more likely to have established a self-standing Korean church than to be part of a larger church or parish. They are also more likely to own their own building than either Salvadoran or Chinese congregations. Salvadoran Protestant congregations are newer (65 percent were founded since 1991) and smaller than those associated with the other ethnic groups, probably reflecting the demographics and timing of the Salvadoran migration. Other differences persist across national/

regional origins, even among Protestants; but most of these, again, can be traced to the demographics of the immigrant groups themselves. Immigrant congregations, nevertheless, tend to be larger than the average Protestant congregation in the United States; and they are notably younger, on average. The profile of Catholic parishes serving immigrants overall tends to match that of Salvadoran Protestant congregations, except in size; the regular participants in such Catholic parishes tend to be even younger and poorer than their Protestant counterparts, but they include more college graduates (see table 2.5).

Gender breakdowns among these worship communities are mixed. Korean Protestant congregations have the highest percentage of female members, almost two-thirds. With the exception of the Muslim communities, more women than men participate in most immigrant worship communities. A very small percentage of worship communities are led by female clergy. Just two of the Catholic groups and eight (5.4 percent) of the Protestant ones have female religious leaders, but the percentage was much higher among Salvadoran congregations (15.4 percent) than other ethnic groups. (Just 9.4 percent of American congregations are headed by women, according to the NCS data.) The picture is considerably different when it comes to lay leadership within the community. Relatively high percentages of worship communities report that women are in the majority of lay leadership positions within the community (see table 2.6). Over 40 percent of African, Korean and Salvadoran worship communities say that their leadership is majority women (as opposed to just 20 percent of the Chinese and 31 percent of the Indian communities). Two of the four Sikh communities report a majority of women in leadership, while 41 percent of both Catholic and Protestant churches say the same. Only two mosques and two Hindu communities have a majority of women in leadership roles. It seems striking that a majority in all these traditions (just short of a majority of worship communities, in the case of Protestants) report over 25 percent female leadership. Nevertheless, women are less likely to be found on the committee or board that makes the major decisions for the worship community (where such exists). Only among Catholics and Protestants (and in

TABLE 2.6. Female Lay leadership by Religious Tradition (Percentage of Worship Communities)

	Catholic	Protestant	Muslim	Hindu	Sikh
0–25 percent females in leadership role	9	11	14	11	0
26–50 percent females in leadership role	50	49	71	68	50
51–100 percent females in leadership role	41	41	14	22	50

TABLE 2.7. Women on Governing Bodies of Worship Communities (Percentage of Worship Communities)

	Catholic	Protestant	Muslim	Hindu	Sikh
0–25 percent women	11	44	86	44	68
26–50 percent women	58	34	7	56	33
51–100 percent women	32	30	7	0	0

one mosque) do women make up a majority on such committees (see table 2.7). In over 50 percent of Catholic churches and Hindu temples, women make up somewhere between 26 and 50 percent of the parish council or board. In 86 percent of the mosques, they are less than 25 percent of the membership. The same is true of 44 percent of Protestant churches. The religious communities do far better in this regard than Congress and our elected bodies in general, but they are far from egalitarian regarding gender.

This profile of the churches, mosques, temples, and other religious communities serving Washington area immigrants suggests that most differences among them reflect underlying differences in the populations served. Nevertheless, religious tradition counts in explaining some of the variation. And some differences among worship communities serving immigrants seem peculiar to the ethnic group in question. There are also distinctive organizational arrangements among these worship communities. Some immigrant groups have established large numbers of self-standing, largely monoethnic congregations. Others have been incorporated as separate ethnic worship communities into larger congregations or parishes. And still others are integrated into a larger, multiethnic worship community. Each arrangement has distinctive implications for the role of the community in the civic and social incorporation of immigrants. In the next section, we will look more closely at these distinctions.

ORGANIZING THE IMMIGRANT WORSHIP COMMUNITY. The churches, mosques, temples, and other worship communities that have come to serve immigrants have organized themselves to do so in keeping with both their own organizational imperatives and the conditions of the immigrants they serve. In some cases, we find self-standing congregations dominated by one immigrant group. In others, established congregations accommodate a significant immigrant population with separate worship services. In still other cases, sizable immigrant populations worship side by side with members of other ethnic and racial groups, some of them immigrants themselves, others native-born. In some cases, these "multicultural" worship communities are the

TABLE 2.8. Organizational Arrangements by National Origin
(Percentages)

	African	Chinese	Korean	Salvadoran
Self-standing congregation	46	60	88	61
Part of larger congregation	54	40	39	12
Worship separately[a]	29	100	88	100
Worship together with others[a]	71	0	12	0

[a]Includes only those worship communities that are part of a larger congregation

result of older, established congregations incorporating immigrants into their worship life; in other cases, they have been created by immigrants themselves, and they include, besides the American-born children of immigrants, small numbers of native-born adherents to their faith. How the immigrant groups we have studied differ in this respect, and why, is the subject of this section. Later, we shall consider more closely the implications of these different organizational responses for the civic and social incorporation of immigrants.

We found significant differences across regional and national origin groups in the degree to which they are part of self-standing "immigrant" worship communities or are part of a larger congregation. As other researchers have noticed, Korean Protestants are much more likely than many other immigrant groups to worship in self-standing, largely monoethnic churches. Both relative affluence and a plethora of willing clergy and clergy candidates seem to account for this trait (Kwon 2004; Warner 2001, 31–33). Thus, while a majority of Salvadoran and Chinese Christian churches were self-standing congregations, some 88 percent of Korean congregations had this characteristic. Over half of the African worship communities, on the other hand, were incorporated as part of a larger parish or congregation, and, of these, over 70 percent worshiped together with others in a "multicultural" congregation. Only 1 Korean group out of the 65 surveyed was part of such a congregation, and none of the Salvadoran or Chinese groups. Nevertheless, as we saw earlier, there seemed to be a tendency for the larger African national and ethnic groups to establish separate worship services and even separate congregations when their numbers permitted.

Looking at patterns of organization across religious traditions presents a fuller picture (table 2.9). Just 27 percent of the Catholic worship communities are self-standing congregations. The remaining 73 percent are part of a larger parish. Nevertheless, it is striking that in all these cases, the immigrant group worships separately. Though "multicultural" arrangements incorporating new immigrants are not unheard-of among Catholic churches, they are relatively

TABLE 2.9. Organizational Arrangements by Religious Tradition (Percent)

	Catholic	Protestant	Muslim	Hindu	Sikh
Self-standing congregation	27	73	100	100	100
Part of larger congregation	73	27	0	0	0
Worship separately[a]	100	60	n/a	n/a	n/a
Worship together with others[a]	0	40	n/a	n/a	n/a

[a]Includes only those worship communities that are part of a larger congregation

rare, given the Catholic Church's insistence on accommodating the cultural practices of immigrants (U.S. Conference of Catholic Bishops 2000). At the same time, it is relatively difficult for committed clergy and lay people to found a new parish. Many bishops are loath to support a nonterritorial "ethnic" parish. Bishops typically insist that members of an immigrant community worship in the context of an existing parish, even if that means that participants will have to commute long distances to do so. Finding clergy who speak the relevant language(s) is often a problem, and dioceses generally do not support new parishes financially. On the contrary, parishes must raise significant sums in order to win the diocese's endorsement for a new building (Foley 1998).

The situation is reversed among most Protestant denominations and traditions, where the founding of new congregations often depends principally on the willingness of clergy to serve them. Clerical "entrepreneurs" may attempt to build congregations from a few converts, and many do. This ease of foundation is reflected in our data. Thus, 73 percent of the Protestant worship communities are self-standing immigrant congregations, while just 27 percent are part of a larger congregation. In 40 percent of the latter cases, on the other hand, the immigrant group worships together with others in a multicultural congregation, often because the immigrant group is too small to constitute a self-standing congregation of its own. Denomination may also play a role here. Among churches serving Africans, most of the 15 multicultural congregations are affiliated with Protestant denominations where a more hierarchical church polity prevails (primarily Lutherans and Episcopalians), making foundation of separate ethnic congregations more difficult.

Our data on the ethnic composition of these congregations seem to confirm the importance of the size of the immigrant group in determining what sort of worship community serves it. Forty-four percent of congregations serving Africans, for example, use English only in worship services, reflecting both the importance of English as a national language in many African countries and the multicultural character of many of these congregations (see table 2.10). The vast majority of congregations serving Chinese, Korean and

TABLE 2.10. Language of Worship among Worship Communities by National Group (Percentage of Worship Communities)

Language spoken at service	African	Chinese	Korean	Indian	Salvadoran
English only	44	7	0	0	4
One ethnic language	5	68	62	15	87
Multiple ethnic languages	0	20	0	39	0
English and one other	18	0	39	31	9
English and multiple other	33	7	0	15	0

Salvadoran immigrants, by contrast, employ a single national language—either Cantonese or Mandarin in the case of the Chinese. Ethnic concentration also varies across the worship communities serving our study groups. Well over 90 percent of Korean worship communities are virtually monoethnic, with between 76 and 100 percent of their members being of Korean descent. This is true of just 24 percent of churches serving the Salvadoran community (which typically include other Hispanics) and 26 percent of those serving Africans.

The Muslim, Hindu, and Sikh communities add new dimensions to this picture (see table 2.11). Despite a long history of Middle Eastern and South Asian migration to the United States, migration to the Washington, D.C., area from these and other areas where Muslims, Hindus, and Sikhs are numerous has been relatively recent. There were no older worship communities, accordingly, into which the new immigrants from these traditions might have been incorporated. All their worship communities are self-standing. At the same time, both Muslim and Hindu communities display another sort of multiculturalism from that we saw among African Christian immigrant congregations. Muslim worship communities typically employ Arabic (or in some cases Farsi) as the language of prayer and English otherwise, to bridge the multiple linguistic backgrounds of worshipers. On the other hand, some 54 percent of worship communities serving Indians employ more than one ethnic language, sometimes together with English, sometimes without, reflecting the enormous linguistic diversity of the Indian subcontinent, as well as the status of Sanskrit as sacred language. Most mosques in the area are ethnically diverse, identified with more than one national origin group. Just 3 of the 12 mosques in our sample are monoethnic in the sense used earlier; half of them report that the largest single nationality represented in the community makes up less than 25 percent of regular participants. Hindu temples, not surprisingly, are overwhelmingly Indian in national origin; but most are multiethnic in terms of the languages and regions of India represented, despite recent trends toward

TABLE 2.II. Language of Worship among Worship Communities by Religious Tradition (Percentage of Worship Communities)

Language spoken at service	Catholic	Protestant	Muslim	Hindu	Sikh
English only	5	13	0	0	0
One ethnic language	68	55	0	0	50
Multiple ethnic languages	0	2	0	56	0
English and one other	18	22	79	22	50
English and multiple other	9	8	21	22	0

greater differentiation. Both Muslim and Hindu worship communities, but especially the former, may also include significant numbers of converts of Euro-American or African American backgrounds. Their multiculturalism is thus the inverse of that of the mainline Protestant churches serving African Christians.

Such differences are relevant to questions about the contribution of worship communities to the social capital available to immigrants as well as to the sorts of civic skills they might acquire through participation in a worship community, as we shall see in subsequent chapters. To round out our profile of the immigrant worship communities that are the subjects of this book, we close with brief histories of these groups in the Washington area.

SALVADORANS IN WASHINGTON, CATHOLIC AND PROTESTANT COMMUNITIES. In 2000, the census reported over 100,000 Salvadorans in our study area. As late as 1960, very few Latin Americans had settled in the Washington area. The first Spanish mass was celebrated in 1962 by Father Virgilio Zeroli in a small chapel in downtown Washington, D.C. In the next year, a monthly Spanish mass began at the Shrine of the Sacred Heart, a large parish in the central city near the Mount Pleasant community. At that time, about 15,000 people of Hispanic descent were living in that part of the city, many of them Bolivians. As more Hispanics arrived in the area, they spread from the District of Columbia to the surrounding counties in Maryland and Virginia. Then in the 1970s Hispanics flooded in, fleeing political conflict in El Salvador and Guatemala, the earthquake in Nicaragua, and droughts and economic hardship in Peru and Bolivia. By 1972, the Archdiocese of Washington was providing services in Spanish in 10 parishes. As of 2005, more than 64 Catholic parishes in our study area featured Spanish masses; a few additional parishes reported high percentages of Hispanics, but the dioceses were unable to provide religious services in Spanish for them. Most Hispanic Catholics belong to large multicultural parishes, but worship services, and often an infrastructure of committees and organized groups, are offered separately for Spanish-speaking members.

The history of Protestant churches is more recent and more modest. In 1970, the first two Hispanic Pentecostal congregations were organized in central Washington. Later the Protestant congregations spread into the Maryland and Virginia suburbs. The new churches included both free-standing congregations and Spanish-speaking congregations within existing Protestant churches (Menjívar 1999). In the 1980s, Pentecostal groups grew up throughout the suburbs. Many were planted by pastors working for Central American missions or other missionary bodies. For example, in 1981, the Apostoles y Profetas mission established a Pentecostal church in the District of Columbia, and in 1987 and 1988 they began new churches in suburban Virginia and suburban Maryland. Similarly, Hispanic Methodist congregations emerged in 1987 in Bethesda, Maryland, and in 1989 in the Virginia suburbs. Congregations belonging to established denominations such as the Methodists and Baptists existed mainly as separate groups within existing churches rather than as free-standing churches in their own right.

KOREAN PROTESTANTS: RELIGIOUS TRANSFORMATION AND PROLIFERATION. The Washington, DC., metropolitan area is home to 45,835 Koreans, according to the 2000 census. Half live in Virginia, and a third in Maryland. Very few live in the District of Columbia. The Washington Korean community is the fourth largest in the United States, after Los Angeles, New York, and Chicago. The population of the Korean community was approximately 50 in 1950, 400 in 1960, 3,000 in 1970, 35,000 in 1980, and over 45,000 in 2000 (Chai 1993, 31).

Korean churches in the Washington area are relatively new. The first one was organized in 1951. (In Hawaii, by contrast, the first Korean church was established in 1903, and in Los Angeles in 1904.) Korean churches in the Washington area grew quickly. There were 2 in 1960, 5 in 1970, 50 in 1980, 113 in 1990, and 192 in 2000 (Kwon 2004). From the beginning, Protestants predominated, partly because of the large numbers of Protestants who immigrated but also because of the high rate of conversion to Christianity upon immigration that is evident in the Korean community. The early Korean churches were located in the District of Columbia, but all moved into the suburbs later, since that is where the vast majority of Koreans live today. There are currently only two Korean churches located in the District of Columbia, and one of them is a mission church oriented to serving homeless people. There are five Buddhist temples, and four Catholic churches (just 2 percent of the Korean worship communities in the area). Of the roughly 32,000 Koreans regularly attending church, around 12 percent are Catholic. As of 2000,

42 percent of the 192 Korean Christian churches in our study area were Presbyterian, 30 percent Baptist, 7 percent Methodist, and 19 percent other denominations or nondenominational. Most Korean Protestant churches are small. Average weekly attendance was 160, but over 65 percent claimed fewer than 100 members. The Catholic churches are much larger, averaging 1,283 Koreans attending weekly. Both Protestant and Catholic Korean churches are largely single-ethnic, serving Koreans only.

From the beginning of its growth period in the 1950s, the Washington Korean community formed many community associations, mostly neighborhood groupings and businessmen's associations. Korean immigrants tended to look at their churches as community organizations of the same kind, offering meaning, support, and social ties to the newly arrived. The Korean churches have been important community as well as religious centers. Some pastors we interviewed saw this as a problem, noting that the early Korean churches resembled social clubs more than true Christian churches, which the pastors had to infuse with theology, spiritual growth, and missionary zeal. One veteran Presbyterian pastor commented:

> When I began to serve the church, I had a hard time to transform the social-club-like group to a church-like one. I remember that every time our church members had a worship service, most of them gathered at a member's home afterward. Many of them enjoyed drinking and smoking there. It was very hard for me to stop their bad habits, because I understood the difficulties in the lives of immigrants. But I began to educate them that churches should be different than social clubs. It took me quite a long time to straighten up our church. If I had failed to correct their bad habits and ideas about church, our church would have disappeared long ago. But our church has grown steadily once it became a church-like church. From that time on, I focused more on Bible study, prayer meetings, and missionary activities. They held the members together and contributed to growth.

Even though the majority of Koreans belong to denominations such as the Presbyterian, Southern Baptist, or Methodist, the denominational ties are seldom strong, and in the case of the Presbyterians, there are periodic attempts to gain more autonomy within the denomination or even to withdraw entirely and form a new Korean Presbyterian denomination. Many of the Methodist churches have withdrawn from the larger United Methodist denomination to join the Korean Methodist Church, a denomination with headquarters in Seoul. A Korean Church Association and a ministerial association both join

Protestants across denominational lines, but neither maintains contact with Catholic (let alone Buddhist) counterparts.

Of the six immigrant groups we studied, the Korean community has developed the highest level of civic organization. Koreans have the most business and civic associations, as well as several social service agencies and church-related organizations; and church leaders were often instrumental in founding the social service agencies. But ties between churches and other sorts of organizations, including social service agencies serving the community, have weakened as organizations have asserted their independence and financial support from churches has diminished.

SERVING AFRICAN IMMIGRANTS. As we saw earlier, Washington has long been an important destination for African immigration to the United States. Large numbers of Ethiopians, Eritreans, and West Africans have come to Washington in recent years, fleeing civil wars and seeking economic opportunities. Africans make up 11 percent of the foreign-born population in the area, as opposed to just 3 percent nationwide. Roughly half of these are from West Africa, primarily Nigeria and Ghana. Most of the West Africans speak English. Many are self-employed or have professional-level positions, though employment niches for Africans include taxi drivers and parking lot attendants. Relatively large numbers live in the District of Columbia itself, though Africans are also dispersed throughout the inner suburbs like the majority of other recent immigrants.

Because of the diversity of national origins and ethnicity among West African immigrants, distinctively African churches were slow to develop in the Washington, D.C., area. Starting in the late 1970s, Nigerian Catholics from the large Igbo tribal group began to meet for a monthly mass in their own language at the Catholic University of America (see the more detailed account in chapter 6). These meetings eventually evolved into the Nigerian Catholic Community recognized by the archdiocese and headquartered at Holy Names Parish near Howard University in Washington, D.C. Other Nigerian Catholic communities have since appeared, connected to other parishes. A much smaller group from Francophone Africa also meets at Holy Names. Similarly, Igbo Episcopalians established a relationship with St. John's Episcopal Anglican Church in Mt. Rainier, Maryland (close to the D.C. border) in the mid-1970s and began holding regular services there. Among mainstream Christian denominations, however, the more general pattern has been one of accommodating sizable, multiethnic African communities within a larger worship community. Instead of separate services in their native languages, Africans participate in a multicultural community led by a white or African American pastor that stresses both unity and respect for the diversity of cultural expressions within the community. Such worship communities may include Asian and Latin American immigrants as well as Africans.

Independent African churches, primarily Nigerian and serving one or the other of the two largest ethnic groups, Yoruba and Igbo, serve another sizable proportion of the African immigrant community. These are often Pentecostal in inspiration, and sometimes notably syncretistic, but some have developed important ties to American churches in the evangelical tradition. The language of worship is largely either Yoruba or Igbo, though some efforts are made to accommodate non-Yoruba and non-Igbo worshipers, and most members are fluent in both their native language and English (which is the language of government and business in Nigeria).

THE CHANGING FACE OF THE CHINESE DIASPORA IN WASHINGTON, D.C. Though there has been a small Chinese population in Washington, D.C., since the 1800s, the city's Chinatown was only settled in its current location in 1936, with some 800 residents. The Chinese population remained small until the 1960s, when immigration reform opened the doors to significant flows of immigrants from Asia. Where the majority of Chinese in the region had been descendants of Cantonese laborers brought to this country in the 1800s, Chinese immigrants after 1965 were primarily from Taiwan, the Chinese diaspora (chiefly Vietnam), and more recently mainland China. As a result, Cantonese (spoken in much of southern China, including Hong Kong, and the Southeast Asian diaspora) has competed with Mandarin (the official dialect in both Taiwan and the People's Republic of China) as the language of choice in the community for some time.

Most Chinese are not Christians, but Christianity appears to claim the largest single block of Chinese immigrants in the United States. In contrast to the 700 Protestant churches in the nation, the number of Chinese Buddhist temples and associations is less than 150 (Yang 1999, 7). We found some 24 churches serving Chinese residents in the area, two of these Catholic, the rest Protestant. In addition, we encountered two Buddhist temples and one syncretist Tianhou temple (serving mainly ethnic Chinese from Indochina).

The first church to serve the Chinese population was a mission established in 1935 by leading mainline Protestant churches in the District of Columbia. The church evolved into the Chinese Community Church, one of the leading Chinese churches in the area and the only Chinese church still in the District of Columbia. Chinese Community Church has an active community center providing services to area residents, Chinese and non-Chinese, in cooperation with the District of Columbia and the federal government. Its members include prominent Chinese business men and women and government officials, and it enjoys ties with most of the Asian social service agencies in the city. The church's membership, nevertheless, includes a high proportion of relatively poor immigrants.

Other Chinese churches emerged slowly, starting in 1958 with the establishment of the Chinese Mandarin Church, which eventually moved to suburban Maryland as the Chinese Christian Church of Greater Washington, D.C. Most of the remaining Chinese churches were established in the 1980s and after (Yang 1999, 7–9). The majority are Protestant and conservative evangelical in orientation. Most are nondenominational, in contrast to the Korean churches, which generally have formal ties to one or another Protestant denomination. Where the Chinese churches do have denominational ties, it is most often to one or another Baptist convention or the Presbyterians.

The Chinese population in the area, as in the rest of the United States, is generally well-off, with many professionals and successful business people among them. Most churches, nevertheless, are mixed, with notable percentages of members at both ends of the income spectrum. Most Chinese churches have had to accommodate increasing numbers of Mandarin speakers as immigration has increased from Taiwan and mainline China. Some do so by offering separate Cantonese and Mandarin services; others offer services in English, which also serve the growing numbers of second- and third-generation Chinese.

THE DISTINCTIVENESS OF THE MOSQUES. Controversy rages over the size of the Muslim population in the United States. Estimates range from 2 to 9 million, but few are based on systematic evidence. Census data on the foreign-born cannot help a great deal, as we have no reliable way of determining whether the immigrant population reflects the demographics of the sending countries. Even sophisticated estimates based on reported attendance at mosques founder on the tendency of religious organizations to overreport participation, and mosque attendance is, at best, an unreliable indicator of religious belief. The best estimates to date depend on survey data. These place the total number of Muslims (including American-born converts to Islam) between 1.2 and 1.9 million persons (Kosmin and Lachman 1993; Smith 2002).

A nationwide survey of mosques done in 2000 estimated that slightly over 1,200 mosques were in operation, and half of them were founded after 1980 (Bagby, Perl, and Froehle 2001). The authors estimated that the number of Muslims associated in any way with the religious life of mosques averaged 1,629 per mosque, making a total of approximately 2 million Muslims associated with mosques, undoubtedly a sizable overestimate, due in part to the tendency of many Muslims to frequent more than one mosque (see Smith

2002). The average number who participated regularly was 340. Mosques had fewer paid staff than Christian churches; in the 2000 survey, 55 percent had no paid full-time staff persons at all. All mosques include diverse ethnic groups, but 64 percent nationally have one dominant ethnic group.

The Washington, D.C., area has seen a notable growth in the presence and visibility of the Muslim population over the last 30 years. Just two area mosques predate the 1980s, and most were founded in the 1990s. Increasing numbers of immigrants from predominantly Islamic countries also point to a growing Muslim population. Iran and Pakistan accounted for over 4 percent of the foreign-born population in the area in 2000, and we can assume that a significant number of immigrants from India and Nigeria are Muslim (one of the two oldest mosques in the area is predominantly Nigerian). Evidence from our survey of religious leaders suggests that much of this population is well-off economically, but the Muslim population in the area includes refugees from Afghanistan and elsewhere who are decidedly poor.

With a few exceptions, mosques in the area are multiethnic. A Turkish mosque, the Nigerian mosque already mentioned, and a couple of Afghan communities are separate from the rest of the 13 mosques surveyed in their language of choice and the clear dominance of one national origin group. Even the prosperous mosque associated with the Iranian community emphasizes its openness to all believers in Islam. Though it continues to use Farsi in prayer services, sermons and the everyday business of the mosque are carried on in English. Other mosques may have a dominant national origin group that plays a major role in governance and decision-making, but in their worship services and everyday activities they are broadly multicultural. In all of these cases, Arabic is the language of prayer, while English is the language of sermons, business, and other activities.

Despite efforts of members of the Wahabi sect of Islam to exert influence over the Islamic education and the mosques themselves (reputedly with the financial support of the Saudi Embassy), most mosques are notably middle-of-the-road and even latitudinarian theologically. Conservative sentiment that insisted that the Muslims must always remain in exile in a non-Muslim society has been superseded in most mosques by the position that Muslims are in the United States to stay and must find ways to participate actively in a pluralistic society. Similarly, while traditional norms, such as the veiling of women, continue to be enforced in most mosques, the diversity of traditions coexisting in the mosques makes it possible for Muslim women to adapt those norms to Western circumstances, in many cases donning a scarf or modest veil only for prayer services or on mosque premises.

Washington area mosques thus display a cultural and theological pluralism that is sometimes lacking in parts of the country where heavy concentrations of Muslim immigrants from individual countries make for more
homogeneous communities. Whether the mosques in the area will go through
a period of ethnic homogenization as the size of immigrant communities from
particular countries grows remains an open question.

The first mosque constructed in the Washington, D.C., area opened in
1957 to serve the downtown diplomatic community. It is located on a prominent avenue near dozens of embassies, and it was financed by Middle Eastern
governments for the embassy population. Of the 17 mosques in our study area,
all the others are in the suburbs. Most of these started out as prayer centers—
simple spaces where Muslim men could meet their obligation to attend Friday
prayers. They quickly became community centers, however, providing not only
religious education to children and converts but a variety of programs and
services for participants. Though men dominate the leadership in virtually all
of these worship communities, women play important roles in the many activities of the mosque and have been important in establishing working relationships with community agencies and institutions.

Mosques have no definite membership lists. No mosque can report that it
has a certain number of parishioners or members; all it can do is report weekly
attendance at prayers and estimate the total number of people who participate
in any of its events over a one-year period. Based on data from mosques in the
Washington area, weekly attendance is similar to that of Catholic parishes,
which average 1,000 families.

HINDUS AND SIKHS. Indian immigration to the United States has increased
rapidly since 1965. In the Washington, D.C., area, the Indian-born population
saw a threefold jump from 1990 to 2000, with 21,697 Indians reported in
1990 and 62,887 in 2000. The boom in technology-related businesses in the
area has undoubtedly contributed to the rapid growth.

Indians in the United States commonly refer to themselves as "Indian" in
public, but among compatriots they identify themselves by their state, region,
or language group. They are Gujarati (from the Indian State of Gujarat) or
Tamil (from Tamil-Nadu or the larger Tamil ethnic region of south India),
south Indian or north Indian. But Indians also differ by religion, which is
sometimes the primary identity invoked. Besides India's majority Hindu population, roughly 12 percent of the 1 billion people of India are Muslim, living
primarily in the northern parts of the country. Sikhs, concentrated in the
Punjab region, make up a little less than 2 percent of the population, while

Christians, including three denominations reaching back centuries and each claiming the Apostle Thomas as their founder, make up 2.3 percent of the Indian population. The best estimates of the number of Hindus in the United States hover around 1.1 million, or 65 percent of the total "Asian Indian" population (Smith 2002, 581–82). This suggests higher rates of immigration on the part of other Indian religious groups, and both Indian Christians and Sikhs appear to be well represented in major urban areas in this country. Both ethnic and religious diversity introduces a centrifugal force impeding unity in the Indian community. On the one hand, early efforts to establish Indian worship communities often aspired to pan-Indian inclusiveness, sometimes attempting to include all the religious traditions of the subcontinent under one roof. At the same time, as we shall see, just as in the case of African Christians, the larger the Indian community, the more likely it is for relatively homogeneous worship communities to form along religious and linguistic divides.

We focus here on Hindu and Sikh worship communities in the area. Hinduism is one of the oldest surviving religions in the world, dating back over 4,000 years. It is polytheistic, decentralized, without a single authoritative leader, without a geographic center, and without a single authoritative holy book. Rather, Hinduism draws on an broad collection of age-old sacred texts, temples, rituals, and identities, with new entrants to the theological and devotional repertoire arising all the time.

Hindu temples differ from Christian churches in that they have no concept of "congregation" or "member." They are houses of prayer, where individuals or family groups may circulate, praying before one or another deity, with or without the services of a priest. On the occasion of major festivals, on the other hand, public ceremonies led by priests may involve hundreds of devotees. In the United States, temples may also be community centers providing a gathering place and religious education to adults and their children. Hinduism has no prescribed weekly communal prayer or worship. Many Hindus have altars in their homes and perform prayers at home as well as at the temple. There is no obligation to pray at a temple at all—much less to do so regularly. Most temples have a core devotee community, yet many Indians visit multiple temples. In the United States, the core community includes a lay board of directors who raise funds, manage the property, hire priests, and oversee activities. This stands in contrast to the situation of most Hindu temples in India, where priestly families are generally in charge of temple affairs.

The other major setting for Hindu worship is the ashram, a spiritual community, usually led by an acknowledged holy man (or sometimes a woman) rather than a priest, and devoted to spiritual training. In the United States, ashrams may be centers of worship as well as retreat and education centers.

Services tend to be more communal in these settings, with more the flavor of an American Protestant-style "congregation," including a shared meal following the service.

The first Indian temple in the Washington, D.C., area was begun in 1965, though it was not formally registered until 1976. For the first 10 years it was a loose fellowship of students and young professionals, and its leaders invited Jains, Sikhs, Parsis, and other Indians to its social gatherings. Another early community, though led by Indians from the state of Gujarat, also attempted to be as inclusive as possible, inviting members of other religious traditions to its events on a regular basis. Over time, however, these pan-Indian worship communities were supplanted by others, as various groups of devotees split off to form their own societies—the Jains, South Indian Shaivites, Gujaratis, and others. The newer worship communities tend to be less inclusive and, in at least one case, less tolerant of other religions and more nationalistic than the original organizations. In 2001 there were 10 Hindu temples in our study area, several of which were very large, and two ashrams.

Sikhism started as a reform movement within the Hindu tradition, founded by Guru Nanak (1469–1539), a contemporary of Martin Luther. Nanak was born a Hindu but joined a Sufi order, and then struck out on his own, teaching that there is but one God and that all humans are equal. Nanak's teachings put special emphasis on compassion and service, and he encouraged equality among his followers through the institution of the communal kitchen, which persists today in ritual form in the communal meal following Sikh services. A series of gurus led the movement after Nanak's death, culminating in Guru Gobind Singh, the ninth guru, who created the "Universal Brotherhood of the Khalsa" in 1699 as a response to the crisis of persecution faced by Sikhs at the time. Under Gobind Singh's discipline, ritual baptism committed male Sikhs to five outward signs of the faith: unshorn hair, covered by a small turban; a small comb symbolizing cleanliness; a steel bracelet; a sacred undergarment; and a small sword, reminding devotees that they are "God's soldiers" (Singh 1994, 167).

Partly as a result of Indian prime minister Indira Gandhi's targeting of Sikhs in the early 1980s, an important, if minority, movement among Sikhs today advocates a separate Punjabi homeland for Sikhs.[7] Though religious violence between Hindus and Sikhs has quieted since the 1980s, the repercussions of these events in India continue to color Sikh politics in the United States (as we shall see in chapter 4).

The first Sikh gathering in Washington was for Sikhs in the Indian Embassy community and a few university students. The first worship center, named the Sikh Cultural Society, grew out of this group in 1964. It tried to be inclusive of all Sikhs, yet it eventually splintered. The first split was over caste divisions (even though Sikhism opposes castes), compounded by personal rivalries. Later divisions were over theological and political issues. In general, the parent congregation was more theologically and politically liberal than the break-off groups. The schisms have continued to the present day, made easier by the constant growth of the Sikh community due to immigration.

The Sikh gurdwaras are smaller and more communal than the Hindu temples, but several have congregations in the hundreds. Most have twice-weekly meetings for worship and fellowship. The buildings are essentially meeting centers, not temples, and they have no idols or shrines. Instead, the altar gives pride of place to the "Guru Granth Sahib," or sacred book of the Sikh religion, which consists of the body of hymns composed by the nine historic gurus. People may come and go for the service, which may last two hours or longer and consists of ritual chanting of the hymns. Families take turns preparing and serving the ritual meal that follows the service. As in the case of the Hindu temples, a board of directors, normally elected by the community, manages the property and affairs of the community and hires professional singers and religious teachers (*granthi*).

Conclusion

Whether we consider the circumstances of their immigration to the United States, their levels of income and education, or the characteristics of their religious institutions, the new immigrants are diverse, and far more diverse than the immigrants of the last great period of immigration to this country. This makes generalization about "the new immigration" difficult. While a large number of contemporary immigrants are poor and occupy the bottom of the income and job ladders, others have moved readily into professional jobs and enjoy high levels of both income and prestige, thanks to educational and professional training in their home countries. Despite racial and ethnic stereotyping, which affects poor and privileged non-Western immigrants alike, immigrant communities with high numbers of professionals enjoy advantages that poorer immigrant groups simply do not have. Even among poorer immigrant communities, moreover, the relatively privileged immigration status of all Cuban and many Southeast Asian refugees contrasts sharply with the official reception of immigrants from Haiti, Central America, and Mexico, most of whom have arrived without official sanction.

These differences will have an impact as we examine the roles of worship communities in the social and civic incorporation of the new immigrants. But the character of these worship communities, based in part on their own religious traditions, will also influence how and what they do for those who participate in them. Some recent work on immigrant worship communities has argued that we are seeing their "Americanization" under the impress of the congregational template (Warner 1998, 2000; Yang and Ebaugh 2001). Our reading of the evidence does not support so sweeping a judgment (we take up the question in more detail in the conclusion). More important, the existing differences among worship communities appear to us to have had a powerful impact on how and to what extent they provide their members with social capital, involve them in civic action in the larger society, train them in skills relevant to civic engagement, and help shape identities that articulate a distinctive sense of their place in America.

Both religious tradition and the efforts of religious and lay leaders contribute to distinctive organizational cultures across immigrant worship communities. Where the Sikh *gurdwara* has a distinctly "congregational" feel, with its emphasis on community life, regular worship services, and communal meal, the Hindu temple is primarily a house of worship, where individuals and families come and go and services at fixed times draw only a small proportion of devotees. Korean Protestant churches are generally quite small—typically with fewer than 100 members—and have the feel of Becker's "family-style" congregation, while most Catholic parishes draw hundreds of worshipers at Sunday masses but have limited contact with most of their members beyond that. Such differences will often be crucial in explaining the distinctive profiles of the worship communities examined here. In the next chapter, we begin this closer look at the evidence, considering how and to what degree different worship communities provide their members with social capital.

3

Sources of Social Capital

Religious institutions can be a prime source of social capital for recent immigrants. They are the primary voluntary institutions in the lives of many immigrants, and they may be the primary locus of face-to-face relationships outside the family. Local worship communities can provide both adults and youth with extended social networks that offer psychological support, trust, and acceptance (reinforcing such networks), and access to educational and job opportunities and other sources of material resources. They may help connect immigrants to social services, legal assistance, and community organizations of all sorts. They may also help integrate them into larger networks, with whatever access to opportunities and resources these might provide. Religious solidarity and identity can serve to strengthen bonds among participants, and the authority of religious leaders can help draw them into contact with the larger community through volunteer service and other acts of citizenship.[1]

The notion of social capital, as we saw, has been diversely defined and applied. For our purposes, social capital is best seen as access to resources thanks to regular networks and interactions. Not all social capital is equally valuable. People may enjoy rich ties with others, but those ties may link them to only modest or poor resources. Nor is social capital necessarily constructive from the point of view of the larger community or the polity. The effects of association for democratic citizenship, as Mark E. Warren has carefully shown (2001), varies according to the sorts of association and the circumstances in which they operate. Our first task will be to try to discern to what degree participants in these various worship communities possess social capital of any kind. This depends upon two factors: first, to what extent does participation in a worship community produce ties among members, with people beyond the immediate community, or both? Second, how valuable are the resources to which the networks it engenders or embodies give access? For example, we should ask: Is this the sort of congregation depicted by Nancy Ammerman (1997), where sociality is as important as spiritual uplift? Or do participants come and go without much contact among themselves or with the institution as a whole, intent primarily on the act of worship or prayer? But we will also want to know whether members are uniformly poor, with few links, personal or institutional, to a wider set of resources. Or is the community economically and educationally diverse, featuring members who have or can readily gain access to important resources for fellow members? Finally, we should ask: Does the worship community itself maintain linkages with a resource-rich environment? Or do religious leaders have a relatively closed and resource-poor circle of institutional contacts?

In the discussion that follows, accordingly, we will pay particular attention to the sorts of linkages immigrants are likely to encounter within their local worship community, the resources that might accrue from participation in the worship community, and the degree to which the community itself provides both key resources and linkages to resources beyond the community. Each of these is important for assessing the "use value" of whatever social capital might be available in a given community: if the resources at the disposal of community members are poor, the community's social capital will be poor, no matter how intensive the social bonds among members. If the community itself provides extensive services, it will be relatively rich in social capital, even if social bonds are weak. And if immigrants can make connections to people and resources beyond the community thanks to their participation, they will enjoy relatively rich social capital, whether or not they enjoy tight bonds with many people within the community.

Tight, Lite, and Missing Social Networks

Social capital starts with social networks, and it is widely assumed that worship communities are apt at providing members with valuable social ties. Indeed, in the growing literature on religion in the lives of immigrants, it is often taken for granted that immigrants turn to religious institutions for fellowship. But to what extent do local worship communities actually provide such fellowship?

Fellowship is more likely in smaller worship communities or in communities in which people have opportunities to participate in small, face-to-face gatherings. In chapter 2, we noted differences across religious traditions and ethnic groups in the size of worship communities. Even the larger congregations, however, may be broken down into smaller, more intimate groups that provide opportunities for building social networks and bonding social capital. Our survey of religious leaders asked whether the worship community has "cell groups, devotional groups, or other faith-sharing groups that meet regularly." Respondents from Catholic, Protestant, and Hindu communities overwhelmingly replied in the affirmative. But the percentage of adult members who took part in such groups was quite low among Catholic, Hindu, and Muslim worship communities, where most communities reported that fewer than 25 percent of their members participated (table 3.1). Christian churches have more such groups than Indian worship communities, either Hindu or Sikh, or mosques. And among Christian churches, Protestant churches of whatever nationality have a higher percentage of participation than Catholic parishes—an average of 47 percent, compared with 26 percent. Only 2 out of 12 Catholic parishes reported more than 50 percent participation in such groups.

The Protestant congregations often involved a high percentage of members in smaller Bible study or prayer groups. This was particularly true among Korean congregations, where it is very common for the community to be broken into "cell groups" according to age, family circumstances, or profession. In many Korean churches, virtually all members are incorporated into such cells,

TABLE 3.1. Interaction and Social Networks in Worship Communities of Five Religious Traditions (Percentage of Communities)

	Catholic	Protestant	Muslim	Hindu	Sikh
Number of cases	22	150	14	9	4
Congregation has cell groups, devotional groups, or other faith-sharing groups that meet regularly	100	91	14	78	25
(If yes:) Average percent of regular adult participants who take part in them regularly	26	47	17	25	a
Average number of groups, meetings, classes, and events for special purposes that took place in the last year	4.5	7.6	7.6	4.8	8.5

a Too few cases to analyze

which meet weekly or biweekly in a member's home for Bible study, prayer, discussion, and a Korean meal. The practice is also quite common among Chinese Protestant congregations. Most of the African churches, by contrast, had rates of participation of less than 30 percent (see table 3.2).

Besides groups created for expressly religious purposes, many worship communities have other sorts of regular group meetings. We asked respondents whether any groups, meetings, or classes focused on one or another of a number of purposes had taken place within the past 12 months. Answers varied from none to 19 different sorts of groups, from gatherings to clean the building to job training classes and political discussion groups. While we have no indication of how frequently any of these groups met, the number mentioned gives us a rough measure of opportunities for face-to-face engagement in the life of the community. Virtually all worship communities had at least one program; but Sikh congregations, Protestant churches, and mosques had the most. Catholic parishes had the fewest, averaging 4.5 such activities, while Hindu communities averaged 4.8.

The degree to which local worship communities provide bonding social capital thus appears to vary widely among communities. It also varies systematically, with Korean Protestant churches much more likely than other worship communities to do so. Catholic parishes, mosques, and Hindu temples are considerably less likely to foster the development of bonding social capital. Thanks to their larger size, these worship communities do provide periodic opportunities for lay people to gather for classes, lectures, discussion, or special projects that can help people get to know one another and, at times, people from outside the community. But these bodies also have many members who simply come and go, with little formal contact with the institution and little opportunity or incentive to build networks within the context of the worship community.

TABLE 3.2. Interaction and Social Networks in Congregations by National Origin

	African	Chinese	Indian	Korean	Salvadoran
Number of cases	39	15	13	65	54
Congregation has cell groups, devotional groups, or other faith-sharing groups that meet regularly (percent of worship communities)	92	80	62	94	94
(If yes:) Average percent of regular adult participants who take part in them regularly	28	48	29	51	45
Average number of groups, meetings, classes, and events for special purposes that took place in the last year	9.3	7.7	5.9	7.3	7.9

How do we explain these differences? Both larger size and the general lack of attention to providing settings for sociability stem from the organizational culture of Catholic, Muslim, and Hindu worship communities as mainly "houses of worship." Though individual mosques, parishes, or temples may assume a different organizational culture, the general structure of the worship community in these traditions is oriented toward providing a place of worship first and foremost. In all three traditions, "membership" is a slippery term. For Catholics, it has been traditionally determined by geography: one is expected to worship in the parish in which one lives. The doors, nevertheless, are open to all comers, and no norms, informal or formal, prevent a perfect stranger from attending a Catholic mass and taking Communion.[2] Nor does the stranger feel any compulsion to stay afterward for the social hour, rarely found in Catholic parishes in any case (and sparsely attended when found). Mosques and Hindu temples are similarly open to all, so long as basic protocols are maintained. Leaders of mosques and temples, moreover, found it difficult to answer our questions about membership, because people came and went according to convenience or for specific celebrations. In each tradition, nevertheless, we found important exceptions—worship communities that emphasized community building, provided opportunities for sociability, and maintained multiple programs to draw people more deeply into the life of the community. To understand the ways worship communities provide bonding social capital and explain differences among them, then, we need to look more closely at some examples.

Bonding Social Capital in Korean Churches

The typical Korean Protestant church is quite small and almost exclusively Korean in membership. At the same time, it is an important source of social capital for newcomers. It provides recent immigrants a place for making friends, locating housing and work, purchasing a car, and finding guidance for such mundane but important aspects of making their way in American society as signing up for social security, getting a driver's license, and choosing a school for their children. Many Korean pastors make it a practice to communicate with potential members while they are still in Korea, helping to orient them for the move. The pastor himself might pick a family up at the airport, find an initial place for them to live, and make serious efforts to connect them to the larger Korean community, in some cases finding them jobs. The tie to a church and its pastor is thus a relatively rich instance of social capital for many newcomers.

Newcomers, once a part of a faith community, find that the most important mechanism for building social bonds is the cell group. All the Korean churches we observed have them. They are formed and supervised by the pastors, who see them as indispensable for spiritual life and church growth. Pastors set up the cell groups according to geography, socioeconomic status, or members' interests. Whatever the criteria, pastors prefer cell groups of similar persons, since groups of this type generate more cohesion and intimacy among members. In most cases, it is understood that the husband's cell group is that of his wife and family, as well, though special gatherings for young people of the second generation may draw away this cohort.

Most Korean churches have fewer than 100 regular members, but even the bigger churches utilize cell groups to provide the sense of intimacy that the smaller churches enjoy. The Korean Christian Center (a megachurch in suburban Maryland) currently has 72 cell groups, while the University Korean Church and Korean Suburban Presbyterian churches (both small) have four and two, respectively. Approximately 65 percent of the members of these three churches participate in cell groups. The cell groups meet monthly, biweekly, or weekly, varying from church to church. Meetings are usually in a member's home, and all have clearly worked-out programs. At University Korean Church, the cells pursue Bible studies, while the Suburban Presbyterian Church's cells engage in worship and fellowship. The cell groups at the megachurch include both Bible study and fellowship.

Besides Bible study, prayer, and discussion, cell group meetings provide a valuable setting for social interaction. The members talk about traditional Korean dishes, job openings, possibilities for opening new businesses, hobbies, and politics in the United States and Korea. Some groups watch sports events and take outings together. All is not love and acceptance, however, and cell groups occasionally erupt in political arguments. For this reason, cell group leaders are carefully chosen and trained, since they will need to control conflicts, mediate disputes, and follow theological guidelines established by the local church. All Korean pastors are aware of potential divisiveness arising from the cell group system, including challenges to their own authority. In one Korean church, the assistant pastor and the cell group leaders meet frequently and develop a close relationship in an effort to support leaders and head off painful schisms. In spite of the danger of conflict, cell groups are used in most Korean Protestant churches, and many Catholic parishes serving Koreans have adopted them due to their obvious value for leadership training, enhancing spiritual growth, building congregation cohesion, and attracting new members. The practice first developed in Korea and was brought to the United States in the 1970s by pastors concerned that Korean churches had become little more than social clubs.

A related phenomenon found in some Korean churches is a system of training programs. The Korean megachurch in our study, for example, has a series of three courses on Bible and doctrine. These courses are recommended but not required. A majority of new members enroll in the first course, but the dropout rate is high, and only about one-tenth finish. Enrollment in the second and third is much lower. Completion of all three is required for candidacy for church deacon, and proven success in serving as church deacon is required for higher church office. The instructors of the courses hope that the new members form friendship groups, and they encourage this by helping people exchange addresses and phone numbers and by giving members assignments requiring teamwork. Friendships often do form in the courses, and they provide newcomers with long-term ties and support.

When churches grow large enough, they organize other sorts of subgroups—first women's and men's associations, then youth groups and senior members' groups. These groups are mostly gender-specific and age-specific, and their meetings are not unlike cell group meetings. However, they are different in that they collect membership dues, meet less often, and are more decidedly social in character. The activities of these subgroups promote fraternity among members. For example, whenever a member has a special family occasion, he or she invites the subgroup members to the gathering. The number of subgroups in a church depends on church size. The Korean Christian Center has more than 30, while the smaller churches we observed each had two or three.

Korean churches in this country have become social centers more than they were in Korea. In America, the Korean churches provide people of Korean descent with a place for information gathering, fellowship, assistance, social status, preservation of cultural heritage, and personal identity. At the same time, the Korean churches, by sponsoring so many internal activities, may impede their members' cultural assimilation and social incorporation into the wider U.S. society. Nevertheless, as we shall see, the superior resources and economic opportunities that many Koreans enjoy mean that social bonds within these communities yield relatively rich social capital and may provide important bridges to individuals, groups, and resources outside the Korean community.

Social Bonding in the Mosque

Most mosques in the Washington, D.C., area are multinational in membership. As we argued in the preceding chapter, this is at least partly due to the relatively small national communities among Muslims in the area. Some mosques acquire identities according to the dominant nationality of their participants. For example, Masjid Al-Muslimeen in suburban Virginia consists of mainly newer Arab and Somali immigrants, while the Potomac Islamic Center mosque has a clear majority of Pakistanis, and the Mustafa Center mosque is over 80 percent Afghan. Nevertheless, most are multicultural, and this suggests two possibilities from the point of view of social capital. On the one hand, greater diversity makes possible a more diverse array of ties and resources, as Granovetter's argument (1974) would lead one to expect. On the other hand, we could expect that mosques would tend to develop subcommunities of adherents along national or ethnic lines. In practice, the two possibilities are in tension. A statement by an occasional female attender at the Mustafa Center illustrates the difficulty of being multicultural:

> I like to come to this mosque because it's close to my home and the people are nice, but I usually feel kind of lonely. I guess the younger Afghans who speak English are at school or work, and most of the older women who come don't speak English. The sermon is also done mostly in Farsi, and the English translation afterward doesn't seem as long or detailed. And a lot of the fliers on the walls are in Farsi, so I can't read them. I know there aren't a lot of people here that aren't Afghan, but I wish the activities were more open to everyone.

Even in the more multicultural mosques of the area, people tend to socialize by family and ethnic group, so that interaction across ethnic lines is limited. But in such settings, common language often serves to bridge differences in national origin (as it also does in many Hispanic churches) and provide the basis for bonding among members. Where that language is English, groups may be more encompassing. But Arab-speakers from the Middle East and Urdu-speakers from South Asia are also able to cross national boundaries in their friendship circles. A Syrian woman at Masjid Al-Muslimeen describes her experience this way: "When I came to America, I didn't know anyone, and Masjid Al-Muslimeen was the first mosque I came to. I don't speak very good English, so I felt happy to be around other Arabs who I can speak with. I've made a lot of friends here, and I feel like I'm part of the community now. We go to the Friday night activities and our kids go to the Sunday school classes. We have family dinners and picnics, and we go shopping together." For those who share widely used languages in the Muslim community, area mosques can provide important sources of bonding social capital.

As in some of the Korean worship communities, many mosques organize small groups or courses to provide religious orientation for newcomers. The Potomac Islamic Center recently established a support program for new converts. It gives new members an opportunity to discuss relevant questions, concerns, and ideas, and at the same time it helps integrate members into the programs of the mosque and the wider community. The Islamic training portion of the program highlights the fundamentals of being a Muslim, such as prayer, fasting, giving alms, and making a pilgrimage to Mecca. Each new member is given a mentor of the same gender who is available to discuss any question, social or personal. The program recently opened a book and video library. A young male convert recalls:

> When I first converted to Islam I didn't know many Muslims except for the ones at college. Since they didn't live in my area, it was difficult to get to know other people here. I was too shy to introduce myself to people at Friday prayer and didn't want to come alone to other mosque activities. People were actually pretty nice, but they didn't really make an effort to get to know me. Maybe it was because they assumed I knew other Muslims already. I was so happy when they created this support group. It opened the door for me to get to know other converts in my situation. We have similar questions and needs. My mentor was always available for me to talk to and was quick to get any resources I needed. Now I really feel like a member of the community here.

In most mosques, as well, groups are organized for more intimate religious education and practice. At the Potomac Islamic Center, at least three groups that we know of meet outside the mosque. One is a Sufi group (Sufism is a widespread mystical movement in Islam). Another is a conservative women's study group made up of predominantly Syrian women. Another is a group of Arab women who form a rather closed circle for weekly religious study sessions. Besides the express purposes for which these groups are formed, they supply typical supports for their members such as passing on tips regarding job opportunities, professional services, child care groups, play groups, or home schooling.

Mosques sponsor periodic social gatherings such as monthly potlucks, youth programs, and Islamic study circles. These gatherings strengthen bonds among the members, though opportunities for bonding vary for men and women. Since Friday afternoon prayers are obligatory for men but not women in Islamic doctrine, the men see each other more often than the women do. However, there are other activities to attend, such as religious study sessions for adults, gatherings of parents of Sunday school students, fundraising activities, and special programs to orient newcomers to American society. Through these means, the women often develop stronger social bonds among themselves than do the men.

All four mosques we studied had abundant opportunities for volunteer work. Volunteers were solicited for building maintenance, coordinating and running educational and recreational programs, assisting social service programs, helping new immigrants with legal paperwork, cooking for fundraising, working at fundraising events and holiday celebrations, ushering at special occasions, and helping in the parking lots. Most of the people who volunteer seem to be repeat volunteers from a core group. The bulk of volunteers were women. Here, too, we find rich opportunities for establishing and taking advantage of social ties, though the number of people involved in such activities is necessarily limited. Social capital in most of these activities is strongly gendered, given the separation of the sexes that prevails in the mosques and the greater availability of women for volunteer work in this community. While a few jobs are reserved for men, many are the work of women, who have often played important roles in making the mosque as much a community center as a place of worship.

Hindu Temples: Weak Ties, Strong Institutions

Of the several categories of worship communities in our study, Hindu temples are the weakest in bonding social capital. A principal reason is theological: temples were never envisioned to forge close-knit congregations of members. Indeed, Hindu temples do not have the concept "member" at all, and there are no membership lists. All that exist are mailing lists, to which new names are added without hesitation (including the names of members of our research group). In India, most temples were established by leading families and maintained by donations from followers. They had no constitution or canon law. Furthermore, the Hindu tradition has no concept of congregational worship in the Western sense. Traditionally, worship was done family by family at a time convenient for them to come. Furthermore, there is no Hindu expectation that a believer will "join" a particular temple. The traditional understanding is that all temples are available, and believers may visit multiple temples as they wish. This conception continues more or less unchanged in the immigrant Indian communities in America. Temple-hopping is a normal and approved practice. There is no obligation to be committed to any one temple, and there is no obligation to attend a temple regularly. The most common pattern is that a family will go mainly for festivals.

For example, we interviewed a family who hires a priest from one temple for a home ritual celebration (called a *pooja*), visits another about once a month, has gone to a third and fourth for big religious festivals, and sends their grandchildren to something resembling a Sunday school at still another temple. Where they participate and how depends on which temple best meets each particular need.

One informant in a large temple estimated that 20,000 people come in the course of a year, but only about 1,000 to 1,500 arrive weekly. Families usually enter the temple as a group, without speaking to other families. They circle the interior of the temple, pausing at most shrines to pray. A typical family devotion was described by one of our researchers:

> I observed a family's routine one Saturday morning. It is typical. The family included a set of middle-aged parents with their two young children and an elderly man. They entered and took off their shoes, and each washed their feet and hands in the designated area. They walked into the temple, stopping first at the Kartikkeya idol. The elderly man stayed at the front praying by quietly reciting Sanskrit prayers and completing a complex set of gestures, while the woman prostrated herself on the floor. The man and his children walked all the way around the idol, touching each side. Before moving on, the man did a different set of gestures and prayers, then herded his kids to the oil lamp burning in the altar where each family member "brought the light to their eyes" by placing their hands in front of the flame and sweeping the "light" or "blessing" to their eyes. This sequence was repeated over and over at each altar—skipping a few. The family did not speak to each other except to scold the children occasionally. They passed a small group of Krishna devotees who chanted in front of his altar. At the Venkateswara altar, the family sat down briefly, along with other devotees who crowded the area, while another family ritual was going on. They waited until the end and then took various forms of blessings distributed by the priests—a liquid that is sipped and then wiped across the hair, a few raisins and nuts, a flame that swept to one's eyes, the brief placing of "God's crown" on their forehead by the priest, and lastly a pinch of color applied to the forehead. The woman bought a $7 ticket for a sponsored ritual from a volunteer, then ushered her family to the Lakshmi altar, where a priest had been summoned to meet them. He recited some prayers in Sanskrit and blessed each family member with the different forms of blessings—as well as the onlookers. The family

then exited the temple, put on their shoes, and went downstairs to buy lunch.

Hindu worship communities in the Washington area are divided increasingly according to adherents' language and region of origin. Within the Indian community, individuals define themselves by state (for example, Gujarat or Mysore), region (North or South), or language. To compound the diversity, the Hindu religion has about 20 major gods, which are partly identified by region, so that some are prominent in the South and others in the North. For a Hindu in America, to be "ecumenical" means to recognize all the major gods. A few Hindu worship communities in the Washington, D.C., area are ecumenical in this way, but not the majority. Most temples are defined by region and devotion to a few gods.

About half of the Hindu temples aspire to be pan-Indian, though, with one exception, they do not attempt to include Jains, Buddhists, Sikhs, or Indian Christians.[3] The biggest temple, which we will call the Dravidi Temple, was described to us as a "nonpolitical Indian-American temple" and "the God mall." While originally a South Indian temple, it has reached out to North Indians also, and now about one-fourth of the devotees are North Indians. It has an advantage in being located close to a major university and easily reached by the numerous Indians in the area. There is little opportunity for the majority of the devotees to feel like part of a community. It is run assuming the traditional Hindu style of family-based worship, in which families come for devotions to the gods at all times of the day. The temple does not have a weekly congregational gathering, and the large majority of the devotees do not volunteer to help, though a small core of volunteers sit on the board of directors, participate in fundraising, and oversee festivals and other community activities. Opportunities to build social bonds are thus limited to those with a special interest in the life of the temple. The main other avenues for devotees to meet others is by joining special devotional groups or by taking their children to one of the educational programs.[4]

Another temple, which we will call Temple Parthi, provides an interesting contrast to the majority of Hindu institutions in the area. Temple Parthi draws mainly worshipers from the Indian state of Gujarat. The temple has communal worship three times a day, as well as the family and individual devotions already described. In these worship services, all devotees who are present gather in front of the main altar while the priest performs rituals of devotion. Then hymns are sung, everyone parades around the main idols, and blessings are bestowed by the priest in the form of water thrown over the congregation. On Sunday evening, this temple has its biggest event of the week, a service of devotional songs sung by 60 to 100 people seated on the floor prior to the regular communal worship. After the service, dozens of people stand in the hallway and outside talking and socializing. The smaller size of the core community, a common ethnic background, and regular Sunday gatherings all promote stronger social ties. This temple is also a major sponsor of Hindutva (Hindu fundamentalist) activism, providing a Sunday school and summer camp to inculcate the youth of the community in a particularly militant form of Hinduism. Stronger social ties here are a direct expression of the politico-theological commitment of the temple.

Hindu ashrams are distinct from temples, in that they embody distinctive spiritual movements whose purpose is to deepen devotion and train lay people and aspiring monks in a particular spiritual discipline. The Hare Krishna movement is the most familiar example in the Western context, but a number of spiritual movements have established ashrams in U.S. cities. Unlike the temples (but resembling the Temple Parthi community in some respects), the ashrams sponsor regular devotions as well as classes for adults, children, and youth. The well-attended Wednesday evening *pooja* at the Ramakrishna Mission, for example, features a largely communal celebration in which a number of lay men and women, as well as aspiring monks, play leadership roles; the whole community participates actively in the singing, and, at the end of the ceremony, the congregation processes around the image of Shiva. Some leave at the end of the service, and a few stop to worship before one or another image, but the majority go the neighboring cafeteria to share a ritual meal. Though more than 100 people of all ages are present, participants know one another and stop to meet and greet each other outside the hall or in the cafeteria at the end of the service.

Both religious and political activism thus may shape the religious life of a Hindu worship community in ways more conducive to building bonding social capital than the predominant practice in Hindu "houses of worship" allows. In the cases of Temple Parthi and Ramakrishna Mission, theological undercurrents in Hinduism come to the foreground, sharpening the theological focus of the group and mandating forms of worship and sociality that promote group solidarity and exchange. These worship communities take on much more the coloration of Becker's "family-style" and "community" congregations, as a result. They place much more emphasis on establishing social bonds among their members, encouraging regular membership and inculcating communally-held norms and ideas among them. In these respects, they resemble less the traditional Hindu temple than Sikh congregations, where ritualized worship and ritual fellowship combine in forming close communities. But a look at the Sikh community can also give us insights into the sometimes close relation between social solidarity and group conflict.

Community and Conflict: Sikh Congregations

As we saw in the last chapter, Sikhism is a late development in the Hindu tradition, emphasizing community, service, and devotion to one God. Sikh congregations do not have ornate temples, nor does an image of God occupy a central honored place in their buildings. Instead, attention is focused on the words of the seven gurus who decisively shaped the tradition, enshrined in a sacred book, the Guru Granth Sahib, that is the center of worshipers' attention during most of their regular worship services.

Sikh congregations have twice-weekly gatherings overseen by learned teachers. These gatherings include devotional chanting led by professional singers or lay men, sermons, speeches, announcements, and then a meal for everyone. They last several hours, and some families have a habit of arriving midway through to catch the last prayers, announcements, and the meal. Regular attendance at the weekly gatherings is considered important for "good" Sikhs, and families rotate duties in the kitchen preparing the ritual meal. Each Sikh congregation possesses a list of members and feels a sense of community, though the congregations in the area average some 300 people in size. At the Sahib Foundation, one of the large congregations, there is a nonchalant social atmosphere that is partly religious, partly social. Due to the large size of the congregation, when visitors arrive, they may not even be noticed or greeted. But regular members know and greet one another as they leave their shoes at the door or linger in the hall leading to the larger rooms devoted to worship and the communal meal. At the Singh Society, a smaller congregation, most attendees at the Sunday gatherings seem to know one another, and there is much chatting during the group meal and afterward. Children go to each other's houses afterward, and parents spend a long time talking and coordinating plans with each other.

Despite the religion's repudiation of caste and doctrine of inclusiveness, Sikh congregations have split acrimoniously on caste lines and over issues such as the roles permitted so-called cut-hair Sikhs, that is, men who have Western-style haircuts and don a turban only for ritual occasions, if at all. Periodic elections of board members are often the occasion for such splits, which can escalate to struggles over ownership of the building and angry confrontations between factions. During our fieldwork, the police were called in at one prominent congregation to dislodge families who had occupied the building in an effort to wrest control from the elected officers. The emphasis on solidarity that is a prominent part of the Sikh religion thus cuts both ways, encouraging a tightly knit community (and ritual and social practices that embody that ideal) while providing the grounds, both ideological and social, for bitter divisions. Events in India have played an important role in some such divisions, particularly in the early 1980s, when violent conflicts between Sikhs and Indian security forces led to Sikh calls for an independent "Khalistan" on the soil of the Indian state of the Punjab. Sikhs in Washington rallied to protect themselves from charges of terrorism launched by the Indian government and echoed by some politicians here, but they also divided over support for Khalistan; some accused the original Sikh Cultural Society of being "pro-Indian," and at least one congregation formed around advocacy for an independent Sikh homeland.

Such conflicts illustrate the two sides of bonding social capital in any group. On the one hand, dense social networks provide participants with a wide variety of supports. On the other, they often sharpen awareness of boundaries between "us" and "them" and a tendency, consequently, for personal, theological, and political differences to generate bitter divisions around definitions of who belongs and who does not. Becker's discussion of "family"- and community-oriented congregations underlines some of the liabilities of tightly knit worship communities emphasizing solidarity. In contrast to the more process-oriented community congregations in her study, she found conflicts in family congregations quickly escalating around personality and perceptions of differences over who was an "insider" or "outsider." Pastors were often the targets of these conflicts, just as conflicts in the Sikh community often center on leadership choice (Becker 1998). And divisions often led to lasting acrimony between congregations, hampering the efforts of most Sikh leaders to promote better understanding of Sikhs in American society. Bonding social capital is thus not an unambiguous good, even from the point of view of social solidarity.

It's Who You Know That Counts

So far we have looked at the sorts of networks that immigrant worship communities promote and their extent. But social capital must be measured not just by the degree to which people belong to social networks but by the sorts of resources to which those networks give access. Network density being equal, more advantaged worship communities will provide richer social capital to participants. More diverse communities, moreover, are more likely to provide a richer variety of resources and opportunities via the social networks within them. Finally, such advantages as higher educational and income levels among members and more diversity among them may provide participants with greater social capital even where social networks are not particularly dense. This is one important implication of Mark Granovetter's argument (1974) that "weak ties" may be more advantageous in the end than stronger ones.

Today's immigration differs markedly from that of the beginning of the last century, not only in the diversity of regions of the world represented but in the widely varying levels of education, income, and wealth current immigrants enjoy. While large numbers of immigrants today are still poor or struggling to get by on low-wage jobs and marginal small businesses, others have highly remunerated technical or professional positions. Some immigrant worship communities serve primarily poor and middle-income immigrants, while others are made up of significant numbers of those who are very well-off. Most of the latter are mixed in the incomes and educational levels of their members.

As we saw in chapter 2, the demographic profile of the "typical" worship community varies significantly across ethnic group (see table 2.3). Most Korean congregations, for example, have relatively few members living in households earning less than $25,000 a year. Only 3 of our 58 cases could really be counted as "poor" congregations, in the sense that most of their members are poor. Among Salvadorans, by contrast, 40 percent of our cases, 20 of the 50 churches, serve a membership whose majority is poor. Chinese and Indian worship communities are even less likely to have high percentages of poor members than Korean churches, while churches serving the African community are somewhere in between. At the same time, a third of the Chinese worship communities report that 20 percent or more of their members live in households earning more than $100,000 a year, as do half the Indian communities and 11 percent of the African churches. Just 1 out of 49 churches serving Salvadorans can match these percentages.

Similar differences are visible across religious traditions (see table 2.4). Almost 28 percent of Catholic immigrant communities could be said to be poor, as opposed to just 16 percent of Protestant churches and 9 percent of the mosques. All of the Hindu and Sikh communities reported few members living in poor households. Meanwhile, the same communities have a high percentage of members living in households earning over $100,000 a year—5 out of 9 Hindu communities and 1 out of 3 Sikh congregations report that over 20 percent of their members enjoy such high incomes. While most Catholic and Protestant communities have few such households represented among their members, 2 of the 17 Catholic communities and 11 of the 92 Protestant churches have a high percentage of relatively well-off members, as do 18 percent of the mosques.

The income of the membership is only a proxy for the sorts of material resources that social networks might enable members to utilize. And it leaves out of account the resources outside the immediate worship community to which intra-community ties might link members. How can we measure the degree of bridging social capital that community members might enjoy thanks to their participation in the community? We can start by presuming that worship communities with larger numbers of well-off members would enjoy a wider range of valuable connections outside the community. We might also suppose that communities with a higher percentage of college-educated members would have a greater range of outside linkages. In both respects, worship communities vary significantly by ethnicity and religious tradition. Almost 93 percent of Salvadoran churches report that fewer than a quarter of their adult membership have a college degree, while 80 percent of Chinese churches and 85 percent of Indian worship communities say that over half their adult members are college educated. Korean and African congregations are more mixed, with just 22 percent of Korean churches and 39 percent of those serving Africans reporting high levels of college education. Most mosques likewise have high percentages of the college-educated, while 72 percent of Catholic communities and 43 percent of the Protestant churches report less than a quarter college-educated (see tables 2.3 and 2.4).

In practice, this means that the resources available to members thanks to the economic and social position of fellow members potentially vary considerably among worship communities. Poor communities are much less likely to be able to provide members access to substantial resources via social networks than more mixed communities, no matter how strong the bonds among members. Similarly, communities with mainly poor members and few of the college-educated are unlikely to have the "bridging" ties that could provide members with access to resources and opportunities beyond the community. For the richer or more mixed worship communities, the amount of social capital that members enjoy depends upon the sorts of ties likely to develop among members. That is, we have to ask about the likelihood that common membership in a given worship community would provide poorer as well as better-off members access to the resources at the disposal of wealthier members. Examples include not just direct financial assistance in cases of special need but access to job and business opportunities, education, technical assistance, advice, and useful information of all sorts. Such access depends very much on how widely members interact among themselves, regardless of class, level of education, or immigration status. It depends, in other words, on the extent of "bonding" social capital in the community.

Turning back to our earlier findings regarding social networks, we would expect that Catholic, Hindu, and Muslim worship communities, despite higher levels of resources among the membership in some of these communities, will be less likely to spread these resources widely, simply because interactions among members are fewer in these communities and opportunities for crossing class and income barriers accordingly less likely to arise. Among the more mixed Korean and Chinese Protestant churches, by contrast, social capital would be high, thanks to the organizational culture of those communities, and would contribute in important ways to immigrant adaptation.

Our ethnographic studies partially confirm these expectations, at least as regards the Korean and Chinese churches. As we saw earlier, these churches are accustomed to provide high levels of informal assistance to newcomers and needy members. The cell group structure that is popular among both Chinese and Korean churches, moreover, facilitates informal sharing of information and opportunity. Because cell groups are often made up of people similar in occupation or education, they are particularly good settings for more established members of the community to provide direct assistance to newcomers with whom they share interests and background.

Similar mechanisms are at work in many of the small evangelical and Pentecostal congregations serving Salvadorans, we found, but almost always in conditions of relative resource scarcity. In the more multiclass African congregations, as in multiethnic churches serving Africans, the smaller, more intimate cell group structure is rare, but we encountered remarkable efforts to use the setting of church to provide opportunities to members. In one Nigerian independent church, at a Thanksgiving Day celebration, for example, the pastor called upon some 48 business owners, members of the church's Haggai Business Network, to come forward in church and describe their businesses. Invitations to contact individual owners regarding business opportunities were as frequent as calls for customers.

Worship Communities as Social Capital

The social capital of a worship community, however, is not just the sum of the social networks and resources of its members. It must also include the resources a community is able and willing to bring to bear as an organization on behalf of the needs of members and nonmembers and the organizational linkages it enjoys. We will look in more detail in the next chapter at the role of worship communities in providing social services of all sorts and their linkages to the larger community. To round out our description of worship communities as sources of social capital, we will sketch the broad outlines here.

First, local worship communities provide a variety of resources to their members through formal and informal programs designed to address their spiritual, social, psychological, educational, cultural, and material needs. Our survey focused primarily on the formal programs worship communities support or sponsor. In general, and in keeping with previous research, we found that larger worship communities provided a greater number and range of opportunities for members and nonmembers to meet their needs and advance their integration into American life. The large Catholic and Muslim communities were likely to sponsor citizenship classes, for example; and several Catholic parishes sponsored job training classes and afterschool programs for children. Mosques were highly likely to have programs devoted to helping immigrant members understand how American agencies and institutions such as the school system worked, and they paralleled efforts on the part of the Muslim community to educate school officials, teachers, and local police about Muslim customs. Catholic, Muslim, Hindu, Sikh, and mainline Protestant communities were also more likely than other Protestants to participate in or support social service, community development, or neighborhood organizing projects; and mainline Protestants, Catholics, and Muslims supported more such projects than others.

The larger communities, irrespective of wealth, thus provide an array of social, educational, and cultural services and opportunities. Most worship communities also make their space available for outside groups—from a Boy Scout troop or chapter of Alcoholics Anonymous to a health education program or tax clinic. In many cases, both members of the worship community and others in the neighborhood benefit from such programs. While a majority of worship communities from most of the religious traditions represented here host such groups, the number of groups hosted tends to be higher among Catholic, Muslim, and Hindu faith communities than among Protestants. Among Catholic communities, especially, these programs include community services such as health lectures or immigration clinics. Thus, worship communities that tended to display less "bonding social capital" nevertheless provided more resources and opportunities for education, training, and orientation to American life. Any attempt to draw up a "balance sheet" of contributions to the incorporation of immigrants among religious bodies would have to take these efforts into account.

Finally, worship communities may enjoy ties with a wider network, which can give them access as institutions to resources and opportunities for their members beyond the resources of the local community. They might also provide opportunities for members to take advantage of those ties or extend their own ties. We will look in more depth at such ties in the next chapter. Here we sketch the ways they serve as sources of social capital for members of the community and the varied sorts of ties that worship communities enjoy. Some immigrant worship communities are themselves part of a larger parish or congregation, which serves as their host. This provides one obvious resource in the form of a settled place to worship. Nevertheless, the relationship may be structured in a variety of ways, some of them involving considerable tension. In some Catholic dioceses, for example, many immigrant congregations are mere renters in a parish space dominated by a native-born congregation and pastor. Even where the immigrant group has been established as part of a larger parish (as in all of our cases), there may be acute tensions between the two (or more!) communities using parish facilities. Still, the tie provides certain resources to the immigrant community, or it would not last long. It also provides a setting in which the problems of incorporation may be fought out, if rarely to everyone's satisfaction. Though such battles may exacerbate divisions and sharpen prejudices, they also demand engagement on the part of at least some members of the immigrant community. In this sense, they are incorporation in practice.

Other ties include denominational and quasi-denominational affiliations and membership in ecumenical organizations on the local and national levels. These ties sometimes reach into the lives of ordinary members of the worship community, as well as providing opportunities for religious leaders to interact with their counterparts in the larger community. In this respect, the most insular groups appeared to be the smaller, more conservative Protestant congregations. Korean pastors, for example, have their own pastors' association and association of Korean churches; but these are restricted to Korean Protestant churches. Nevertheless, high percentages of Korean churches report joint worship services with communities outside their denomination and ethnic group. While such experiences provide only limited opportunities for interaction, they are expressions of integration that should not be ignored, and they provide opportunities at some level for members of different faith communities and ethnic backgrounds to work together.

The importance of this bridging social capital is hard to measure, but in general its impact depends upon the sorts of resources and opportunities that such ties provide. Immigrant Catholics and mainline Protestants can draw on a wide range of resources even where they are members of an overwhelmingly poor parish, thanks to the linkages that Catholic and mainline Protestant leaders enjoy in denominations long committed to social service and community involvement at the diocesan and national levels, in some cases tied to full-fledged social service agencies such as Catholic Charities or Lutheran Social Services. Individual pastors may not take advantage of such linkages, but they are available for entrepreneurial local leaders. Smaller evangelical churches, by contrast, are often relatively isolated or tied to denominational or associational structures that provide little help with social services. Differences rooted in religious tradition thus count importantly in explaining different levels of bridging social capital among worship communities. But so, too, does the socioeconomic background of the immigrant groups represented in those communities, sometimes in paradoxical ways. Hindu temples, for example, are little involved in the social service realm, in part because of the nature of the temple as primarily a house of worship, but in large part because most Indian immigrants are relatively affluent. Private giving, not active charity through the worship community, appears to be the norm in the Indian community. Churches that both serve needy communities and enjoy significant denominational and other linkages are likely to provide a wide range of opportunities for participants and neighbors to gather, learn English or acquire a skill, iron out legal problems, or organize around pressing issues of the day. For middle-class worship communities, by contrast, ties to the wider world provide opportunities to give or volunteer for charitable causes and religious work outside the community but bring little back to the worship community itself.

Conclusion

Local worship communities foster social capital among their participants in a variety of ways, and they differ among themselves in how and to what extent they do so. Smaller Christian churches and some larger ones promote intimate relationships among members and provide multiple opportunities for interactions that build upon and build up social capital. Larger worship communities must work self-consciously to provide opportunities of this sort, either through the "cell group" structure we found in Korean Protestant churches or through the many committees and activities in some of our larger Catholic parishes and Muslim communities. A self-conception of church as a "family" often underlies strong bonding social capital, especially among the smaller communities. But social capital effects depend upon structures that encourage sociality among members, whatever the rationale. Worship communities that function primarily as houses of worship rarely build up such structures, and larger worship communities committed to building community among their members through varied activities rarely reach more than a small portion of those who attend worship services. Bonding social capital is built largely through repeated face-to-face encounters.

Such structures are largely a feature of the default organizational culture that characterizes a given religious tradition. But each religious tradition also embodies alternative visions that can affect the organizational culture, and thus the level of social capital, within a particular worship community. The Hindu ashram, for example, differs markedly from a typical temple in emphasizing communal worship and fellowship among members who share a common devotion to a particular manifestation of the deity and a guru. Among Catholics, the post–Vatican II emphasis on participation of the laity has led to more community-oriented parish structures, while Catholicism's social justice tradition sometimes promotes wide-ranging efforts to address the needs of the poor. Korean churches, regardless of denomination and size, have adopted the cell group structure as a way of deepening faith while enhancing social solidarity within the community.

The value of the social capital present in these worship communities also varies widely. While poorer communities may provide a great deal in the way of social solidarity and low-cost material support, they cannot link members readily to opportunities for advancement in the larger community. They may even become a sort of ghetto for immigrants, reinforced by exclusivist religious ideology and intense social solidarity. But worship communities with predominantly poor members may also provide access to a wide range of opportunities if the community itself is well connected, through denominational ties or thanks to the initiative of religious and lay leaders. In poor communities, bridging social capital can outdo bonding social capital as a source of support and opportunity for many immigrants.

Bonding social capital will be richer where tightly knit communities are more diverse socioeconomically. Korean, African, Chinese, and Indian communities in our sample all featured considerable diversity. The more intimate Korean and Chinese communities appeared to be particularly good at mobilizing resources for newcomers and members in need. Among the Hindu communities, by contrast, the relative wealth of the membership did not necessarily translate into greater care for less fortunate members, due to the very loose structure of social relations entailed in their house of worship organizational culture. The socioeconomic characteristics of the membership thus have important effects on the social capital available to members, but they interact with religious tradition and organizational culture in the type of social capital they produce.

Social capital, finally, may be an important resource for newcomers in a strange new world. The friendships and shared resources that immigrants encounter in their places of worship may ease the difficulties of adapting to the new setting. The worship community may serve as a "haven in a heartless world" for many. For others, social ties struck up in the worship community may provide opportunities for material advancement in their new lives. In either case, the social capital that immigrant worship communities provide may have little relevance for immigrants' incorporation into the civic life of the nation. To get a better sense of the contributions of immigrant worship communities to civic life and to the civic incorporation of immigrants, we will have to look beyond the social capital they provide. In the next chapter, we consider the civic presence of worship communities themselves and its contribution to immigrant incorporation.

4

Immigrant Worship Communities in the Public Square

Look around a typical American community and you will see churches, an occasional synagogue, and, increasingly, mosques, Hindu
and Buddhist temples, Sikh gurdwaras, and other meeting places
for a wide range of worship communities. Though religious groups
gather in members' homes or rent out a storefront, where possible they make their homes in imposing buildings that stand out
for their architecture and choice of location. Far more numerous than
the occasional Masonic temple, much more visible than the offices
of a community's nonprofits, worship communities occupy a prominent place in America's civic landscape. They may also be prominent civic actors, though the degree to which they concern themselves
with community affairs or play an active role in shaping them
varies enormously.

In this chapter we look at the varied roles that immigrant
worship communities have assumed in the larger community
and their implications for the civic and social incorporation of
immigrants. As we saw in the last chapter, the social capital that
worship communities embody, nurture, and maintain can help immigrants cope with life in a new land; but, unless that social
capital includes significant linkages to opportunities outside the
immigrant community, it may do little to incorporate immigrants
into American society. Nor does the availability of social capital per
se tell us much about the contribution of worship communities to
the civic incorporation of immigrants. To discern that, we need to

look further. First, we need to see to what degree immigrant worship communities assume a role in American civil society, involving their members collectively in civic affairs. Second, we need to see to what extent such civic incorporation provides members of the community with the sorts of linkages to the larger society that can genuinely contribute to their individual civic and social incorporation. And, finally, we need to look at the contributions of the worship community to both its members' repertoire of civic skills and their self-image as civic actors. This chapter takes up the first two of these tasks. In chapters 5 and 6, we will investigate worship communities' contribution to the development of civic skills and civic identities among their members.

Varieties of Civic Action

Worship communities may occupy prominent places in our civic landscape, but the character of their participation in civic life ranges from virtually nil to deeply and persistently engaged. At the more engaged end of the spectrum, they can play a leading role in local affairs by active involvement in the political process. Religious traditions seldom mandate political activity. Rather it is an extension of the universal mandate, found in all world religions, to serve one's neighbor and to be charitable to the poor. All religions demand charity and goodwill, but political action is another matter. The traditional Baptist view, for example, put primary emphasis on building a community of the redeemed whose battles are with spiritual enemies, not political ones. A good Baptist stayed well clear of the public square, even when it came to settling legal disputes with a neighbor (Greenhouse 1986). Other religious traditions have seen political action as an integral part of their purpose. The Synod of Catholic Bishops said in 1971, in a widely quoted statement, "action on behalf of justice and participation in the transformation of the world fully appear to us as a constitutive dimension of the preaching of the Gospel" (Synod of Bishops 1971, no. 6). Liberal Protestant denominations have made similar statements, articulating political positions on a variety of issues, either as denominations or members of the National Council of Churches of Christ or the World Council of Churches. But public pronouncements are one thing and local action is another. Few local worship communities have political action as a priority.

Much more frequently, worship communities assume roles in the larger society through charitable activities and the ties with government agencies and other community organizations that these entail. Sometimes these activities are directed toward needy members of the worship community and its neighbors. At other times, the worship community addresses societal needs beyond its immediate setting. In either case, such activities can lead to involvement on community boards and task forces and efforts to influence public policy. They can also provide opportunities ("bridging social capital") to members of the worship community, as either consumers of social services or participants in the community's civic efforts. Many worship communities sponsor programs of this sort and cultivate the ties that often go with them. But many others can boast of little or no civic involvement. In this chapter, we will explore the evidence we have gathered on the civic involvement of immigrant worship communities and explain differences among communities.

Past research on the involvement of worship communities in civic action has focused principally on Christian churches and, to a lesser extent, Jewish synagogues and temples. Two consistent findings have emerged from this research. First, theologically liberal congregations are more likely to provide social services and engage in civic activities of all sorts than are conservative ones (Chaves, Giesel, and Tsitsos 2002; Wuthnow 2004, 52–57). Although volunteerism is high among members of conservative churches, members are much more likely to devote their energies to tasks internal to the church than to the larger society (Wuthnow 1999). The second finding has been that historically black churches engage in more social action than white churches. The reason commonly offered is that African Americans feel social injustices more keenly and thus encourage their church leaders and members to be involved in justice issues (Cavendish 2000; Harris 1999; Pattillo-McCoy 1998).[1]

What should we expect in the case of immigrant worship communities? On the one hand, we might encounter less civic engagement, since immigrant worship communities are often conservative in theology. On the other hand, we might expect more social action, since many immigrants personally feel the injustices in American society and, like African Americans, are motivated to work to redress them. Immigrant worship communities, moreover, include members who could benefit from social services that connections to the wider community provide. What does the evidence tell us?

Civic Activism

Our survey revealed striking variations among worship communities in civic activism, ties to the wider community, and involvement in social services and community betterment. Roughly half of all worship communities report at least one political activity, but Hindu temples were highly unlikely to sponsor or host political activities of any sort, while Sikh congregations were the most likely to do so (though the number of cases is too small to generalize). We asked religious leaders whether opportunities for political involvement were ever announced at services; whether voter guides had been distributed in the last year; and whether the community had sponsored or hosted events or meetings to discuss politics, register people to vote, lobby elected officials, or participate in a march or demonstration. Responses varied significantly across ethnic groups and religious traditions (see tables 4.1 and 4.2). To our surprise, almost 40 percent of Korean churches reported distributing voter guides, and close to 30 percent announced opportunities for political involvement from the pulpit. But 15–24 percent of worship communities serving other national origin groups also distributed voter guides, and roughly a quarter announced political opportunities at services. Encouragement of political activity was highest among Catholic, Muslim, and Sikh groups, with more than 50 percent of worship communities making political announcements, versus just 26 percent of Protestant churches and none of the Hindu temples. The use of voter guides was more evenly distributed across religious traditions, but Catholics and Muslims stood out here as well.

Other sorts of political activity likewise varied across groups and religious traditions. Voter registration activities were common, with roughly a quarter of all worship communities hosting them. Chinese churches stood out in this regard; nearly 50 percent of them held voter registration activities. But on other measures of political involvement, the Chinese churches were not involved, or rarely so. More than a quarter of Korean churches sponsored events aimed at lobbying public officials, but they were highly unlikely to host groups discussing politics or participating in a demonstration. We found much more

TABLE 4.1. Programs of Civic Activism in Immigrant Worship Communities by National Group (Percent)

	African	Chinese	Indian	Korean	Salvadoran
Number of cases	39	15	13	65	54
People at worship services were told of opportunities for political activity	34	20	23	29	26
Distributed voter guides	24	20	23	39	15
Held groups or meetings for these purposes:					
Citizenship class	21	33	0	15	20
Register people to vote	28	47	23	25	20
Discuss politics	28	0	23	5	20
Lobby elected officials	36	0	23	26	11
Participate in a demonstration	21	13	15	5	24
Conduct an assessment of community needs	55	33	8	52	48

TABLE 4.2. Programs of Civic Activism in Immigrant Worship Communities by Religious Tradition (Percent)

	Catholic	Protestant	Muslim	Hindu	Sikh
Number of cases	22	149	14	9	4
People at worship services were told of opportunities for political activity	50	26	57	0	75
Distributed voter guides	36	25	36	22	25
Held groups or meetings for these purposes:					
Citizenship class	46	15	43	0	0
Register people to vote	41	23	43	11	50
Discuss politics	41	11	21	11	50
Lobby elected officials	32	20	21	0	75
Participate in a demonstration or march	46	11	50	0	50
Conduct an assessment of community needs	62	48	36	11	0

consistent involvement in political activities of all sorts among African and Salvadoran churches. Among the African churches, multiethnic churches (mostly mainline Protestant) in which Africans worship along with others engaged in more political activity than the congregations of Africans only. More of the multiethnic churches distributed voter guides, had meetings to discuss race relations, and participated in marches and demonstrations. Widespread political activity in the Salvadoran churches is due to the relatively high proportion of Catholic parishes among them; indeed, Salvadoran Protestant churches were among the least likely to engage in political activities. Overall, Catholic worship communities were twice to four times as likely to sponsor voter registration programs, hold meetings to discuss political issues, and organize people to participate in a demonstration than Protestants; and they were half again as likely to lobby public officials. Muslim worship communities were almost as likely to sponsor all of these sorts of activities, while it was a rare Hindu temple that featured any of them. Sikhs, again, stood out as the most politically involved in all these ways.

Immigrant worship communities are apparently more civically active than the average American congregation. In comparing our sample of Christian churches with the NCS, we found that immigrant churches, both Catholic and Protestant, are more involved in civic activism than the average American Catholic parish or Protestant church (see table 4.3). It would make sense to suppose that both the immigrant condition and "home country" concerns promote greater civic engagement. The importance of establishing a place in American society, the legal difficulties surrounding immigration, the need for

TABLE 4.3. Lay Participation in Worship Services in Immigrant Worship
Communities Compared with NCS Sample (Percent)

	Catholic		Protestant	
	Immigrant	NCS	Immigrant	NCS
Number of cases	22	77	149	1123
People at worship services were told of				
opportunities for political activity	50	33	26	25
Distributed voter guides	36	13	25	18
Held groups or meetings for these purposes				
Register people to vote	41	16	23	7
Discuss politics	41	7	11	5
Lobby elected officials	32	12	20	3
Participate in a demonstration or march	46	25	11	7
Conduct assessment of community needs	62	54	48	35

specialized social services for immigrants, as well as continuing concerns
about homeland politics may all push immigrant worship communities toward greater civic involvement. We will see examples of all of these motives
for involvement shortly. But before we turn to these examples, we should look
at nonpolitical forms of civic involvement, especially the contributions immigrant worship communities make toward providing social services for their
own people and for members of the larger society.

Charitable Choices

Religious communities are often deeply involved in their communities through
social services, community development efforts, and participation in community
organizations and boards. Some offer a variety of social services to members and
nonmembers, from food distribution to counseling programs, job training, legal
aid, and citizenship classes. A few invest heavily in such services, while others
have little in the way of formal programs. Whether or not to provide social
services is both a theological and a practical question. Shall the focus be on
worship and religious education above all else? Or should the community engage
in meeting the needs of its members and the larger community in significant
ways, and if so, how great a priority should such activities be given, taking into
account competing demands on members' time, energy, and money? Theology
and the organizational culture of the worship community do not act alone in
deciding such questions. Rather, organizational culture interacts with the peculiar identity of each faith community, the sense of security and self-confidence

in the new land that community members feel, their own needs and resources, and theological and cultural preferences as to who outside their own membership most deserves their help.

Social services may be *formal*, as in the cases of afterschool tutoring or food distribution programs, or *informal*, as when a pastor calls upon members to help another member find an apartment or a baby sitter. Both may help the newly arrived find their way in the new land. But they have different implications for the incorporation of the worship community into the larger American society. Our survey asked about formal services, but our case studies revealed how important informal services are in the everyday life of many immigrant worship communities

Charity for Whom?

Faith communities vary in the groups they target for help. We can divide them roughly into three. The first target group is the most obvious—needy people in the worship community itself and, sometimes, their immediate neighbors. A second target of concern are others of the same ethnicity or religious background. This is manifest, for example, in community service programs serving an ethnically or religiously defined clientele; but sometimes the focus is on the needy abroad to whom worship community members feel connected by ties of ethnicity and/or religion. Third, some worship communities focus their attentions especially on the needy outside their immediate purview, on the homeless or other poor residents of the larger community.

Most worship communities sooner or later provide for needy members of their own. They may be recently arrived from the home country, or they may have been residents in the United States for a long time but in temporary dire straits due to sickness or unemployment. All the faith communities we have studied were ready to help these families, but in varying degrees and ways. It appeared common, for instance, for potential immigrants from Korea to establish contact with a pastor in a Korean church in this country before making final plans. Pastors would offer to pick people up at the airport, help them find an apartment and a job, and assist with immigration papers. They would call upon their members to help out, drawing on their own social capital to do so. Similarly, in some of the evangelical Salvadoran churches, pastors speak from the pulpit about the plight of a family in need and ask those present to take up a collection to pay the rent, cover the deposit on a new apartment, or help out with health costs. Pastors themselves often saw to it that needy members got the necessary help. These sorts of gestures can be quite important in helping immigrants adapt and survive in their new surroundings, and they can be potent means for drawing in and holding onto members in a worship community. They do less to integrate immigrants into the larger society, and they involve the worship community itself only occasionally in seeking out or exploiting linkages beyond their walls.

Formal programs may be directed solely to members of the worship community or to neighbors, fellow ethnics outside the immediate community, or the needy in general. Many communities have all they can do to attend to the needs of their members, though their programs may be formally open to everyone. A few manage to provide a variety of services to members, their neighbors and friends, and others. Many put a primary emphasis on helping members of their own ethnic or religious group. For example, the Community Service Department of the Maryland Korean Christian Church, a "megachurch" in the suburbs, established service to fellow Koreans and other Asian immigrants as its first priority. Most of the Muslim communities, likewise, targeted the majority of their programs to their own membership and to other Muslims, particularly needy immigrants. Depending on the scope and level of services, this sort of community involvement may entail little contact with agencies outside the worship community, or it may motivate a host of connections to other worship communities, government agencies, community groups, and nonprofits.

While most social service activity is directed locally, many immigrant worship communities keep in mind the needs of their conationals abroad. Salvadoran Catholic churches sent large donations of money to El Salvador after a disastrous earthquake there in 2001. Quite specific "transnational" ties between individuals and institutions in both countries often shape such contributions.[2] In the case of the earthquake relief, some Salvadoran leaders preferred to deliver the financial help personally, since they wanted to be certain that funds were distributed in the towns from which the church members came. In some cases, missionary activities and aid are intermingled. One Chinese Christian church provides discrete aid to clandestine Protestant communities inside mainline China, and many Korean congregations take up collections for missionary and relief activities among North Korean refugees living illegally in Manchuria.

Such activities should not be seen as purely charitable or purely missionary in impact. Not only do missionary and charitable activities sometimes mesh; in many cases, such causes are simultaneously the subject of media, educational, and advocacy campaigns directed at U.S. audiences and public officials. Aid for one's own and involvement in homeland causes thus spill over easily into greater civic activism in the United States.

The third target group is needy people in the Washington, D.C., area, regardless of ethnicity. These people, albeit deserving, are not as visible or as urgent as the first two groups. Immigrant faith communities serve the needy stranger largely through contributions to religious or secular social welfare programs. They provide contributions and volunteers to programs feeding the homeless in Washington, D.C., the Red Cross, Habitat for Humanity, AIDS campaigns, and other familiar causes. In general, the wealthier worship communities fit this typically middle-class American pattern of involvement. Poorer immigrant worship communities either provide mainly informal services for their own members (and potential members) exclusively; or they sponsor a range of services for their membership and needy neighbors. We will explore later the factors affecting such differences.

Finally, the events of September 11, 2001, sent a sense of shock and goodwill through all the faith communities. All of the communities we studied raised funds, wrote to political leaders, held meetings, or engaged in projects such as blood drives to help the September 11 victims. Some mobilized defensively against the threat of backlash directed at their own ethnic group. These efforts, coupled with the more everyday engagement in social services in which they were already engaged, put many communities into closer touch with other worship communities and agencies; and, in many cases, immigrant worship communities have forged important partnerships as a result, deepening their integration into American society.

Partnering in Community Service

Jo Anne Schneider has looked in some detail at partnerships between worship communities and social service agencies, drawing on both data gathered explicitly for our study and data from her research on other communities across the United States (Schneider 2003; Schneider and Foley 2003). Congruent with findings in previous studies, our data show that worship communities are more likely to partner with other organizations to provide services than to do so exclusively on their own (Chaves and Tsitsos 2001). Delving more deeply into the character of these partnerships, however, Schneider finds three patterns of relationship. First, local worship communities play a significant role in the founding of social service agencies, whether through the direct involvement of religious leaders or as a spinoff of relationships formed among lay members of a congregation concerned about some social need. Second, while some agencies retain their religious moorings, others lose their ties with religious bodies as they professionalize and enlarge the scope of activities. The requirements associated with accepting and administering government funds may have something to do with this, but another factor is the combination of declining interest on the part of religious leaders and a need for autonomy on the part of agency directors.[3] Such agencies may continue to receive small donations from worship communities, and they may rely informally on volunteers from one or another worship community for part of their volunteer staffing, but the relationship with worship communities has ceased to be institutionalized. Third, an important subset of social service agencies were founded by and for racial or ethnic minorities and sometimes draw on volunteers from worship communities, but these rarely have formal ties to the worship communities themselves.

One illustration of the changing character of such relationships is the case of the Korean social service agencies that today play an important role in the Korean community. One Presbyterian pastor explained their origins in this way:

> Because of language barrier and cultural unfamiliarity, most Korean immigrants encountered difficulties in communication with local and federal government authorities. Korean Protestant churches and the church leaders played a role of mediator or facilitator in solving the impending problems the immigrants encountered immediately after immigration. As an example, currently the two most important Korean community service organizations were initiated by two Korean church leaders. The Korean Community Service Center of Greater Washington, which is the largest ethnic social service organization in the Korean community, was originally initiated by a pastor of the United Korean Presbyterian Church in the early 1980s. Another Korean social service organization, the Korean-American Service Center, located in Silver Spring, was also originally initiated by a pastor (Rev. Ham) of a Korean Church in Montgomery County in need of the community members' social service organization. The Korean churches were the only social service organizations that were able to take care of the problems of the early Korean immigrants. Church was the core of the community since the beginning of Korean immigration to the U.S. (Kwon 2004, 262)

Currently, however, just a handful of churches make significant donations to these agencies, and church contributions are only a small proportion of their total funding. For some time, virtually none of the members of the boards of these organizations have been clergy. Moreover, half of the Korean agencies have no history of church affiliation, though most of the leadership of these organizations attend Korean churches.

Apart from questions of affiliation, however, nonprofit agencies and worship communities interact in a variety of ways. Three patterns emerge. In the first, worship communities may refer the needy to an agency for specialized assistance. Both larger churches and mosques in our sample and smaller, resource-poor worship communities referred people to agencies they were aware of. Most of these agencies offered an array of services, including emergency relief. Both nonprofits with roots in the Anglo-American and African American communities and those associated with specific immigrant groups took referrals from worship communities. In a second pattern, worship communities complemented their own services with support from nonprofit agencies. In some cases, the worship community simply played the host to a program, such as a Red Cross blood drive, organized and managed by the nonprofit. In other cases, a worship community and nonprofit partnered to provide specific services at the site of the worship community. In the third pattern, finally, worship communities chose particular nonprofits as outlets for their charitable energies, providing limited funding, volunteers, and in-kind donations to their operations. While virtually none of the agencies Schneider looked at depended to any significant extent on one or another worship community, such contributions were a regular part of the life of most nonprofits engaged in general social service provision. For the charitable agencies, service to the needy was their main reason for existence; but we must keep in mind that for the worship communities it was almost always a low priority relative to spiritual nurture of their members and religious outreach to others.

Patterns of Community Service

As in the case of explicitly political community involvement, immigrant worship communities differ enormously among themselves in the level and kind of social services they provide. Our survey suggested that, among the immigrant groups in our study, the Korean and Chinese churches are the least active in providing or supporting formal social services, while Indian worship communities and churches serving Africans are the most active (see table 4.4). Over half of Salvadoran worship communities provide or support social services or community development efforts. But differences among national and regional origin groups turn out to be less interesting than differences across religious traditions.

For example, the African communities in our sample are unique, in that roughly half are in multicultural worship communities, in which African members worship alongside American whites and/or African Americans, who often make up the majority in the congregation. Most are mainline Protestant

TABLE 4.4. Worship Communities Sponsoring Social Service or Community Projects in the Last Twelve Months, by National Group

	African	Chinese	Indian	Korean	Salvadoran
Number of cases	39	15	13	65	54
Percentage of congregations that have supported social services, community development, or neighborhood organizing projects in the last 12 months	76	40	85	29	54
Number of social service projects or programs supported, if any	3.2	1.2	2.0	2.3	2.4
If any social service projects supported:					
Money spent on the projects or programs in the last 12 months (percentage of worship communities)					
$1,000 or less	8	40	43	31	29
$1,001–$10,000	35	60	29	46	48
$10,001 or more	58	0	29	23	24
Percentage of congregations who had a paid person spend more than 25% of time on the projects	35	17	0	11	50
Percentage that had anyone from the group do volunteer work for the projects	100	100	100	88	87
Percentage with projects supported by outside funds	31	33	10	4	43
If yes, percentage that had funds from foundations, businesses, or United Way	60	a	a	a	69
Percentage that had funds from local, state, or federal government	30	a	a	a	31

[a]Too few cases to analyze.

churches. In such cases, the data we gathered on community involvement describe the *entire* worship community—not just the African portion. This affects comparison of "African" worship communities with those serving other national and regional origin groups. The African worship communities in our study, for instance, were the most active in providing social services. But 84 percent of the mixed-ethnic congregations with significant African members reported participating in social service projects, compared with 68 percent of the stand-alone, African worship communities.[4] The higher percentages of "African" worship communities involved in social services may thus have less to do with the ethnic composition of the churches than with the fact that most of the multiethnic churches are mainline Protestant or Catholic.

As we have noted, mainline Protestant and Catholic parishes are generally more civically involved than evangelical and independent Protestant churches. Our data confirms that this is true in the realm of social services as well as more generally. As table 4.5 shows, on average, Catholic parishes are involved in more social service delivery than Protestant churches. Sixty-four percent of them report some sort of involvement, versus just 52 percent of the Protestant churches. Muslim worship communities, Hindu temples, and Sikh congregations appear similar to Catholic parishes, but due to small samples we cannot be certain. Catholic parishes, compared with Protestant churches, spend more money and invest more staff time on social service. Mainline Protestant churches, moreover, are different from other Protestant churches.[5] Mainline churches had more outside funding than the others. Together, mainline Protestant and Catholic churches participated in significantly more social programs and hosted more outside groups, including social service providers, than more conservative Protestant churches.

TABLE 4.5. Worship Communities Sponsoring Social Service or Community Projects in the Last Twelve Months, by Religious Tradition (Percent)

	Catholic	Protestant	Muslim	Hindu	Sikh
Number of cases	22	149	13	9	4
Percentage of congregations that have supported social services, community development, or neighborhood organizing projects in the last 12 months	64	52	62	79	100
Number of social service projects or programs supported if any	3.5	2.3	4.0	1.7	2.5
If any social service projects supported:					
Money spent on the projects or programs in the last 12 months (percentage of worship communities)					
$1,000 or less	10	24	63	25	68
$1,001–$10,000	50	43	25	25	33
$10,001 or more	40	33	13	50	0
Percentage of congregations who had a paid person spend more than 25% of time on the projects	43	28	50	0	0
Percentage that had anyone from the group do volunteer work for the projects	100	91	100	100	100
Percentage with projects supported by outside funds	50	22	40	14	0
If yes, percentage that had funds from foundations, businesses, or United Way	63	67	0	100	a
Percentage that had funds from local, state, or federal government	38	28	100	0	a

[a]Too few cases to analyze.

In terms of the number of social services and social programs that worship communities participated in, patterns that seem to distinguish national and regional origin groups also tend to disappear when we break down the data by religious tradition. We asked how much money the worship community spent, if any, on social service and community development projects or programs in the last year, and also if any staff persons paid by the group spent more than 25 percent of their time on one or more of the projects. The African congregations spent more money and devoted more staff time to social services than any of the others, but the overall numbers are also striking. Fifty-eight percent of those African churches that sponsored programs (and three-quarters of all the African churches did so) spent more than $10,000 on them, and 35 percent devoted considerable staff time to them. The Chinese, Korean, Salvadoran, and Indian worship communities spent a good deal less, on average, and invested less staff time. Worship communities also differed in their ability to acquire outside funding for social service and community projects. The Salvadoran, African, and Chinese churches were by far the most successful, and among the African churches, the mixed-ethnic churches received more than the African-only churches. The Salvadoran and African churches drew 60 percent or more of outside funds from foundations, businesses, and the United Way, with another 30 percent or so coming from local, state, or federal government (see the last three lines of table 4.4).

Such differences tend to disappear, however, when we look at the data by religious tradition. We have already noted that Catholic and mainline Protestant churches tend to be more civically involved than more conservative Protestant churches. Of the five religious traditions surveyed, Catholics, Muslims, Hindus, and Sikhs were more likely to support social service or community development programs than Protestant churches. Meanwhile, 40 percent of Catholic churches and 50 percent of Hindu temples spent over $10,000 in the past year on such programs. Catholic parishes and Muslim worship communities often provided paid employees to work in social service and community development projects. Protestant churches did so rarely, and Hindu temples and Sikh congregations not at all. And half of Catholic parishes and 40 percent of the mosques received outside funding for these efforts, compared with just 22 percent of Protestant churches and 14 percent of the temples.

Immigrant worship communities compare favorably in these respects with the average American church. Immigrant churches, both Protestant and Catholic, support more programs and spend more on them than the average American Protestant or Catholic church (see table 4.6). They also receive much more financial support from outside. This is true regardless of size.

TABLE 4.6. Social Services Sponsored by Immigrant Worship Communities Compared with NCS Sample

	Immigrant congregations			American congregations		
	Small	Medium	Large	Small	Medium	Large
	100 or less	101–500	501 or more	100 or less	101–500	501 or more
Number of cases	71	87	42	780	375	65
Percentage supporting social service, community development, or neighborhood organizing projects within the last 12 months	42	57	79	49	67	85
Of those:						
Percentage who spent $10,000 or more on social service programs	7	33	54	3	13	38
Percentage who had congregation members volunteer	90	92	100	43	62	81
Percentage who received support funds from outside the congregation for social service	30	26	25	10	11	16

Large or small, the immigrant congregations in our survey provided much more in the way of social services than their counterparts.

Besides social services and community development initiatives, worship communities almost universally organize groups for various purposes, and many provide classes and training sessions for their members or host organizations that make such opportunities available to the larger community. We will look at this phenomenon in more detail in the next chapter, but for now it is important to underline the ties these activities forge with the larger society. Classes on citizenship, English as a second language (ESL), job skills, tax preparation, and so on often rely on relationships with outside agencies. In many cases such relationships are initiated by the latter, who see in worship communities an ideal way to reach immigrants. Many worship communities also provide forums where representatives of the local police, municipal or county government, the school district, or other government offices can meet residents and explain their programs. Finally, worship communities typically provide what Sara Evans and Harry Boyte called "free spaces" where community organizations of all sorts can borrow or rent facilities to conduct meetings, workshops, and community events (Evans et al. 1986). The worship community may play little direct role in these activities, but in making its facilities available, it contributes significantly to American civic life.

Our survey showed that, among those immigrant worship communities that owned their own buildings, most hosted outside groups of one sort or another. African and Salvadoran churches were especially prone to do so, and half of these hosted six or more groups over the course of the last year, but so did a large number of the Korean churches. All of the religious traditions except the Sikhs hosted outside groups, and most hosted numerous groups. Among Catholics and Protestants, self-help groups like Alcoholics Anonymous were especially prominent; but all religious traditions frequently hosted community service and youth groups such as Scouts, followed by educational programs, health and human services, neighborhood groups, social clubs, and art, music, and cultural groups (see tables 4.7 and 4.8). Religious groups not affiliated with the worship community also rented or borrowed space.

TABLE 4.7. Hosting Community Programs, by National Group (Percent)

	African	Chinese	Indian	Korean	Salvadoran
Percentage who rented or gave space in their building to outside groups	90	43	55	65	75
If yes, percentage renting or giving space to 6 or more outside groups	54	0	83	58	50
Percentage renting or giving space to self-help organizations, like Alcoholics Anonymous	52	a	a	22	65
Percentage renting or giving space to community service programs	50	a	a	67	87
Percent renting or giving space to other groups:					
Political group	11	a	0	0	10
Neighborhood or community group	19	a	0	12	10
Immigration services	11	a	0	0	0
Ethnic association	22	a	17	4	0
Advocacy and aid (foreign)	7	a	0	0	0
Specialized advocacy group (domestic)	11	a	0	0	14
Health and human services (local)	22	a	0	0	19
Scouts and other youth groups	33	a	17	8	43
Art, music, and cultural groups	33	a	33	8	0
Educational programs	37	a	0	23	24
Athletic clubs and activities	15	a	17	12	10
Social groups and clubs	26	a	83	8	10
Outside religious groups	22	a	33	12	10

[a]Too few cases to analyze. In the bottom of the table N = 3 for Chinese and N = 6 for Indians. Due to the small samples, the data are only suggestive.

TABLE 4.8. Hosting Community Programs, by Religious Tradition

	Catholic	Protestant	Muslim	Hindu	Sikh
Percentage who rented or gave space in their building to outside groups	78	72	58	86	0
If yes, percentage renting or giving space to 6 or more outside groups	62	39	72	83	0
Percentage renting or giving space to self-help organizations, like Alcoholics Anonymous	60	40	0	17	0
Percentage renting or giving space to community service programs	87	62	43	50	0
Percent renting or giving space to other groups:					
Number of cases	14	63	7	6	4
Political group	7	6	0	0	a
Neighborhood or community group	7	14	14	0	a
Immigration services	0	5	0	0	a
Ethnic association	0	11	14	17	a
Advocacy and aid (foreign)	0	3	29	0	a
Specialized advocacy group (domestic)	14	6	0	0	a
Health and human services (local)	29	11	43	0	a
Scouts and other youth groups	57	21	0	17	a
Art, music, and cultural groups	7	16	0	33	a
Educational programs	43	25	14	0	a
Athletic clubs and activities	2	14	0	17	a
Social groups and clubs	14	14	43	83	a
Outside religious groups	7	16	29	33	a

[a]Too few cases to analyze.

Explaining Civic Engagement

Immigrant worship communities, we have seen, differ in the degree to which they play roles in the larger community and the sorts of roles they play. We have already looked at some important sources of variation, but understanding the differences uncovered here requires that we return to the variables we explored in the last chapter: organizational culture, the socioeconomic characteristics of the community and the circumstances of immigration, and religious tradition. We can see these factors at work by looking at some examples of civically active worship communities.

Local, National, and Transnational Activism: St. Francis of Assisi Parish

Saint Francis of Assisi is one of the most politically active of the Catholic parishes serving Salvadorans. It stands in stark contrast to Nuestro Señor, an energetic but inwardly oriented evangelical church where we also conducted fieldwork. Saint Francis is a large, multicultural parish still dominated by the Anglo-American parishioners who were once its principal members. The Hispanic community—mostly Salvadoran but including Cubans, Bolivians, Peruvians, and other Central Americans—grew large enough some years ago to prompt the pastor to appoint a native Spanish-speaking associate pastor, who has assumed effective leadership of a Hispanic worship community. The latter worships separately from the older congregation during two masses on Sundays, a Saturday evening mass, and a Sunday evening Catholic charismatic celebration. Relations between the pastor and his associate are good; they are rather more strained between activists in the older Anglo community and the Hispanics. Nevertheless, the parish members attempt to work together in a number of ways.

Saint Francis's main vehicle for civic action is participation in broader political committees, especially a network of Catholic parishes in Northern Virginia called Social Action Linking Together (SALT). SALT groups in the member churches give their attention to issues, not political candidates. They work together by researching legislative issues at the local and state level, selecting priorities for action, and advocating for them with political leaders. Most recently, the SALT group at Saint Francis worked on a project to reduce homelessness. One autumn, for example, they conducted postcard-writing campaign called "Home for the Holidays," in which volunteers wrote to their respective legislators in support of state funding for rental housing assistance for homeless families. Saint Francis's SALT group has both Anglo and Salvadoran members; the majority, however, are Anglo. The parish team at Saint Francis is trying to get more Salvadorans mobilized to participate in SALT, and for this purpose they have been pushing for more attention to immigrants' rights issues.

A second instance of civic action is the personal work of Father Mesa, the Hispanic associate pastor. Father Mesa is a very visible leader in the area, often sought out by the media as a spokesperson for Hispanic immigrants. He actively lobbies officials on behalf of immigrant causes. For example, he took a very proactive role in identifying possible Salvadoran candidates to stand for election to represent the local district in the state legislature. Moreover, he has organized workshops to help his Salvadoran parishioners fill out forms to renew the special "temporary protected status" granted Salvadorans by the INS. His team has also organized seminars to teach parishioners about the new immigration guidelines. Father Mesa repeatedly urges his parishioners to vote. Some of our field notes on one homily will illustrate his approach:

He then talked about the upcoming elections and told the people that those who could vote had the responsibility to do so, for themselves as well as for "your brothers and sisters who can't and who need a government that would take our community seriously and pass that amnesty that has been asked since 1986—and nothing has happened about it so far." He went on: "We need to pray to God so that we will get a government that respects our community. The undocumented need this amnesty and the government needs to understand that they are not criminals, that these are all hard-working people who deserve dignity and the right to work without raids. We need to stop the number of INS raids! ... I'm not running a political campaign ad here. All I want you to understand is that if you can vote, then you should exercise that right. Go and vote! Vote for whomever you consider is best, but vote! Only by voting is our community going to become more powerful."

The bilingual parish newsletter also included a section on the importance of voting in the November elections. Father Mesa never mentioned candidates, but he repeatedly urged and prayed that the amnesty bill in Congress would pass so that "our people and their dignity be respected."

Father Mesa is also the founder of a nonprofit organization that draws on parish members and local supporters for a variety of charitable endeavors. Originally conceived as a way to bring children in need of expensive medical treatment from El Salvador to the United States, the Foundation, as it is referred to in the parish, now engages in a variety of social service programs within the parish. It has organized workshops on housing, health, and legal issues and manages special programs for the sick, the elderly, and prison inmates. Father Mesa has maintained and strengthened transnational ties to El Salvador (though he himself is not Salvadoran) through frequent trips. Shortly before our research in the parish, he went to several communities affected by Hurricane Mitch and the 2001 earthquake to deliver donations from the Hispanic community to their home towns.

In addition to the work of the Foundation and Father Mesa's direct community involvement, the parish provides counseling services in Spanish and English through its Lumen Christi Center and a wide variety of other services through its Social Justice Committee. For example, the committee had recently joined forces with a local nonprofit to offer tax preparation workshops for Spanish-speaking members of the parish; and it was reviewing a proposal from a landscaping company to conduct training sessions for potential employees. The pastor was also seeking funding to hire a part-time bilingual staff member to coordinate a health and domestic violence program.

Interviews with staff at St. Francis and our own survey make clear that this parish stands out among Catholic parishes. Both the leadership of the pastor and that of Father Mesa have been important in transforming the parish. One staff person commented: "There are other nearby parishes that come nowhere close; people don't pour in mass the way they do here. Look at Saint Paul and Holy Rosary, they barely respond to the needs of the Latino community. Saint Paul—even located in the heart of 'Arlandria,' near what the Salvadoran im-migrants dearly refer to as 'Chirilagua.'[6] . . . The problem there was that the previous pastor was very close-minded and he pushed people away." Leadership is thus important in transforming what could otherwise be a typical "house of worship" sort of parish to one that is much more devoted to building community and meeting members' needs through a variety of programs by forging ties to Catholic and non-Catholic agencies that serve community needs. Local parish leadership draws on significant potential within the Catholic tradition. Finally, the scope of involvement reflects the character of this immigrant community, many of whose members are undocumented, relatively poor, and in need of training and orientation in the skills necessary to get by and advance in American society. The precarious situation of Salvadoran immigrants in the United States informs Father Mesa's activism on their behalf and his promotion of civic responsibility among those who already citizens.

Circumstances of immigration are not enough by themselves to promote active engagement in the larger society, as the example of Nuestro Señor shows. Nuestro Señor is a member of one of four Salvadoran evangelical denominations active in the Washington area; but its social and organizational ties are almost exclusively concentrated on fellow congregations of the same denomination. Most of its 300 members, including the pastor, are recent immigrants from rural El Salvador, with limited education and training. Most subsist on low-wage jobs in the area. Congregational life is vigorous, with services virtually every night of the week and an all-day Sunday service and communal meal that occupies the energies of dozens of members each week. The focus of activity and preaching is on building the community and maintaining one's life in keeping with the dictates of the Bible. Members are attracted through family and friends, and several have found spouses in the congregation. They seem to be held by the intense expectations of the community and the constant round of activity. But the congregation, as such, plays scarcely any role in the larger society, nor does it partner with other organizations to provide for its members.

Despite its relatively large size, at around 300 active members, this is clearly a "family"-style congregation, where relationships, community life, and religious education come before everything else, indeed crowd out most everything else. Strict attention to personal salvation and the demands of community life under the gospel shape the culture of this congregation and circumscribe the lives of its members in ways that a Catholic parish could never duplicate, given the fluid boundaries of the typical Catholic house of worship.

Civic Engagement at Arm's Length: The Korean Churches

Like Nuestro Señor, most Korean churches, even those affiliated with mainline Protestant denominations, see themselves as conservative and evangelical. Starting in the 1970s, Korean pastors began to reshape their churches, transforming what had been mainly social clubs for Korean immigrants into more "churchly" institutions with greater emphasis on religious education and spirituality (Kwon 2002). By and large, these efforts have been successful, despite significant tensions within some churches. Nevertheless, Korean churches are also civic actors in a number of ways, while remaining focused on the religious and relational dimensions of their organizational cultures.

The largest of the Korean churches we looked at, a "megachurch" in the Maryland suburbs, has a Community Service Department devoted to promoting community service and recognizing the achievements of Korean Americans in the larger community.[7] The department—really a small group of volunteers—rallies members of the congregation to come to ceremonies marking the achievements of prominent Korean Americans. It also oversees efforts within the church to help needy members, especially those who are handicapped. Through the department, the church brings volunteers to work with a Korean Mennonite church that has a mission to inner-city African Americans in Washington, D.C.[8] Every year it stages a bazaar, featuring a flea market, food sales, public service presentations, and other services. Special efforts were made to draw in the church's Hispanic and African American neighbors, and the "Medical Mission" of the church offers a variety of free medical services to visitors. The bazaar in 2001 also featured a talk on public safety issues by a local police captain. Brochures advertising the event were distributed in English and Spanish in the neighborhood, though most of the participants were Koreans from the congregation.

These are the sorts of activities that one might expect of a large, relatively prosperous, suburban church. Charitable activity is directed outward, to needy members of the larger Korean community and beyond, through an inner-city mission, and to African American and Hispanic neighbors. Members of the Community Service Department invoke evangelical, charitable, and community-service motives in justifying their work. Religious tradition, the community-style organizational culture of this church, and its relative affluence make possible a degree of community involvement that is consonant with that of larger, mainline Protestant churches around the country.

The majority of Korean churches in the area, however, are small. Over 90 percent of the Korean congregations in the Washington, D.C., area had fewer than 500 members. Over 65 percent of them had fewer than 100 members. These smaller congregations are often focused exclusively on their inner life, with occasional calls for contributions to missionary activities abroad or for help for Koreans at home or in exile in Northern China. Much of the outreach activity of these churches is devoted to church growth. Most churches form "cells," or subcommunities, even within a relatively small congregation, and some of these cell groups are active in recruiting new members and, occasionally, community service. One pastor of a medium-sized Korean United Methodist church noted that he and his congregation had participated in a number of community-service activities, including social services for the mentally ill, the homeless, and victims of domestic violence, but that they could do much more. Challenged by the criticisms of an African American scholar he met at a social service conference he attended, he reflected, "I think we cannot overestimate the importance of churches' participation in social service activities. I always think we are quite behind." The small size of these congregations, however, combined with the family-style organizational culture characteristic of much evangelical Protestantism, militates against active community involvement. A well-organized secular Korean community, moreover, now provides outlets for the community-spirited efforts of Koreans that churches once satisfied.

Facing the Challenge of September 11: Sikhs, Hindus, and Muslims in the Public Square

The September 11, 2001, attacks on the World Trade Center and the Pentagon produced a wave of shock, grief, and sympathy in worship communities of all sorts, not just in the United States but around the world. In the Adams Morgan district of Washington, D.C., immigrants testified to their horror at the events and their support for the United States in a dozen languages on a temporary paper wall hung from the fence of a local church. Worship communities throughout the area mobilized to send money, material donations, and letters of condolences to the families of the victims and the agencies that were serving them. But some immigrant worship communities felt the dangers lurking in public anger at the attackers, identified almost immediately as of Arab and Muslim origin. Particularly among immigrant groups whose members might be mistaken for Muslims, fear of the backlash, which soon emerged, was mixed with emotions of national solidarity in the face of the attack.

Immigrant communities whose members, buildings, and organizations became targets of anti-Muslim sentiment responded in remarkably different ways. In the Washington area, Sikhs mobilized almost immediately, and the various Sikh worship communities, otherwise deeply divided among themselves, came together in a campaign to educate the public on the distinctiveness of the Sikh religion and Sikhs' desire to share the sufferings of Americans over the attack. The Hindu communities, by contrast, did nothing to publicly distance themselves from the attackers, and most Hindus felt little sense of threat, despite the fact that several Hindu temples were vandalized in other parts of the country in the weeks following September 11. Muslim worship communities immediately felt the threat but did little to organize as a group until well after the attacks. Many Muslims stayed home from worship community activities, and some mosques curtailed services. Eventually, though, a number of area mosques joined a Federal Emergency Management Administration (FEMA) project offering counseling, orientation to services, and other assistance the Muslim community needed post–September 11. And some mosques became much more actively engaged with the larger community, both politically and in community service, than before the attacks.

THE SIKH RESPONSE. The first Sikh worship community, the Sikh Cultural Society, was established in Washington, D.C., in the 1960s by Indian professionals, many of whom had come to Washington to work with international agencies. As the community grew, its composition changed, and new congregations formed as it split. Starting in the 1980s, an increasing number of Sikhs were from poorer households, and some came as refugees from the political violence that followed Indira Gandhi's efforts to capitalize on religious tensions in Punjab state as a political tool. The violence fostered growing separatist movement among Sikhs in the Punjab and around the world. Support for an independent "Khalistan" has waxed and waned among Sikh communities. It is stronger in some than in others and has been a factor in some of the division in Sikh congregations. At least one Washington area congregation was created in protest at what its leaders saw as the lackadaisical attitude in their former worship community toward the situation in India.

Partly as a result of these concerns, this gurdwara, or congregation, which we will call the Guru Granth Sahib Center, has been at the forefront of attempts to educate the Washington area public on the nature of the conflict and the inherently peaceful character of the Sikh religion. This congregation has also forged important ecumenical ties in the area, and its leaders participate in a wide variety of local charitable and community boards and events. Ethnoreligious identity and homeland politics, ironically but certainly not for the first time in American immigrant history, thus have contributed to deeper civic involvement in U.S. society. One former board member of this congregation founded the Sikh Media Watch and Resource Taskforce (SMART) in 1996. This organization is committed to the fair portrayal of Sikhs in American media and to ensuring that Sikhs understand civic and political rights in America. It has created packets teachers can use in their classrooms to educate Americans about Sikhism, and pamphlets that Sikhs can give to their non-Sikh friends in school, office, or neighborhood.

A second organization, the Sikh Council on Religion and Education (SCORE), founded later by leaders of the same congregation, is also a media watchdog but is more committed to public policy work and lobbying than SMART; SCORE describes itself as a think tank working to represent Sikhs in various public forums; and it has advised government departments and supported antidiscrimination legislation. For example, in November 2001, SCORE worked with other Sikh groups to lobby the Department of Transportation to clarify its policies and educate airport screeners about the rights of Sikhs to wear turbans as an article of religious faith.

Despite often bitter divisions among them, Washington area Sikh congregations came together in an unprecedented show of unity to deal with the perceived threat of backlash from the events of September 11, 2001. Sikhs in the Washington, D.C., area knew that with their turbans and beards, they were liable to be mistaken for Arabs or Muslims. Young Sikh professionals in New York immediately mobilized a website called the Sikh Coalition to track hate crimes, and within a few days the first reports started rolling in. At the Sahib Foundation in suburban Maryland (another congregation), the list of hate crimes, harassments, and attacks against Sikhs (and some Hindus) were printed and posted in the central hallway. Five days after September 11, 125 incidents were reported from around the country, including the murder of one Sikh.

The Sikh Cultural Society quickly organized two candlelight vigils on Wisconsin Avenue in the District of Columbia. Another congregation hosted a memorial service at the Washington Monument. Speakers at the memorial service said over and over that Sikhs are not terrorists or followers of Osama-bin Laden but are proud and patriotic Americans, and so they should not be attacked by non-Sikhs simply because they wear a turban or long beard.

"We condemn terrorist acts as cowardly and reprehensible," said one speaker. "We have sworn allegiance to the star-spangled banner. Let us all be tolerant. Do not target other Americans out of sheer anger."

Most remarkable, however, was the coming together of the ordinarily fractious Sikh community. Already on the evening of September 11, 2001, leaders of the various congregations were on the telephone arranging an emergency meeting. The series of meetings that followed included the heavy participation of high school and college-age youth, who often chided their elders for wanting to distance themselves from Muslims more than expressing the shock and horror of the Sikh community at the events of September 11 and their solidarity with Americans of all creeds. Youth organized a vigil outside one of the gurdwaras, with a candlelight march and placards mourning the dead. They also reacted strongly as infighting broke out again among the leadership of the congregations. Despite disagreements, the ad hoc committee oversaw the printing of thousands of American flag stickers, which were distributed at Wednesday night and Sunday services for people to put on their cars. They mailed a letter to school district superintendents expressing concern at the bullying of Sikh children at school. They successfully courted the media to cover dozens of "mistaken identity" cases of hate crimes against Sikhs. And banners were printed and hung outside each gurdwara proclaiming: "Sikh Americans Join All Americans in Prayer." The community sponsored two full-page advertisements in the *Washington Post*, which was controversial among members of the committee because the leadership had taken charge of the ad campaign to more sharply differentiate Sikhs and Muslims and focus on hate crimes against Sikhs more than sympathy for the victims.

Sikh young adults argued that Sikhs should stop focusing on defending their own community and start helping in the relief effort. When the leaders brushed off the young persons' desire to raise funds or to volunteer for relief work, the Sikh youth called an all-Washington-area youth meeting to organize themselves. They decided to raise money for the Red Cross through a car wash, bake sale, yard sale, community cleanup, and promotion of a festival. They started a letter-writing campaign to congresspeople and school principals, urging them to condemn hate crimes. They organized a telephone bank to phone politicians, telling them about the intolerance visited upon Sikhs. At the same time, they decided to write letters of thanks to the rescue workers in New York and at the Pentagon and letters of solidarity to the Muslim community. They organized a large number of candlelight vigils to express Sikh solidarity with the victims of September 11. They distributed handouts saying "We are uniting together as a diverse community to collectively mourn the loss of our families, friends, colleagues, and innocence."

Despite the infighting, Sikhs remained concerned and active for many months after September 11. At the same time, their activism apparently had little lasting effect in spurring greater community involvement. One of the more active congregations fell into a bitter factional fight following the mobilization to defend Sikhs from backlash, and members' energies were taken up with that. At other congregations, particularly the activist pro-Khalistan Guru Granth Sahib Center, the heightened levels of community involvement occasioned by September 11 soon declined. Nevertheless, congregations continued to encourage members to participate in service activities and promote a positive image of the Sikh religion in the larger community.

MUSLIM RESPONSES. The Muslim response was much less organized, at least initially, but no less motivated by concern over the backlash. Nevertheless, as early as the day of September 11, one prominent mosque was encouraging its members to give blood and was setting up a fund to help the victims and their families. This same mosque also discouraged Muslims from wearing religious attire in public and asked all members of the community to report suspicious and discriminatory behavior. Vandalism at one mosque on September 12 prompted immediate calls to local media and decisions among many mosques, Muslim institutes and schools, and businesses to temporarily close down.

American mosques have been politically active in various ways for many years. No mosques endorse political candidates, but the mosques we visited repeatedly urged congregants to vote in support of Muslim American and international Muslim issues. The Potomac Islamic Center, the more cosmopolitan of the mosques we studied, repeatedly urges its members to join the political process in the United States, to vote, and to become involved in American institutions. It organizes drives to get members to register to vote; it repeatedly urges individuals to sign petitions (typically for Muslim rights in the United States or for causes in Muslim communities overseas); and it pushes members to attend conferences to become trained for leadership in the larger community. Occasionally it has sponsored debates between local candidates. The mosque has striven to maintain a good relationship with the mayor's office and police department in the city where it is located, and members have organized programs to educate local school officials about Islam and the cultural practices of Muslim students. The mosque has also sponsored workshops for their members to educate them about local government services and relations with local agencies. Some of the members have held positions in congresspersons' offices and even in the White House, and prominent figures in the community are tied to national Muslim organizations.

Nationwide, Muslims in the United States organized a large political mobilization in the 2000 U.S. presidential election. Some organizations had urged a bloc vote for George W. Bush in opposition to Joseph Lieberman, the Democratic vice-presidential nominee who was seen as too closely tied to Israel. George W. Bush and his father were not favorites among American Muslims, but they were considered to be the lesser of two evils. A smaller group of Muslims (primarily Arabs) voted for Ralph Nader in 2000. Nader is of Christian Lebanese descent, and many Arabs felt that the chance of having a future Arab Christian as president would be beneficial to them since they care about many of the same issues—such as Palestine. Secular organizations representing Muslims did much of this political organizing, not mosques, but many individual Muslims were active in both secular organizations and mosques; and some of the most active members of area mosques were also active sponsors of local and national representative organizations and lobbying groups.

Organizations such as the American-Arab Anti-Discrimination Committee (ADC) and the Council on American-Islamic Relations (CAIR) were more active and visible in the days and weeks following September 11 than the mosques themselves. The mosques tended to their own communities' needs and fears. They took part in the effort to protect American Muslims principally through participation in interfaith worship services for the victims and, after a number of months, public outreach efforts. Some of the political connections that area Muslims had forged, however, paid off when President Bush visited the Islamic Center of Washington, D.C., on September 17 and met with Muslim leaders from the area. His speech recognizing Muslims as part of the fabric of American society was widely seen as an important achievement for Muslims in this country and a significant antidote to the heated anti-Muslim feelings that emerged after September 11.

The events of September 11 changed life in all mosques. Though the initial response to the dangers the events posed for the Muslim community was muted and gained the most political visibility through national-level organization, the massive detentions of foreign-born Muslim men and increasing threats to civil liberties posed by the Patriot Act prompted area mosques to work harder in defense of Muslim rights. The final wake-up call came in March 2002, when federal agencies, including the INS, the Federal Bureau of Investigation, and the Department of the Treasury, raided a series of Muslim homes and organizational offices in the Washington, D.C., area, carting away truckloads of files and computers. The justification for the raids was that the organizations and the people who ran them were laundering money to funnel it possibly to Al-Qaeda. The Muslims in the Washington area were outraged at the charge, maintaining that the organizations that were raided were opposed to Al-Qaeda. Many mosques held meetings, gave press conferences, and invited government officials to discuss the accusations and tried to allay their fears.

Notes from one meeting at a Shiite mosque are illustrative: "During the program first an African-American Muslim spoke of civil rights abuses and paralleled those occurring against Muslims with those against African-Americans in the 1960s. Then a representative of the American Muslim Council [a national-level advocacy group] discussed the allegations [against] the groups in detail. After a question-and-answer session, participants took part in writing letters to congressmen asking them to uphold the civil rights of Muslims." At all three of the larger mosques we studied, imams and lay leaders made themselves as available as possible for interviews by the media. One mosque bought advertisements in local newspapers identifying themselves as Americans and condemning the terrorist attacks. Both mosques organized informational open houses for area non-Muslims to attend. Booklets were printed and handed out to attendees. Imams stressed the commitment of Muslim immigrants to their new home, as in this sermon in November 2001:

> This [America] is not a temporary resting area. This is our home, and
> we need to create the best possible atmosphere for our families
> and children. Many Muslims suffered after September 11th be-
> cause of the backlash, and we were saddened and angered. Well, we
> should be angry at ourselves for not doing a better job showing
> them what Islam and Muslims are really about—what we believe,
> how we act, and that we are normal and nothing to be afraid of. That
> we care about them too. We must make our presence known in
> our communities by volunteering our time, helping our neighbors,
> participating in neighborhood projects for the betterment of our
> communities. This is the way to change things.

Mosques also played a role in the increasing mobilization of local Muslims in marches and demonstrations protesting U.S. policy toward Israel and Iraq. All of the mosques in the area sent groups to attend a massive demonstration in downtown D.C. on April 20, 2002, which had as many as 100,000 attendees, joining Muslim and non-Muslim protesters from around the country. One woman member of a local mosque commented, "It is our duty to attend these demonstrations. I'm so upset about what's happening to the Palestinians. We need to make our voices heard. I went to the one on Saturday [April 20, 2002] with my whole family, even my little ones. It's better to make it a family event, otherwise no one ends up going." All of the mosques stressed over and over that the backlash incidents after September 11 and the government raids are examples of what can happen to members of the Muslim community if they do not become politically active.

As many as a third of the congregants in the mosques we studied became politically active in some way after September 11. Many congregants spoke of the need to identify excellent spokespeople for Muslims and to promote them for elected positions. The Potomac Islamic Center created its own civil rights division, devoted to researching legislative issues, selecting priority items for action, and advocating for them. At the Center, sermons and announcements, e-mail notices, and brochures urged everyone to phone and write their congresspeople and to build positive relationships with them. The main issues the members were interested in were the human rights situation in Palestine, opposition to war on Iraq, and civil rights in general.

Volunteering for social services also accelerated immediately after the attacks, most notably for fundraising drives and blood drives for the victims. The Potomac Islamic Center increased involvement through volunteering at senior citizen centers, running marathons for benefits, serving food at soup kitchens, and participating in community cleanups. Masjid Al-Muslimeen held fundraisers for the fire and police departments in the area. Both mosques organized meetings with government officials concerning civil rights issues. One small Muslim organization that had been working with battered women in the community extended its work to sponsoring meals for the homeless and arranged to cosponsor weekly food preparation with an activist Christian congregation, drawing on local mosques for volunteers.

Not all mosques have been politically and civically involved to the same degree. Though our sample is limited, both the survey results and case studies suggest that three factors encourage civic action in some mosques more than in others. The mosques with more second- and third-generation immigrants tend to be more active than those primarily composed of first-generation members. Mosques with members with higher incomes were also relatively more active than others. Mosques in which the genders mingle more freely seem to allow more pooling of skills and efforts than mosques that keep men and women rigidly separate and women's roles limited. We might speculate that this is partly because of better communication where men and women work together and partly because in the former mosques, the women have more influence and are more likely to take on volunteer efforts. Comparatively speaking, mosques are much more diffusely organized than the Sikh gurdwaras, with their ritual family meal accompanying major worship services and their tight sense of community. But conflict over focus, strategy, and personalities repeatedly splits gurdwaras, as Penny Edgell's work would lead us to expect, while the more diffuse structure of mosques and "community-style" organizational culture allow a variety of approaches to civic engagement to flourish.

The more community-style mosques—typically also the more affluent ones—are thus homes to a variety of efforts to promote outreach beyond the Muslim community, provide services to Muslims and non-Muslims, and mobilize for civic action. Other mosques, especially those serving recent immigrants, are more likely to adopt a house-of-worship format consonant with the function of the mosque in most countries-of-origin or to concentrate services on the community of worshipers. Our observations in the field and survey results bear out these expectations. In the face of threat, theology appeared to become the handmaiden of survival, as most imams stressed that American Muslims had to become full participants in a pluralistic American society and not sojourners awaiting the restoration of the Caliphate, yearning and working for the (re)establishment of an Islamic social order somewhere else.

THE HINDU TEMPLES. In contrast to the quick-response efforts of the Sikh community and the eventual wide-scale mobilization of area Muslims after the events of September 11, the Hindu community in the Washington area responded minimally, neither adopting an organized posture of self-defense nor moving on a large scale to announce its solidarity with the victims. Individual Hindus responded with horror and expressions of solidarity, like all Americans, but the temples in the area sponsored few events or activities. Most Hindu temples consider themselves to be apolitical, though it is a central teaching of one of the most revered Hindu texts, the *Ramayana*, that lay people have an obligation to be active participants in the world. At the temples we observed, there was no political activity regarding American political issues during 10 months of observation. By and large, the only expressly political activity we encountered revolved around the religious conflicts in the Indian state of Gujarat in 2002, in which Hindus and Muslims clashed in bloody fighting after destruction of a historic mosque on a site holy to both Hindus and Muslims. Temple Hindi sponsored a public forum in a high school, in which representatives of various religious groups condemned the violence and asked for mutual tolerance. Temple Gujarat, by contrast, which was home to an active branch of the Hindu fundamentalist movement, saw the massacres of Muslims in Gujarat State as an act of Hindu self-defense.

In the wake of September 11, small gestures were made at several local temples. Temple Hindi sponsored a fundraiser and mailed a check for $1,000 to the Red Cross to help care for September 11 victims on behalf of the community. Dravidi Temple posted a sign offering the temple's condolences to all of the victims and took up an offering to be distributed to victims by a non-profit agency. Temple Parthi hung a large American flag on the door as a sign of solidarity and as a possible deterrent against vandalism by antiimmigrant hooligans. Though Hindu temples elsewhere suffered vandalism and individuals of Indian descent were harassed, temples in our study area did not organize in self-defense as the Sikh congregations had, nor did participants in worship services express significant alarm.

At the oldest and most encompassing of the Hindu worship communities, speakers gathered for the public ceremony surrounding the annual celebration of Diwali, or the Festival of Lights, soon after September 11, compared the Hindu god Ram's epic battle over evil with the Bush administration's "war on terrorism." Kathleen Kennedy Townsend, Maryland's lieutenant governor at the time and a prominent invited speaker, recalled that over 250 persons of Indian descent died in the World Trade Center attacks and declared that diversity is America's strength in combating evil. Anil Chadhauri, from the office of cultural affairs of the Indian Embassy, emphasized the parallels between Ram's defeat of Ravana and America's war on terrorism: "The battle [between good and evil] is still on. India is shoulder to shoulder with the United States in its war against terrorism." While the politicians present looked on, an 11-year old boy read his patriotic poem decrying September 11 and praising the American effort in Afghanistan.

By and large, however, the public response among Hindus was muted, and where it appeared, it was sponsored by civic and community groups, not temples. A half-page advertisement placed in the *Washington Post* on October 15, 2001, by some Hindu civic and community groups, for example, was not initiated or organized by any of the Hindu temples, nor were any of the temples listed as contributors. The main sponsor of the ad was the National Federation of Indian American Associations. The ad was a message to the American public offering condolences and solidarity:

We, the Indian-Americans of the Greater Washington area, express our deepest sympathies for the victims and families of the September 11, 2001 terrorist attacks on America. For decades, our brothers and sisters in India have suffered death and destruction from terrorism, which has claimed the lives of over fifty thousand ordinary, innocent people [presumably a reference to the struggle over Kashmir, thus a subtle reference to Hindu-Muslim strife]. The civilized world condemns terrorism and those who harbor terrorists. From the land of non-violence and Mahatma Gandhi to the Land of the Free, we stand by President Bush in his fight against global terrorism. UNITED WE STAND, one nation, under God, indivisible, with liberty and justice for all. (Emphasis in original)

The Hindu temples thus demonstrated their character as principally "houses of worship," organized not as surrogate "families" or around efforts to build diverse communities or as civic actors, but providing a setting for both individual and communal worship and education. It is perhaps characteristic of this sort of organizational culture that the fullest expression of reaction to the events of September 11 should come at a large-scale public event, in the presence of prominent Hindu and non-Hindu guests. Here public acknowledgment of the Indian community's reaction to September 11 would be appropriate. In the everyday life of the temple, however, such concerns were not only subordinate to worship and religious education, but they had little occasion to be expressed at all, as worshipers came and went on a mainly religious calendar.

The one exception to this pattern was Temple Gujarat, where the fundamentalist Vishwa Hindu Parishad (VHP) movement dominates temple life. In India, the VHP calls for Hindu dominance in national culture and is closely associated with the Bharatiya Jana Sangh party (BJP), which rose to national prominence in the 1980s. Both are offshoots of the Rashtriya Swayamsevak Sangh (RSS), which has been widely associated with the assassination of Mohandas Gandhi on the eve of India's independence. The Washington, D.C., chapter of the VHP has joined forces with the international arm of the RSS, the Hindu Swayamsevak Sangh (HSS), to sponsor Sunday schools for Indian children to preserve Hindu culture and advance the nationalist cause. One of these schools is hosted by Temple Gujarat, which also cohosts a HSS/VHP summer camp where children practice disciplined marching and "speed yoga" calisthenics, both designed to toughen Hindus for the nationalist struggle. Though most of the young people who attended these programs resented their parents' attempts to impose Indian values on them and spoke disparagingly of their elders' racism, they could also echo the VHP line. In a wide-ranging discussion that touched on the riots in Gujarat and relations with Pakistan, one young woman exclaimed, "You see, in history Hindus were a passive race. Muslims took our jewels and temples and land, and then the Brits took over everything. This generation is stronger though, and we're fighting back."

Conclusion

The extent and type of civic engagement in these worship communities varies enormously. This should surprise no student of American religion. Neither American churches nor civil society more generally, much recent rhetoric to the contrary notwithstanding, exhibits a uniform pattern of civic engagement. Worship communities are civic actors in varying degrees and ways. One of the determinants of greater civic engagement, particularly the provision of formal social services, is the size of the worship community. More profoundly, though, worship communities serving the new immigrants differ in the level and kind of civic engagement they display, thanks to variation in the circumstances of immigration of their members, their organizational culture, and the theological tradition they draw upon.

The Hindu temples we have just considered offer little to nothing in the way of formal social services. That is the case in part because of the circumstances of immigration: most members are quite well-off, and their demand for services, accordingly, is low. But it is also because these institutions are organized primarily as houses of worship. They devote little attention to building a sense of family or community among their members. They sponsor few activities above and beyond worship. In a few temples, the political preoccupations of the VHP find resonance, insofar as they express themselves through religious education; but otherwise the temples remain apolitical.

Among Salvadoran churches, circumstances of immigration explain one of the main preoccupations of political activism, namely, immigration laws affecting the status of many Salvadorans in this country. But other factors explain why only some churches and not others actually have a civic presence and encourage their members to become involved. The version of evangelical Protestantism espoused by many of the small Salvadoran churches discourages political involvement and lays particular stress on building up the community of the saved. Individual pastors could take up the social justice tradition within Catholicism and the United Methodist churches we studied to shape distinctive local responses: some pastors engaged directly in civic affairs; some promoted naturalization, voting, and advocacy on immigration issues among their members; some churches sponsored food pantries and ecumenical activities; and many gathered charitable contributions for the needy in El Salvador. But not all pastors were persuaded of the importance of these sorts of activities. Most Catholic parishes stopped well short of political engagement; some churches were only minimally responsive to immigrants' needs, focusing largely on worship and religious education—bespeaking the house-of-worship organizational culture that is typical of Catholic parishes. Others, like St. Francis, actively promoted community among immigrant and Hispanic American members and sponsored numerous social services, in keeping with a more community-oriented vision of parish life.

The character of political engagement, where it occurs, also varies a great deal among these worship communities, responding to the sorts of political issues that most catch the attention of the immigrant communities and their leaders. In some cases, worship communities were politically engaged, but primarily with home country causes. Among Korean Protestants, such civic engagement has long focused mainly on events on the Korean Peninsula. In the 1980s and 1990s, many churches were preoccupied with supporting the prodemocracy movement at home. By the time of our study, some disillusionment had set in, and the focus of external concern was with the famine in North Korea and the fate of North Korean refugees in China, many of whom were being clandestinely housed and supported by underground Korean Protestant organizations in Manchuria. We did not encounter churches involved in lobbying the U.S. government around these issues, in large part, perhaps, because secular Korean American organizations in the area were active but also, it appears, because of the largely apolitical stance of most area pastors, whose conservative evangelical training stressed attending to the religious life of the family of God over civic engagement. To the extent that Korean Protestant churches promoted civic engagement, it was through collections for local charities, most of them Korean-run, but a few of them with a wider clientele. In this respect, the Korean churches resembled other middle-class, conservative churches.

In some cases, though, homeland concerns also prompted civic engagement. The Guru Granth Sahib Center is a case in point. There, outrage over Indian government treatment of Sikhs in the Punjab led to well-organized efforts to educate the media and the general public on the Sikh view of the conflict and on the Sikh religion. The congregation itself originated in these efforts and in its founders' identification with the cause of an independent Sikh Punjab, or "Khalistan." Sikh leaders active in defense of the Sikh religion sought to demonstrate the ecumenical and charitable faces of Sikhism by joining the Washington Interfaith Conference, promoting Sikh participation in blood drives, AIDS walks, and work with the homeless, and playing an active role in community affairs. Homeland politics thus promoted domestic civic engagement, and Sikh nationalism reinforced American citizenship, a pattern that is probably as old as ethnic organization in the United States. We saw a similar phenomenon at Father Mesa's St. Francis Catholic parish. And the larger, more prosperous mosques also combine concern for homeland causes and domestic political and civic engagement. Expanding possibilities for legal dual citizenship will undoubtedly make it more and more common to see ethnic and religious groups civically engaged at both ends of the transnational continuum; but, again, this is nothing new.

Finally, immigrant worship communities are more likely than the average American church to provide multiple formal social services, expend significant resources on such efforts, and draw on outside resources to fund them. But they vary greatly in the sort of presence they maintain in the larger community. Many smaller churches provide no formal services and enjoy few links to secular or faith-based social service agencies; but they take care of members and those whom members bring to their attention on a regular, if informal, basis. Others, particularly the generally larger Catholic and mainline Protestant worship communities and the larger mosques, provide formal services to their members and neighbors or work closely with agencies that do so. These same worship communities may also host multiple community organizations, and in some cases pastors or prominent lay people play active roles in civic associations and local politics. Finally, many of the relatively affluent worship communities—Korean and Chinese Protestant churches, Sikh congregations, and Hindu temples—focus their charitable activities on supporting Washington area causes and programs for the needy, donating money, clothing, or food, and supplying volunteers to agencies serving people outside their immediate communities.

Less a spectrum than a set of three distinctive types, this pattern reflects larger patterns of civic engagement among American churches. Level of income, organizational culture, and religious tradition all influence which category of civic engagement a given worship community will fall into. Those with poorer members, or located in poorer neighborhoods, are more likely to sponsor formal social services, especially when the congregation is economically mixed or has access to resources outside its walls. Among the relatively affluent Chinese congregations, for example, the First Chinese Christian Church, located in Washington's small Chinatown neighborhood, where new immigrants often find cheap housing, stands out as the most committed to sponsoring a range of social services. But having a relatively poor clientele does not ensure that a worship community will engage in formal social service delivery or link up with local agencies that do, as the example of Nuestro Señor showed. An organizational culture that is focused on creating a close-knit "family of God"—even in a church of 300 members—precludes the sort of effort that formalized social service programs might entail. In this evangelical Protestant church, both organizational culture and religious tradition, moreover, encouraged members to look out for one another and provided ample opportunities to do so, without recourse to formal organization.

More affluent worship communities may devote considerable resources to charitable causes, even when they are not otherwise organized to encourage civic engagement, as the example of the Hindu temples suggests. Occasional special collections provide outlets for the charitable impulses of worshipers and ensure that the temple or gurdwara or church acquires a reputation for generosity in the larger community. A more active civic presence, however, takes special effort, and usually springs from a worship community that is larger, open to multiple initiatives among members, and theologically (or politically) motivated to assume a greater role in the civic arena. Such worship communities fit the "community" style described by Becker. Such congregations appeared among all the ethnic groups we studied, but they sprang from the theological, and sometimes political, commitments of leaders and lay people who drew on their respective religious traditions to justify civic engagement alongside the strictly religious functions of worship and spiritual education. They were common among mainline Protestant churches, but they could be found in Catholic parishes, mosques, and Sikh communities; and some of the Hindu temples had the nuclei of such forms of organization in cultural groups, religious education for children, youth groups, and other subgroups. Community-style worship communities need not be politically active, but most of the civically engaged congregations had this sort of organizational culture to build on.

The civic presence of immigrant worship communities is thus enormously varied—as varied as that of American worship communities more generally. The variation springs not from ethnic or even mainly religious differences but from differences in the specific circumstances of the immigrant and ethnic community that each worship community serves, its organizational culture, and the religious tradition its leaders draw on to shape the community's common life.

The character of a worship community's civic presence can certainly influence its members' own engagement with the larger society, through both example and the larger body encouraging and giving members opportunities to become involved in civic activities. But worship communities, like other sorts of voluntary associations, may also shape members' civic engagement through training in the sorts of skills necessary to participate actively in civic life. We take up this theme in the next chapter.

5

Building Civic Skills

Attending a worship service can be a lonely affair, or it can be a source of deep and lasting friendships. An individual or even a family might attend a mosque or temple or church for years without becoming significantly involved in the life of the worship community. Others, however, are drawn in, rapidly or more slowly, eventually participating as active members in the life of the community. Individual personalities and family styles undoubtedly play a role in how this plays out; so does the organizational culture of the worship community. But wherever worshipers become participants in community life, they acquire and practice skills that will serve them in civic life more generally.

Recent research has confirmed that churchgoing has as one by-product the training and encouragement it often provides to members for civic involvement. Verba, Schlozman, and Brady's (1995) study of the bases of civic engagement in the United States found that persons active in churches received education in skills such as public speaking, leading meetings, and planning events. Churches, along with the workplace and unions, were especially important for poorer and less well educated members of the community, increasing their abilities to become civically active alongside those who enjoyed the privileges of higher education and income. At the same time, local worship communities provide important settings for the mobilization of civic participation, whether through the informal contacts worshipers enjoy among themselves, as a direct response to religious teaching and sermonizing, or through organized efforts to get members involved in the public sphere (Rosenstone and Hansen 1993; Verba et al. 1995). Worship communities may not have as their central purpose the teaching of civic skills or mobilization for public participation, but they often provide both training and motivation for civic engagement in the course of the everyday life of the community.

Worship communities differ among themselves in these respects, just as in others that we have considered. Some encourage relatively little lay involvement, vesting governance in a priest or small coterie of lay or religious officials and confining participation, even in worship, to a limited number of people. Others self-consciously promote community involvement, actively train lay leaders, and enthusiastically promote civic engagement beyond the worship community. Between these poles, worship communities vary widely. Organizational culture plays a large role in generating the differences among communities, but we will find that the leadership styles of religious and lay leaders, backed by alternative theological traditions, also account for many of these differences. And, as we saw in the last chapter, the circumstances of immigration for a given group, especially the salience of homeland causes, can have an important role in how strongly communities encourage civic engagement.

This chapter looks at the ways immigrant worship communities help their members acquire and exercise aptitudes that can enhance their participation in civic life. Where Verba, Schlozman, and Brady emphasize skills such as public speaking, leadership, organizing meetings, and writing letters, we emphasize as well the abilities to bargain and compromise, create new solutions to problems, and exercise critical judgment. Training for civic engagement should also include experiences that help promote a sense of efficacy, that is, a feeling that one is capable of making a difference, and that provide information and ideas relevant to civic engagement. Participation in all sorts of collective action can contribute to the development of both personal and political skills and a sense of efficacy; but participation in the governance of the worship community is particularly apt to do so. Such involvement may be thought of as "on-the-job training," but in addition, worship communities may offer courses and seminars on skills relevant to public life, such as public speaking. Or they may host organizations that do so, providing their members opportunities to acquire skills that they might not acquire in the course of the community's everyday life. Finally, worship communities may sponsor or host discussion groups, speakers, or informational sessions that encourage members to learn about issues of civic importance and develop their ideas and consciences with regard to them.

Throughout this chapter, we will be interested not only in how worship communities promote civic skills and aptitudes among their members but also in how well they do so and why some do so more than others. "How well" includes asking about the opportunities for women and young people to acquire such abilities. As we explore these issues, we will find some surprising outcomes, such as the high rate of participation in governance and collective action among Muslim women. We start by looking at our survey results, then turn to the ethnographic cases to flesh out the picture.

Arenas of Participation

Worship communities differ among themselves in the number and character of arenas in which members might acquire and exercise civic skills. In some, the worship service is the only occasion for members to come together and participate in the life of the community; and in some such cases, there is little scope for lay involvement. In others, the worship community sponsors a variety of small groups, committees, and special activities where lay people may be actively involved. In some cases, governance is tightly held by a single pastor or small, relatively unaccountable board of directors. In others, there are multiple opportunities to participate in community governance. Finally, some worship communities sponsor or host courses, seminars, projects, and events that can provide lay people with opportunities to develop civic skills.

First Arena: Participation in the Worship Service

Lay participation in worship services varies enormously across religious traditions. In some cases, lay people are excluded from public roles in the service. In others, they play a vital part. In some cases, lay participation is part of a training for religious leadership that is only open to a circumscribed few. In others men, women, and children are all invited to take part in helping to lead the community in worship. Such participation arguably provides training in civic skills in giving participants opportunities to develop and hone their abilities to play a public role with skill and confidence, assume a measure of leadership in a large group, and gain a sense of efficacy. While critical and political skills are largely in abeyance on such occasions, there are settings, as we shall see, where public participation in worship exercises even these.

Our survey and ethnographic studies revealed striking differences among worship communities in lay participation in worship. In the Muslim communities, opportunities to participate publicly were very limited, with just one lay person chosen to lead Friday prayers, but in some communities, efforts were made to recruit young men for the role, and the opportunity to lead Friday prayers was widely shared. Among Salvadoran Catholics, some churches routinely involved a dozen or more lay people in leading the worship services, in roles ranging from lectors to participants in music groups to distributing Communion. Men, women, and even children assumed roles at the altar. Proportionate to the large number of worshipers, the number of lay participants was small; but the sense that lay people had important roles to play was readily conveyed in these churches. In other Catholic churches serving Salvadorans, however, few roles were open to the laity. On average, more lay people—and more women and youth—shared leadership roles in Catholic worship services than in any other religious tradition.

The generally much smaller Protestant congregations also involved a significant number of lay people, including women and youth, in worship services. Salvadoran evangelical churches, for example, sometimes call upon members of the congregation to give "testimony," or an account of their conversion or other religious experience. Lay volunteers often lead the singing or make up the choir in Protestant churches; and some pastors give authoritative positions to lay people whom they view as pastors in training.

In the typical Hindu temple, by contrast, worship is conducted entirely by one or two priests. Lay people may solicit prayers and step forward for blessings, but otherwise they play little role in the service. Not all Hindu worship communities are typical, however. Hindu ashrams often involve selected laity—women as well as men—in conducting worship services as part of the spiritual training that they have undertaken as members of the community. Sikh congregations are similarly varied; some restrict most of the active roles to priests, while others involve lay men in reading from the sacred book, the Granth Sahib, and even recruit boys and girls to perform as members of a chorus to chant the sayings of the Gurus. While religious leaders were overwhelmingly male in all of the religious traditions (in close to 95 percent of our cases), women and youth were likely to participate as speakers, prayer leaders, or lectors at roughly half the rate of lay men in all but the Muslim worship communities.

Immigrant worship communities feature more lay involvement in worship and other leadership roles than the average American church. Our survey results suggest that Catholic churches serving immigrants involve almost four times as many lay people in leading the worship service as the average Catholic parish, while immigrant Protestant churches involve almost three times the number of lay people as their counterparts surveyed in the NCS. Almost four times as many women participate in immigrant Catholic worship

TABLE 5.1. Lay Participation in Worship Services, by Religious Tradition

	Catholic	Protestant	Muslim	Hindu	Sikh
Number of cases	22	150	14	9	4
In the main worship service this past week, how many different individuals spoke, prayed, or read to the group? Mean:	12.7	8.6	1.0	5.9	6.3
If one or more: how many were female? Mean:	5.7	3.9	0	3.0	2.3
How many teens or young adults participated in this service by speaking, reading, singing or performing? Mean:	7.1	4.1	0.4	3.2	1.7

communities as in Catholic parishes generally, and more than three times as many women helped lead immigrant Protestant congregations as in the larger Protestant community. Whatever truth there might be to the notion that immigrant religiosity is more "traditional" and patriarchal, our results suggest that both lay men and women in immigrant worship communities are more likely to enjoy leadership roles in the performance of worship than lay people in the population as a whole. (See tables 5.1 and 5.2.)

The Second Arena: Organizing the Community's Life

Many worship communities, as we saw in chapter 3, have some sort of subgroup structure. Whether these are small groups established to further the religious education and training of members or committees assigned with one or another task in the life of the community, they provide opportunities for lay people to assume leadership roles and acquire civic skills.

As we saw in chapter 2, most Catholic, Protestant, and Hindu faith communities had cell groups, devotional groups, or other faith-sharing small groups. Protestant churches were far more likely, however, to report a high

TABLE 5.2. Lay Participation in Worship Services in Immigrant Worship Communities Compared with NCS Sample (Percent)

	Catholic		Protestant	
	Immigrant	NCS	Immigrant	NCS
Number of cases	21	77	150	1119
Worship leadership				
In the main worship service this past week, how many different individuals spoke, prayed, or read to the group? Mean:	12.7	3.4	8.6	3.2
If one or more: how many were female? Mean:	5.7	1.6	3.9	1.1

percentage of members participating in such groups. Small groups were most common among Korean churches, where the cell group structure became a favorite tool of pastors starting in the late 1970s and early 1980s. In the typical group, a lay person (almost invariably a male head of household) would be chosen by the pastor to head up the group, which meets as often as weekly in one or another member's home. While leaders in some cases have to undergo special training by the pastor, they could also be critical of the pastor's performance, and small groups could become the locus for impassioned discussions of church politics and even revolts against the pastor's authority. Both leadership and critical skills could be honed in such settings. In the case studies we will see some examples.

Most worship communities, we found earlier, had at least one group organized to oversee some activity within the worship community or to pursue some particular interest. These groups ranged from those devoted to keeping the premises clean, to classes and training sessions of various kinds, to meetings on public issues (see tables 4.7 and 4.8). Sikh congregations, Protestant churches, and mosques had the greatest number of such groups, Catholic parishes the fewest; but even there, the average was 4.5 activities per parish. Here, too, lay people frequently find opportunities for leadership. Most of these activities, in fact, are organized by lay members of the community, if our ethnographic studies are any guide.

Women frequently take the leadership in these activities, even where the religious leadership is overwhelmingly male. Roughly half of those who played leadership roles in communities in each of the religious traditions were female. Young adults were less likely to be involved in leadership roles in this way; but a quarter or more of leaders in Catholic, Protestant, and Muslim communities were young adults. (The percentages were 11 and 20 percent for Hindu and Sikh communities, but varied enormously from community to community. See table 5.3.) The percentage of participants who play some sort of leadership role in these communities was surprisingly high: ranging from an average of 13 percent in Catholic parishes to 28 percent among Protestants. Muslim, Hindu, and Sikh worship communities reported, on average, that 15 percent of their regular adult members served in leadership roles.[1]

The Third Arena: Governance

Lay leadership in worship and in the multiple activities of a community's life are important for developing civic skills, but participation in governance is arguably more important. Here members of the community take responsibility for the larger life of the community, participating actively in framing

TABLE 5.3. Lay Leadership in Immigrant Worship Communities
by Religious Tradition

	Catholic	Protestant	Muslim	Hindu	Sikh
Number of cases	22	150	14	9	4
Persons in leadership roles					
Percent of the regularly participating adults who have served in some leadership role in the congregation in the last 12 months. Mean:	13	28	15	15	15
Of these persons, what percent are female? Mean:	51	49	49	47	55
What percent are young adults, that is, under 30 years old? Mean:	27	27	24	11	20
Congregational governance (percent)					
Worship communities with a governing committee	86	91	100	100	75
If yes: how many people are on it? Mean:	14.5	15.1	10.3	10.4	10.0
Percent female	46	43	17	23	13
Governing committee is elected by members	32	52	85	22	33
Governing committee has power over the budget	32	76	93	78	100
Governing committee appoints the pastor	5	41	86	56	100

decisions, and often participating in delicate negotiations or difficult coalition building. Of course, not every governance body has the same level of responsibility. In Catholic parishes, the pastor generally remains in firm control, and parish council members often serve at the pleasure of the pastor, with little authority over the budget or other key decisions in parish life. Many of the pastor-founded Protestant churches are equally, if not more, authoritarian in structure. In other cases, religious leaders serve at the pleasure of the community or of a board of directors, and the latter wields considerable power in the community. We shall have to keep these distinctions in mind as we assess the evidence of our survey.

Most immigrant congregations, regardless of religious tradition or ethnic group, feature a governing committee of some sort. In a majority of Protestant churches and 11 out of the 14 mosques we studied, this body is elected by the community (see table 5.3). By contrast, in almost a third of Catholic parishes, the governing parish council is appointed by the pastor. In other religious traditions, direct election by the community and/or election by some special body prevails. These committees, as we noted, vary considerably in their powers. In Catholic parishes, they have no say in selection of the pastor; but in over 40 percent of Protestant congregations, 55 percent of Hindu temples, 86 percent of the mosques, and 100 percent of the Sikh gurdwaras, the governing body has this power. It is even more likely to have authority over the budget in these traditions, whereas Catholic churches tend to restrict budgetary authority to the pastor. Women are less likely to sit on these committees in all the traditions than they are to assume leadership roles in other subgroups of the worship community. Though the percentage of females on governing bodies approaches 50 percent in Catholic and Protestant churches, the percentage varies between 13 and 23 percent in Sikh congregations, mosques, and Hindu temples. The last numbers are low, but they are a corrective to the prevailing patriarchal image we have of these religious traditions. The higher numbers among Catholics and Protestants also belie dominant images of immigrants as religious traditionalists for whom women play at best a subsidiary role in community life. In fact, a comparison with the NCS figures for female participation in Catholic and Protestant churches in the United States suggests that women are as likely to have a place on governing bodies in immigrant churches as in the average American church.

The Fourth Arena: Training in Civic Skills and Civic Engagement

Opportunities to participate in leading the worship service, take part in small groups and committees within the community, and share in community governance provide indirect training in civic skills. They give people the opportunity to develop and hone skills in public speaking, organizing and conducting meetings, coalition-building and political maneuvering, and critical thinking. They are not directly oriented, however, to civic engagement. Indeed, there is some evidence that the more intensely involved people become in their worship communities—honing civil skills along the way—the less likely they are to participate in the larger civic arena. Some individuals may be multitaskers whose energies overflow from worship community to the larger community, but most people, it seems, feel forced to chose between a demanding worship community and larger civic involvements, as Robert Wuthnow argues (1999). Nevertheless, there are a number of ways worship communities not only encourage civic engagement but actually provide enhanced opportunities to become involved, as we saw in chapter 4. Among these opportunities is direct training for civic engagement via classes and discussion groups.

Worship communities often provide classes and discussion groups for their members, and they frequently host other organizations that do so as well. As we saw in the last chapter, a surprising number of worship communities sponsor programs to register people to vote, discuss politics, lobby elected officials, and participate in demonstrations. The Hindu communities were by far the least likely to do so, a phenomenon we attributed both to the organizational culture of most temples and the view that Hindus already felt an obligation to be civically engaged and did so in other venues.

Beyond these directly political sorts of efforts, worship communities often sponsor other sorts of skills training and civic engagement. Catholic and Muslim communities were most likely to sponsor citizenship classes. More than three-quarters of the Catholic churches had English language classes, as did over a third of the Protestant churches and a quarter of the mosques. Meetings to help orient immigrants to local community services were common among all religious traditions, with Muslim, Catholic, and Protestant communities leading the way. Less common were meetings to discuss race or ethnic relations; but half the Catholic and Sikh worship communities had such meetings, as did between 20 and 27 percent of Muslim, Hindu, and Protestant communities. Not surprisingly, such discussions were particularly important among African congregations; but 20–30 percent of worship communities serving the other ethnic groups also held them.

In all these respects, then—opportunities for lay leadership in the worship service, participation in subgroups within the community, leadership in the governance of the community, and direct training for civic engagement— churches, mosques, temples, and gurdwaras undoubtedly contribute to developing civic skills and promoting civic engagement among immigrants. But these organizations differ tremendously in how much they do, for whom, and with what effect. In order to explain variation among them and to begin to get some sense of the meaning of such training for immigrants, we must look

TABLE 5.4. Training in Civic Skills: Meetings, Classes, and Discussion Groups

	Catholic	Protestant	Muslim	Hindu	Sikh
Number of cases	22	150	14	9	4
Percent of worship communities that, during the last 12 months, have hosted, sponsored, or held:					
Voter registration drive	41	23	43	11	50
Discussion of political issues	41	11	21	11	50
Meeting to participate in lobbying effort	32	20	21	0	75
Meeting to participate in a demonstration	46	11	50	0	50
Meeting to plan an assessment of community needs	62	48	36	11	0
English as a second language classes	77	38	23	0	50
Citizenship classes	46	15	43	0	50
Meeting to orient members to community services	46	41	64	22	25
Discussion of race relations	55	27	21	22	50
Meeting for volunteer work in the community	82	49	50	78	75

more closely at cases. In the remainder of this chapter, we will focus once again on the contrast between Catholic and Salvadoran Protestant churches, then consider the sometimes explosive relations between laity and pastors in Korean Protestant churches, and, finally, look at the rich variety of lay roles and civic engagement in the Muslim community.

Civic Skills and Religious Purposes

Worship communities are organized around religious purposes. Religious organizations do not generally set out self-consciously to generate civic skills. The training relevant to civic life in which they engage is a by-product of their own community life and of efforts to meet their own needs. Even when worship communities provide direct training and encouragement to engage civically, they do so out of motivations that answer to religious imperatives or justifications. Precisely for these reasons, we need to ask about the impact of such training on actual civic engagement. If the "civic skills" generated in the course of community life are mainly focused inward, they will have little immediate impact for civic engagement. If members are encouraged to play an active role beyond the worship community, we can begin to speak of civic impact. The best measures we have of such differences are primarily qualitative ones; so in the following pages, we take up two Salvadoran cases to explore the quality and meaning of the civic skills that worship communities produce.

Nuestro Señor: Multiple Arenas, Little Civic Engagement

We have already explored some of the contrasts between the large Hispanic Catholic community at St. Francis of Assisi parish and the evangelical Protestant community we have called Nuestro Señor. In chapter 4, we discussed the variety of ways the Hispanic community of St. Francis maintained a civic presence in the larger community and sponsored programs to help parishoners and others navigate and participate in American life. By contrast, Nuestro Señor, despite a vibrant community life, had almost no interaction with the surrounding society, and the focus of its members' lives outside of work was almost completely on the life of the congregation.

Opportunities for developing civic skills are nevertheless abundant at Nuestro Señor. Members of the congregation are expected to give "testimony" in the course of the service, and women and children, as well as men, stand before the congregation at every service to tell of their experiences and praise

God in spontaneous song or prayer. Leadership training is incorporated into the worship service. And every Saturday, young people aged from 10 to 30 are encouraged to come to the front of the church to recite scriptures or give testimony. Our field notes describe one such occasion:

> About 40 young members came to the front of the church. The women stood to the right and the men to the left. There were about 25 females and 15 males ranging from 10 to 30 years old. Most seemed to be in the 18-to-30 age bracket, plus a large number of females between 14 and 18. Each person had memorized a sentence or brief passage of the scriptures, and each came to the microphone and shared it with the whole congregation. The males went first. One of them came to the microphone and seemed taken over by emotion, so he had to start his passage several times before he was able to finish it all. He then started crying and moving back and forth. As this was going on, the congregation started shouting, "Praise the Lord!" believing that his behavior was a manifestation of the presence of the Holy Spirit. He eventually returned to his place with the males but kept on crying and praising the Lord during most of the time the young members were speaking and singing in front of the congregation.

The church's program of leadership training for young men is especially directed toward participation in the worship service. Young men 20 to 35 years old are in charge of Friday worship services, including preaching and arrangements. They gain public speaking and organizational skills, and they become visible in the congregation. This is hands-on training in poise, public speaking, and debate. The young men are dressed in suits and give the impression of being apprentice preachers being prepared for service—which in fact they are. Those who are judged suitable on the basis of their commitment, public speaking ability, and spirituality may be elevated to the role of deacon or co-pastor and eventually recruited to head another congregation affiliated with the denomination.

Lay members of the congregation are also called upon to take part in a multitude of volunteer activities, from cleaning the premises after services to working as ushers to organizing the Sunday afternoon meal and bazaar. Roles are largely gender-defined, with men given all the prime leadership positions; but women organize the meals for weekly and special fundraising activities, and their husbands typically help out. The round of volunteer activities, coupled with worship services several times a week and a full day at church on Sundays, can occupy most of participants' leisure time, and several complained that they had no time for English classes or other activities outside of church.

St. Francis of Assisi: Who Learns Civic Skills?

At St. Francis, by contrast, a much smaller proportion of the parish's Hispanic community participates in the life of the parish, despite a multitude of opportunities to do so. Yet many of these opportunities involve active contact with the larger society. Father Mesa's Foundation depends upon about 150 volunteers who run Spanish literacy classes and organize workshops related to housing ("Buying a Home," "Getting a Mortgage," "Tenancy Rights"), health (health fairs offering medical screenings free of charge), and legal issues (immigration law updates). Other workshops focus on fundraising, media relations, financial management, leadership training, and public accountability. Not all volunteers are from the local immigrant community, of course. Many are successful Hispanic business people or professionals who are well established in the area. But these older immigrants and Hispanic Americans take pride in mentoring newcomers and building new leadership through the foundation's and the parish's many social services. Volunteers also staff such parish-sponsored efforts as assisting people in applying for TPS; tax preparation workshops; ESL and literacy classes; and organizing, staffing, and catering for such events as Thanksgiving or Christmas lunches for the congregation at large. A pastoral council and a variety of pastoral commissions also provide volunteer opportunities for active members of the parish, though most of the members are not Hispanic. Through the parish's SALT group and affiliation with the Virginia Coalition for the Homeless, members of the Hispanic community also have the opportunity to work on social and political issues outside the scope of everyday parish life.

Participation in worship services is much more limited at St. Francis than at Nuestro Señor. Young boys may serve as altar boys; but girls were banned by diocesan decree some years ago, and the pastor's brief experiment with ignoring the decree was quickly put down. Nevertheless, both nuns and lay women assume roles at the altar as lectors, and women also help distribute Communion. Women are much more likely to play leadership roles in the charismatic community's worship services, though, where the frequency and intensity of lay participation approaches that of Nuestro Señor. In the larger parish, lay participation in worship is largely passive, for both men and women.

Committees, nevertheless, flourish in St. Francis's Hispanic community, where Father Mesa encourages participation and depends upon volunteers to keep the multiple activities of the community going. Indeed, because of its relative youth and energy, the Hispanic community has far more activities than the Anglo community with which it shares the parish. The latter has a single youth group, while the Hispanic community has three; the Hispanics have formed several choirs, the Anglos only one or two. But it has proven difficult, perhaps precisely for this reason, to integrate the larger Hispanic community into parish life. The pastor's strategy has been to insist on a unified parish council and commissions, with members of both the Anglo and Hispanic communities represented on each. In practice, this means that mainly those Hispanics who are relatively fluent in English participate in leadership posts outside specialized committees overseeing the Spanish-language liturgies and activities. Older Anglos often dominate the governing groups. When the pastoral team attempted to conduct a parish-wide "needs assessment," few Hispanics showed up, and those who did struggled to understand the badly translated questionnaire that formed the basis for their deliberations.

Who Rules?

St. Francis and Nuestro Señor differ in important ways on the question of governance. While Catholic canon law gives the pastor absolute authority in his parish, both theological currents since Vatican II and the pressing needs of large parishes with few priests have generated strategies of governance that depend heavily upon the laity. Many parishes have pastoral teams made up of pastor, assistants, nuns, and sometimes hired lay people who take responsibility for different areas of parish life. The parish council, sometimes called a pastoral council, has long been a feature of Catholic life; in most parishes, including St. Francis, it plays an advisory role in governance decisions within the parish, with the pastor the ultimate authority. In practice, nevertheless, many of those decisions are made by subcommittees or special commissions dedicated to specific areas of parish life. At St. Francis, the Financial Commission is particularly important, as it oversees the parish budget.

Catholic pastors differ on whether to tolerate an elected council or appoint members. In the case of St. Francis, members of the parish council include representatives of the various commissions, at-large members, and members of the pastoral team. Father Mesa made clear the leeway enjoyed by the pastor and assistant in the composition of the council when he commented: "When I got here nine years ago, I found that most of the Hispanic leaders in the parish were of Cuban ancestry and that didn't reflect the reality of our population, so I took it upon myself to replace that leadership with a leadership that would reflect the new demographics of our congregation, which is 80 percent Salvadoran" (interview, September 2000).

The leadership at Nuestro Señor is equally top-down, but it is also more subject to challenge from below. Religious leadership consists of the pastor, a co-pastor, and six deacons. The latter are elected by the congregation, but the current pastoral team preselects candidates for election, drawing especially upon the young men already in formal training for the ministry. The pastor may choose to ask a deacon to step down, or he may postpone yearly elections if the leadership team is doing well. Women have no place in the ministry at Nuestro Señor, however skilled they are at giving testimony and public speaking.

As Becker's model would predict, however, this family-style congregation is not without its tensions. These are apparent in the preaching and public commentary of the pastors, deacons, and some members of the congregation, which frequently discuss the lax discipline of some members of the community and the low rate of tithing among them. At a Sunday service, a woman named Maria recounted a dream she had had that reflected some of these concerns:

> She said that in her dream she was trying to enter the church but the doors were blocked with huge wooden blocks. She had seen in her dream that all the congregation was dressed up fancy with women dressed as though they were attending a prom, with high heels and "horrible, horrible" make-up in their faces. Men and women were selling items in the basement of the church and it looked like a marketplace, not a church. Everybody was very engaged in the selling and buying and they were laughing and enjoying themselves. As this was going on, Maria entered the room with a young girl and a small boy and she noticed there was a short ugly-looking man following her and the children. This man was disgusting and she soon realized that he harbored evil intentions and that he wanted to rape her children. She looked around for support and help from the crowd but found no assistance in a complacent and decadent crowd so she rushed out of the basement to protect the children. (field notes, November 2000)

Another middle-aged woman came forward one day at Nuestro Señor with 13 children surrounding her. Our field notes record the scene:

> She placed herself in the middle, with the girls at her right (with their heads covered by a handkerchief) and the boys at her left. The

children were standing from tallest to shortest. Each child said a few sentences or words of prayer in front of the congregation and they all sang together at the end. After the children's intervention, the woman addressed the group and basically scolded the congregation because only these 13 children were receiving religious education and the congregation had "plenty, plenty more children who could be going to Sunday school." She added that parents needed to make clear that Sunday school "was not a choice but an obligation, that parents had to force them to go if necessary." (field notes, November 2000)

The pastor and other religious leaders spoke frequently on the importance of tithing, and they even recruited a guest preacher to underline the point. His sermon concluded that those who did not pay tithes would be cursed and would not achieve salvation. The pastor followed up on a more conciliatory note, observing that some churches exclude from membership those who did not pay tithes. This was not the policy at Nuestro Señor, he said, but tithing was essential to the health of the church.

From the congregation's side, rumors abounded about leadership conflicts within the church, so much so that pastor and deacons felt obliged to squelch them publically. Countering complaints about the deacons, the pastor preached:

These are people who are sacrificing themselves for the community; they are preparing their sermons at night, sometimes without being able to sleep because they have two or three jobs. I, myself, Brothers and Sisters, I am not schooled. I only have a primary education and this fact doesn't make me less capable of leading the church and listening to the word of God. Religious leaders work through divine inspiration and the Holy Spirit inspires us to deliver our sermons, not information the world has put in our head. You all have to be more obedient. There needs to be more order because this environment of disorder is affecting negatively both the members of the church, the visitors, and the youngsters. Some members have told me that this is the reason why they are leaving the church. The Church has to unite! (field notes, March 2001)

When a rumor swirled that deacons were maneuvering to remove the pastor, one of the deacons stepped forward to resolve the "misunderstandings" and the rumors going around, "because these misunderstandings are demoralizing the congregation." He reported that the pastor and deacons had met to clarify things and that the key issue agreed on was that the ministry and its resources needed better management. He read a formal statement that pastor and deacons had prepared, and he and the pastor asked the congregation to unite behind "the work of the Lord."

Saint Francis also had its share of conflicts, but neither Father Mesa nor the pastor were the objects of challenge. Direct challenges to the authority of a priest or pastor are rare events in a hierarchical organization like the Catholic Church. Conflicts were more common between Anglo and Hispanic communities, within commissions and subcommittees within the parish, and over the quality of some of the lay leadership. Most of these clashes could be resolved, or at least quieted, through the intervention of the religious leadership, whose authority was largely unquestioned. Plenty of critical thinking could be exercised in these conflicts, and in the numerous opportunities for discussion of issues of concern to Catholics and Hispanics, but only in extreme cases would criticism be seriously directed toward challenging the authority of a priest.

At Nuestro Señor, the effort to maintain moral discipline in the congregation, the pastor's hectoring on the subject of tithing, and the gossiping among members about the leadership suggest that this community, apparently so zealous, was in constant tension. However tightly knit socially and even spiritually, the congregation was still a collection of individuals and families with their own needs, desires, and thoughts, some of these in conflict with the idealized Christian community promoted by the religious leadership. Though conflict with the leadership did not take organized form during our period of observation, this congregation, like the family-type congregations in Becker's study, was vulnerable to sometimes convulsive struggles over leadership. But precisely for that reason, it was also an arena in which critical thinking could be honed and exercised. Indeed, the very demand for public "testimony" on the part of worshipers could provide outlets for critical thinking alongside the apparently spontaneous, but closely scripted, narratives and prayers that were standard fare at worship services.

Conflict and Contention

At some of the smaller Korean and Chinese churches, we encountered tensions similar to those we saw at Nuestro Señor. These tensions occasionally exploded into mass defections on the part of members or the replacement of one pastor with another. But the ordinary life of these small churches also provided arenas for exercising critical judgment even on delicate questions of theology and moral deportment. These possibilities are often nourished within the cell group structure, which gives members regular opportunities for discussion outside the purview of the religious leadership. Though some pastors have attempted to incorporate cell group leaders into a specially trained religious leadership, these efforts sometimes backfired when lay people rebelled at the pastor's discipline. In some cases, lay leaders whose tenure antedated that of the pastor have led revolts against the ostensive head of the congregation. Thus, the high degree of respect generally accorded pastors in Korean Christian churches sometimes had the paradoxical effect of exacerbating tensions, encouraging pastors to exercise arbitrary authority and leading lay people to try to replace the pastor rather than use dialogue and negotiation.

In contrast to the Salvadoran evangelical churches, Korean and Chinese churches often have a large proportion of well-educated, economically comfortable members. This can sometimes lead to tensions with pastors, especially those who were trained in Korea, where no college degree is required of seminary graduates. But it also means that the church is not generally the vital avenue for economic and social advancement it once was. Several Korean pastors reported that Korean Protestant churches had been largely "social clubs" up until the 1970s, gathering places where Koreans could foster connections among themselves and find the help they needed to advance in the larger society. Only a couple of secular organizations, often founded with substantial help from pastors, served the Korean community in the 1970s. Since then, Korean business and professional organizations, as well as specialized social service agencies, have proliferated, rendering the church less important to the community. Korean pastors, meanwhile, began to insist on the religious purposes of church life, using the cell group structure introduced from Korea in the 1970s to encourage Bible reading, prayer, and moral discipline (Kwon 2004). With two or three exceptions, few Korean churches have developed into the larger, community-style church exemplified by St. Francis; the majority are quite small (fewer than 100 members) family-style affairs, with a decided emphasis on worship and religious education. As a result, they provide fewer opportunities for developing civic skills than more community-style churches or even a larger evangelical church such as Nuestro Señor.

Even so, the cell group structure that is widespread in Korean churches provides one such setting, calling on the organizational and leadership skills of cell members and offering a regular opportunity for discussion and debate. In many cases, members rotate leadership duties among themselves. Generally, cell groups meet at members' homes over a potluck Korean dinner or a dinner prepared by the host family. After the meal, members gather for Bible study, drawing on a textbook by a favorite Korean preacher or theologian or study notes prepared by the pastor. Members are invited to discuss the Bible passages of the day and move on to implications for their own lives. Cell group members are rarely in complete agreement over matters great or small. Field notes from one such meeting give a feeling of the quality of the exchanges:

The given topic of this day's cell meeting was religious "misguidance." Once the moderator introduced the day's debate topic to the members, one of the members, Mr. Kim, raised a question: "I don't know why we Korean Christians, especially the Protestants, denounce moderate drinking and smoking as a sinful deed. As far as I know, a lot of American Christians do not consider them a sinful deed. I enjoy drinking beer and other alcoholic beverages sometimes when I meet some close friends. Whenever I have a chance to get together with my close friends, they ask me to drink few bottles of beer. I do not consider drinking a few bottles of beer with close friends a sinful deed." The person next to Kim, Mr. Ha, agreed with Kim's opinion: "I drink beer almost every weekend. I am not sure what is wrong with that. I don't get drunk, but I enjoy it. It is very hard to get away without drinking beer on the weekend." The person next to Ha pointed out: "All the drinkers in this room do not consider their drinking habits a wrong and sinful deed." This brought a burst of laughter from a few members. The leader interrupted by stating: "The Bible never judges believers' drinking and smoking habits. But it warns a chronic alcoholic about the negative effects on his or her life. As you might already realize, Koreans in Korea drink and smoke too much, compared to people in other advanced countries. I personally want to avoid judging the influences of drinking and smoking on their life. As medical science continuously reveals so many negative influences of drinking and smoking on peoples' health, I personally think that we Christians do not have any reason to hurt our body for a moment's pleasure."

Mr. Jang responded to the moderator's statement: "I used to drink and smoke a lot before I became a Christian. Personally, I do regret my bad habits, which made my life unhealthy, otherwise [sic] now I would be enjoying a healthier and happier life. If you become a 'real' Christian, I think you will watch all aspects of your deeds and will become happy to follow the rules of our God, let alone, drinking and smoking!" Kim said, "You sound like you are able to tell the difference between the 'true' or 'real' Christians from those who are not. Could you possibly tell me what happened to you when you became 'true' or 'real' Christian by admitting Jesus Christ as your personal savior? What kind of sign or change did you get by any chance when you felt that you became a reborn Christian?"

The exchange continued with an intense discussion of what it might mean to be a "true" Christian, and several members were sceptical of the very concept; but debate was muted on so central a question, and the moderator closed the discussion with the question "Who is able to know someone has experienced a sign of salvation? I think only God knows your state of belief or your own degree of religiosity, and only God can tell who is saved or not. So, it is not necessarily an arguable topic in this Bible study."

Arguments about fundamentals are nevertheless not uncommon. Nor is criticism of pastors, despite the general deference accorded them. The relatively young pastor at University Korean Church, for example, attempted to hold members to a rigorous "Discipline Training Program." His idea was that all the qualified members of the congregation should be equipped for leadership roles within the congregation and that only in that way could the church grow. Only members who have "testified in our religion" are qualified to exercise leadership in the church, according to the pastor, who selected cell group leaders on the basis of his own evaluation of their religious seriousness and insisted that they attend weekly trainings with him in addition to Sunday service and weekly cell group meetings. Many of the older members of the congregation left. (The church declined from 86 to just 35 regular members in the two years of this pastor's tenure.) Korean graduate students and second-generation young people now dominate the congregation. The leadership training appeals to some of these members, but many are planning to return to Korea after completing their studies, and the congregation is struggling to stay afloat.

Such conflicts are not restricted to Protestants. The Sikh community has been wracked with divisive conflicts, as we discussed in chapter 4, and the solution is often the formation of a new worship community. Even among Catholics, struggles over leadership occasionally break out, and at one small Chinese Catholic church, the members successfully petitioned the disocese to replace their pastor. Conflicts are rarely about politics—though Sikhs have split over the role of the congregation in defending Sikhs before the world. Nor are they usually about theology, though questions of pastoral practice can acquire theological overtones. More often they are struggles over leadership style. Conflicts appear to be most acute, as Becker's work suggests, in the smaller, more family-style worship communities where the close interdependence of religious leaders and people, and of religious leaders among themselves, provide multiple opportunities for conflict and the basis for radical solutions. Larger, more community-style organizations permit multiple channels for members' energies and often depend on a leadership team that balances qualities across the team and provides flexibility in addressing problems from below. In such contexts, people hone their civic skills not as weapons for internal warfare but as instruments of collective action. Some of the larger mosques provide yet another illustration of how this sort of worship community trains its members and helps them engage in the larger society.

Training Muslim Americans for Civic Engagement

Mosques would appear, on the surface, to be unlikely places to look for the sort of training for civic engagement highlighted by Verba, Schlozman, and Brady. Traditionally, the mosque is simply a place of worship. Other organizations, such as Muslim charities, channel the charitable impulses and social service energies of Muslims. Imams (and ayahtollahs in the Shiite tradition) dominate the popular imagination as the forceful leaders of the religious community, and they are generally as subject to a rigorous process of training and vetting as any priest or minister in the more hierarchical traditions of Christianity. Nor do laity participate in religious services except as supplicants. Men dominate scenes of Friday prayers in Muslim countries, while women, if they participate at all, do so separately.

This portrait is not altogether accurate, even for traditionally Islamic countries. In the United States, they must be radically revised. Laity, not clerics, control most mosques. Even in the rare case where a cleric assumes the role of executive director of the mosque, the community's assets are controlled by a lay board of directors, who also hire and fire religious specialists. Most mosques are not simply houses of prayer; they are simultaneously community centers, sponsoring a wide array of activities and services. In such settings, moreover, women and youth frequently play key roles. Gender relations vary from mosque to mosque, and though women and men are segregated almost everywhere during worship, women are likely to be visible at Friday prayers in U.S. mosques, in some cases even occupying their partitioned section of the main hall of the mosque side by side with the men.

Worship services provide extremely limited opportunities for participation in the Muslim tradition, though a lay person is typically asked to give the call to prayer. The larger mosques, however, feature a wealth of opportunities for lay participation and leadership in the life of the community. The Potomac Islamic Center, for example, holds classes for new members, parenting and marriage classes, personal finance and tax workshops, conflict resolution workshops, fundraising events for the needy, a counseling program, and building maintenance events. It also held a blood drive in conjunction with the American Red Cross after the September 11 attack, coordinated volunteering at a soup kitchen in D.C., and participated in an interfaith social service program that helps the needy with sustenance and clothing. All of these activities are organized and staffed by lay volunteers.

In the wake of September 11, greater emphasis throughout the Muslim community, but especially in the larger mosques, was placed on outreach and participation in charities that reached the non-Muslim population, such as food drives for the homeless and fundraising for cancer and AIDS research. An excerpt from a sermon at one mosque illustrates the tenor of this effort: "Just as Prophet Muhammad helped everyone in need, whether they were Muslim, Christian, or Jewish, we too have an obligation to help those around us." In the words quoted on page 160, the imam then went on to argue that America is not a temporary home for Muslims and that Muslims should be angry at themselves for not having done a better job of showing Americans what Islam is all about and that "we are about them too." Muslims should be volunteering and helping their neighbors.

The notion that "this is not a temporary resting area," as this speaker insisted, is an important one. It speaks of a growing determination among American Muslims to imagine a permanent place for Islam in a non-Muslim society, a notion that is foreign to strains of Islamic political theology, "moderate" as well as radical, that emphasize the centrality of Muslim rule to the life of the believer. Its appeal is primarily to second-generation (and later) Muslim Americans, and, indeed, the majority of volunteers in the larger mosques come from second-generation and better established members. But the notion also resonates with many immigrants. One member of a smaller, predominantly Afhani mosque expressed the dilemma of many immigrants:

It's really difficult for us to decide where to spend any extra income we save. If we give it to the mosque, it's going to be at the expense of our own families in Afghanistan. Everyone is so poor there, and even if our families are taken care of, they have so many neighbors that are in dire need. On the other hand, we're probably never going to go back home, and we need well-established facilities and services for our children. (interview, February 2002)

In building and maintaining those facilities and services, immigrant Muslims stand to acquire civic skills that will also be important in their integration into American life.

Participation in leadership and governance positions is an arena particularly relevant to developing civic skills. As we saw, all of the mosques are governed by lay boards of directors, most often elected by members of the community. Only in one mosque were board members appointed by the religious leader. Many of these boards are nevertheless top-down sorts of affairs, with founding members occupying board positions for many years and dominating the selection of new members. They have final authority over their budgets in all but one case, and in all but two of the 13 mosques we surveyed, the board appointed the religious leader.

Women and young people play leadership roles, particularly in the larger mosques and those with a higher percentage of second-generation members. They run religious education programs, organize fundraising events, manage youth groups, promote outreach, and manage much of the housekeeping of many mosques, though in the more conservative mosques, these tasks are limited to stereotypically "feminine" concerns. At the Potomac Islamic Center, teen groups are autonomous, relying on adults only for advice. Some of their members have gone on to found a national organization for Muslim youth.

Finally, while civic skills may be nurtured in the everyday life of the mosque, some communities set out to advance the integration of immigrant members into American life and promote good citizenship, particularly post–September 11. In chapter 4, we saw that a surprising number of worship communities encourage members to take advantage of English language and citizenship classes, promote voter registration, urge members to vote, and even seek to orient them in their vote. Some mosques also actively encourage volunteering in civic affairs among their members, and they sometimes sponsor, host, or promote activities designed to give members the capacity to become more deeply involved in civic life.

In the case of the Potomac Islamic Center, the mosque has been a center for the developing political presence of Muslims in American politics, as we saw in chapter 4. In sermons and announcements, the mosque regularly promotes participation in informational and leadership training activities sponsored by other organizations. When the American Muslim Social Scientists organization held its annual conference at Georgetown University in October 2000, for example, the mosque's leadership urged members to attend, and many did. Part of the conference focused on Muslims in America, including emerging legal issues, institution building for Muslim Americans, and Islamic identity in America. One panel that attracted members from the Potomac Islamic Center addressed the issue of educating the Muslim community for skilled leadership. Similarly, workshops held by the Council on American–Islamic Relations in early 2002 on political participation, lobbying, and leadership were also promoted by the mosque's leaders.

Political engagement became more of a priority in many mosques after September 11. Prior to that time, the organization of political activities was coordinated by religious and ethnic interest groups. Now the larger mosques began organizing their own activities, some on their own and others in cooperation with other mosques and other religious and secular groups. Many meetings were organized at which members could hear from and question government officials on civil rights issues.

Through sermons, announcements, fliers, e-mail, and word of mouth, mosque leaders have repeatedly encouraged members to vote, attend politically related workshops and conferences, contact government officials regarding issues relevant to the Muslim community, and run for office. Many congregants have discussed a need to identify articulate spokespersons for the Muslim communities who could run for legislative positions. The Potomac Islamic Center created its own civil rights division to research legislative issues, select priority issues for action, and advocate for those issues. From the onset of the second intifada in the Palestinian territory, in late September 2000, members paid closer attention to notices and announcements for demonstrations in protest at Israeli policy and U.S. support for it. Large percentages of the members of area mosques, as we saw, attended a massive demonstration of an estimated 10,000 participants on April 20, 2002, in Washington, D.C. Area Muslims also mobilized through their mosques to protest Bush administration plans to invade Iraq in late 2002 and early 2003.

As in the case of the Salvadorans at St. Francis, the political mobilization of Muslims responded both to pressing issues of concern to Muslims in this country and to homeland issues. The difference in the case of the Muslim community is that homeland issues are not primarily determined by ethnicity. For many area Muslims, regardless of their ethnicity or country-of-origin, U.S. policy toward Iraq and Israel have long been "Muslim" issues. These issues are closely related to efforts of mosques and lay Muslims to encourage civic engagement, get out the vote, develop a capable Muslim leadership, and enhance relations with the larger society. As we saw in the case of certain Sikh congregations, homeland issues, far from isolating Muslims in American society, contribute to their integration.

Hindu Fundamentalism and Civic Skills

Homeland issues are also likely to stir even the politically quiescent Hindu temples. Hindu temples generally provided sparse opportunities for lay people to develop civic skills, but one temple stands out for its sponsorship of a militant program of civic training for youth. As we saw in chapter 4, Temple Gujarat cohosts a summer school to teach "Hindu values" and train children in Hindu nationalist militancy. In the wake of the riots in the state of Gujarat, where the killing of 69 Hindu militants by a Muslim mob was followed by a widespread pogrom in which hundreds of Muslims were left dead, the VHP held a large public function at Temple Gujarat. Speakers insisted that Muslims had started the violence and had been taught a lesson, while others lamented that members of the VHP had done nothing to combat the picture of Hindu violence that was put out by the American press. Members of the audience were urged: "Get involved, send mass letters to clear up the misinformation, so that we can proudly say we are Hindus." A similar event at the other, more liberal, predominantly Gujarati temple in the area featured very different reflections on the events in India. Hindu, Muslim, and Sikh speakers concurred in deploring the violence, and the Hindus expressed their shame at what had happened and their revulsion at the BJP government for complicity in the massacre of Muslims. (See chapter 6 for a more detailed account.) Nevertheless, though the more liberal temple sponsors a number of social service activities and occasional forums like this one, it does not provide the sort of concrete channels for political education and activism that Temple Gujarat does in hosting VHP functions and a VHP-run Sunday school.

Conclusion

As in other respects, so in regard to the civic skills that worship communities nourish, the extent to which they nourish them, and the ways they put them to use, immigrant worship communities differ enormously among themselves. How do we account for these variations? Country-of-origin or religious identity clearly determine *what* homeland causes are salient to a given worship community and indirectly, therefore, the sorts of civic skills that might be exercised. But not all communities take up homeland causes, and the cultivation of civic skills extends far beyond such overt political engagement. Why do some communities have more opportunities than others? Why are some oriented almost exclusively inwardly, or to members of their own religious tradition, while other encourage civic skills specifically oriented to engaging with the larger society? Why do some encourage some skills but not others?

The answers revolve around the organizational culture of the worship community, the theological tradition on which it draws, and leadership. They also depend not only on the circumstances of migration but also the larger demographics of the worship community, which is itself partly a product of the sort of immigrant stream(s) that have shaped it. We start with this last point. Communities made up mainly of more recent and poorer immigrants will naturally be at a disadvantage in building up the sorts of facilities and services that larger, wealthier worship communities enjoy. As the Afghani worshiper quoted earlier noted, recent immigrants are often torn about how to use their resources, and the more meager those resources, the less is going to be put into a local worship community. The communities that offered the widest array of opportunities for learning and exercising civic skills were not only the largest but also those with higher proportions of members who had resided in the United States for some time. They also tended to be communities with a good mix of income and educational levels.

St. Francis is illustrative. Though the majority of the Hispanic community is Salvadoran, most of whom have only recently arrived and have limited resources, a few members of the community have been in this country for decades. They have high levels of education and are well established. This is particularly true of the board of Father Mesa's foundation, which helps link parish activities to agencies, donors, and civic affairs outside the Salvadoran immigrant community. Father Mesa has tried to nourish a leadership drawn from the majority Salvadoran community, but he depends on the more established members of his board and of the parish to help nourish this leadership and provide the expertise and connections that most recent immigrants lack. Some of the same dynamic is apparent at the wealthy Potomac Islamic Center. Here, too, members of the second generation and well-established professionals have taken the lead in building up the community and bringing it into contact with non-Muslim agencies and organizations of all sorts. They have set a tone of adaptation to U.S. society and civic engagement in the context of defending Muslim interests in this country and advancing the community's foreign policy concerns. The civic skills that are nourished at the Potomac Islamic Center reflect both the ample opportunities for active participation within the mosque and the civic concerns of the lay leadership.

Multiethnic communities also seem to be particularly apt to develop a wide range of civic skills among their members. In the case of the mosques, this may simply be an artifact of our sample and of the situation of mosques in the Washington, D.C., area. Elsewhere, where greater concentrations of

Muslims of one or another ethnicity are found, mosques tend to be predominantly of a single ethnicity. In the Washington area, most mosques are multiethnic, reflecting the geographically scattered Muslim community and the relatively low concentrations of immigrants from any one country or ethnicity. Mosques can afford to be larger, and they have developed a wider range of activities than the few single-ethnicity mosques we observed.

As the Muslim population grows in the United States, the community undoubtedly will build more and more institutions besides the mosques to serve its members. The community can be expected to create more and more social service, professional, and civic associations outside the mosques, just as other immigrant groups have done; and the mosque may become less of a community center than it now is. Korean Protestants have two more decades of growth than the Muslim community in the Washington area, and Korean secular nonprofits now provide most of the social services and many of the social functions that the churches once provided. The Catholic Church has spent more than a hundred years building a social service and voluntary association infrastructure. For now, in any event, the mosque remains the center of community life for most Muslims, and it is an important arena in which Muslims immigrants come together, regardless of ethnicity, and acquire and develop civic skills.

The African worship communities also suggest that multiethnic groups provide a wider range of experiences for developing civic skills. As we noted earlier, the African worship communities are of two basic types—free-standing churches composed entirely of Africans, and Africans worshiping together with other persons in multiethnic churches. The two different settings appear to produce different opportunities for training in civic skills. The multiethnic churches have more meetings to plan to lobby elected officials and to organize participation in demonstrations or marches; they have larger lay governing committees; and they have a higher percentage of women in the governing committees and in leadership roles. One reason might lie simply in the greater resources available to most of the multiethnic churches and their ties to larger, mainline denominations. More important, perhaps, is the greater diversity within these communities, a greater awareness of difference and diversity, and greater efforts, accordingly, to support activities and services for all the various groups within the community.

All of this should not be interpreted as arguing that poorer communities made up principally of newer immigrants cannot contribute to the development of civic skills among their members. Nuestro Señor is a key example. This vibrant community provides opportunities in both worship services and the everyday life of the community for active participation, and a great many individuals assume responsible roles in the community. But the sorts of civic skills nourished at Nuestro Señor contribute only in theory to civic engagement. By and large, members of the community are occupied with the affairs of the church, and the religious leadership does not encourage them to become active elsewhere. No doubt, over time, some of those who are currently disaffected will move on and perhaps away from this sort of intense church community. Then the civic skills developed here may be relevant to other organizations more civically engaged than Nuestro Señor. As long as they remain deeply enmeshed in this "enclave of the saved," however, the civic skills they are acquiring are likely to have little relevance to their integration into American civic life.

As this argument suggests, we must look beyond simple demographics to account for all the differences we have encountered among worship communities. In the case of Nuestro Señor, both organizational culture and theological tradition help account for the pattern of intense cultivation of civic skills coupled with limited relevance to civic engagement. An evangelical theology that puts major emphasis on personal salvation through participation in an intense community of God seems here to discourage forms of civic engagement that draw members out into the larger society. At the same time, Nuestro Señor's Pentecostal flavor also makes for significant differences from the vast majority of the Korean churches. It encourages spontaneous lay participation in the worship service, whereas the Korean churches maintain much more formal liturgies with more limited scope for creativity or lay leadership. The size of the congregation also has an impact. Larger churches in the evangelical and Pentecostal traditions demand the sort of organizational complexity that provides members with many opportunities for active participation and even leadership. The smaller Korean Protestant churches have much more limited scope for internal organization. At best, they might include a youth group, a choir, a board of elders, perhaps women's and men's associations, and a number of cell groups. In most cases we considered, the church was too small to include even this range of activities. Some of the Salvadoran, Chinese, and African Protestant churches and a few small Catholic communities also fell into this category. The "family" flavor of such communities, Becker suggests, is not just an artifact of size but may itself dictate the size of a congregation, encouraging limited growth or fostering contentious division as the community outgrows its preferred style.

Clearly, some communities deliberately choose a more community style of organization. Large-scale "houses of worship" may evolve naturally into more community-style organizations to meet the needs of a diverse membership with significant lay activism. Or they may be transformed by a

community-building leadership. The Potomac Islamic Center combines something of both patterns; St. Francis illustrates the second. In a less common
pattern, a dynamic leader or leadership team may build a small congregation
into a larger, more dynamic organization with numerous activities and avenues for lay participation. Many of the so-called megachurches reflect such a
pattern (Sargeant 2000). Where more family-style communities tend to fis-
sure, sometimes acrimoniously, as we saw in the case of the Korean Protestant congregations, the community-style worship community often proliferates
channels for leadership development, satisfying the need for active engagement
that some members feel while sharing responsibility and thus buffering against
rancorous dissent. These communities are also more likely to forge links with
institutions outside their own denomination or religious tradition and to encourage greater civic engagement among their members. The character of the
civic skills they nourish is, accordingly, going to be somewhat different from
that developed in other settings. Habits of negotiation and conflict management, a talent for coalition building, and the ability to work with other civic
actors outside the immediate religious community are more likely to come out
of such settings than the more family-style worship communities.

Finally, what training in civic skills will mean for civic engagement in the
larger society varies across cases. As we saw, homeland causes can be a major
impetus both to such training *and* to deeper involvement in American politics.
We need not approve of the politics of a particular group to recognize that it is
motivating and preparing people for active citizenship. The more inwardly
facing worship communities, on the other hand, may provide training in civic
skills, but these skills tend to be applied primarily to the activities of the worship
community, which often strives to monopolize members' leisure time. The
typical "house of worship" provides few opportunities to learn or exercise civic
skills. The difference has mainly to do with organizational culture and theological tradition: the family-style worship communities, and especially those
whose theology emphasizes the importance of nurturing an economy of salvation within the religious community over asserting a moral presence in the
world, tend to maintain a small scale, with fewer opportunities for acquiring
civic skills and to focus inwardly. A Catholic church, a mosque, or a temple
under a more conservative leadership may well resemble much more Becker's
"house of worship" than the stereotypical Protestant "congregation" or the
more diverse community-style organization of the sort we have seen. In a
"house of worship," opportunities for active lay participation will be few and
acquisition of civic skills, accordingly, quite limited.

The ways people orient themselves to civic life in the larger society, however,
depend not just on their personal philosophies or theological leanings, not just

on the sorts of civic skills they have acquired and the opportunities they encounter for exercising them, but on how they see themselves in relation to that society. Personal and communal identity influence civic engagement, though both are often ignored in the political science literature. The next chapter takes up this topic, examining the identities that immigrant worship communities foster and their impact on communal and personal civic engagement.

6

Who We Are

Korean immigrants to the United States grew up in Korea as Buddhists or animists, Protestants or Catholics. A certain self-selection means that roughly half were Protestant at the time they left Korea. Yet in the United States, they overwhelmingly join Protestant churches. The religious self-portrait fostered in these churches puts their Christianity well ahead of ethnic considerations. Yet their churches are almost exclusively Korean, and a great deal of their civic and social outreach is oriented toward Korea and the problems of Korean immigrants. As one pastor noted, explaining his reasons for participating primarily in organizations working for the reunification of Korea and the welfare of needy Koreans, "as a religious leader I am obliged to help underprivileged people . . . as a Korean descendent I am also obliged to help fellow Koreans first."

At Nuestro Señor, personal salvation, achieved by embracing Jesus as Lord and Savior, is the center of community life, and those who have not achieved salvation are presumed to be lost. Nevertheless, the pastor was happy recently to open the church for the wake of a young man who was not a member simply "because he was a Salvadoran." Salvadoran identity apparently trumps membership in the church, at least for certain purposes. Indeed, the congregation is almost 100 percent Salvadoran; nevertheless, as an evangelical Christian community, Nuestro Señor is open to all. Meanwhile, at St. Francis, members embrace multiple identities—Catholic, Hispanic, and Salvadoran; Cuban American and Catholic;

Puerto Rican and American. At the mosques, we found similar amalgams: Muslim, Syrian, and Arab; South Asian, Pakistani, and Muslim American; African American and Muslim. Africans are Muslim or Christian, Catholic or Protestant, Ghanaian or Nigerian, but also Twi or Igbo, Fulani or Yoruba, and multiple combinations of these. Indians see themselves as simultaneously Hindus, Gujaratis, Indians, and Americans; Punjabi and Sikh; Tamil, Vaishnavite, Hindu, and Indian American; Hindu, South Asian, and American; the possibilities are unlimited.

Assimilationist sentiment poses a starker choice for new immigrants: either they maintain their cultural allegiance to their home country, or they adapt to that of their new country. Until recently, sociologists have depicted assimilation as the inevitable outcome of the immigrant experience in the United States, and assimilation was thought to be complete when immigrants or their descendants replaced the historical, cultural, and linguistic traditions and memories of their homeland with those of their new country (Park and Burgess 1924; Gordon 1964). In this conception, religious identity was the one exception, at least for those whose heritage stemmed from the "Judaeo-Christian" tradition. According to Will Herberg, a "triple melting pot" stripped immigrants of their ethnic distinctiveness, leaving only the major religious differences that characterized the United States at midcentury—Protestant, Catholic, and Jew (Herberg 1983). Subsequent work on ethnicity, as we saw in the introduction, has rejected the "straight-line" notion of assimilation, recognizing that, for many immigrants and their descendants, ethnicity's importance has ebbed and flowed. The reality is that immigrants make numerous adjustments and accommodations, in a process that is by no means a transition from one, fixed identity to another—a fact that makes empirical research on identity a bewildering task (Alba and Nee 1997, 2003; Gans 1992).

The question of ethnic identity is scarcely settled, and its relations to religious identity have scarcely been explored. Indeed, as Robert Wuthnow has recently noted, the growing religious diversity in the United States has prompted more than a little unease but little scholarly attention (Wuthnow 2004). This chapter cannot pretend to answer all the questions that surround immigrant adaptation to a new culture. But we can draw attention to the complexity of the issue of identity for recent immigrants and the role of religious communities in nurturing, shaping, and mobilizing ethnic and religious identities. What role do immigrant worship communities have in shaping such identities, and what is their significance for the civic and social incorporation of immigrants? What do they mean to the second generation—those born of immigrant parents in this country—and how enduring can we expect the new ethnic (and religious) politics to be in American life? Our survey of religious leaders provides preliminary answers to these questions, but looking at specific cases will once again help flesh out the picture and provide context.

Besides the survey of religious leaders and ethnographies we have been drawing on throughout, we also put to use a unique body of interviews with young people and their immigrant parents, conducted by Lene Jensen as part of our project. (Dr. Jensen's analysis will be published separately.) We will use these interviews to illustrate the complexity of the identities constructed in the context of Salvadoran Catholic and Hindu worship communities. The chapter starts with a look at some of the complexity of the issue of identity that is frequently neglected in popular debates. We report on some of that complexity through a look at our survey data; then we turn to Jensen's interview material. From there, we take up directly the question of the role of worship communities in shaping and mobilizing ethnic and religious identities, via a closer look at a number of case studies.

Religion and Ethnic Identity

Historically, immigrant worship communities have been important sites for strengthening ethnic identities. Indeed, Martin Marty argues that "ethnicity is the skeleton of religion in America" and is a significant basis for many denominational differences (Marty 1972). Religion and ethnicity have been intertwined throughout U.S. history (Greeley 1971; Hammond and Warner 1993; Smith 1978). In the nineteenth and early twentieth centuries, local worship communities were central to that identification, even where larger denominational bodies discouraged ethnic identification and promoted a universalist version of their particular religious persuasion (see, for example, Gleason 1992).

Worship communities reinforce ethnicity first and foremost by providing a common setting in which people of similar backgrounds may come together, "increasing social interactions among co-ethnic members and . . . providing a social space for comfort, fellowship, and a sense of belonging" (Yang 1999, 33). They do so while simultaneously permitting and sometimes promoting a certain "selective assimilation": "Instead of choosing *either* American *or* ethnic identities, immigrants may construct adhesive identities that integrate both together" (17; see Hurh and Kim 1993). The experience of racial stereotyping and discrimination that affects many recent immigrants from Latin America, Asia and Africa, may accentuate ethnic, or sometimes panethnic, identification (Alumkal 2003; Takaki 1989; Waters 1990). Both "reactive identity" of this sort and pride in one's ethnic heritage find outlets in immigrant worship communities.

Though we are accustomed to think of ethnicity as a product of national origin, the question of identity is further complicated by the fact that many immigrants possess a regional, tribal, or linguistic identity that is at least as strong as a national identity. Among Indian immigrants, being from Gujarat or Bihar is often more salient than being from India, and among Nigerians, being a part of the Yoruba or Igbo tribal family may be more important than being Nigerian. When these people come to the United States, they discover that regional or tribal identities are poorly understood by Americans. From the beginning, these immigrants find themselves labeled as Indians or Nigerians, South Asians, Africans, or simply "black"; but that experience does not erase their sense of identity; rather it promotes the assumption of multiple identities. As one second-generation adolescent told one of our researchers, "Americans don't know what Gujarati means, so with them I just say I'm Indian. But when I'm hanging out with Punjabis, I always identify as Gujarati."

Pressures on immigrants to assimilate themselves to broader groupings and become, for example, "Indians" rather than "Gujarati," thus appear to be strongest for small and more isolated immigrant populations (Morawska 1994). This is because small groups cannot easily form their own worship communities and ethnic organizations. But as more immigrants arrive from their home country or region, the specific worship communities and organizations become possible. If the immigrant stream for a particular group is small, group members may well downplay regional or tribal differences in order to form "Indian" temples or "Nigerian" churches. To do this entails a sometimes unwelcome adjustment from regional to national identity. As we saw in the last chapter, our evidence strongly suggests that when the continuing influx of immigrants makes each community large enough to form separate temples, churches, or mosques, they do so. The early Hindu places of worship in the Washington area were often pan-Indian, attempting to incorporate all the principal faiths of the Indian subcontinent. More recent foundations have been along regional and ethnic lines. One of the leading early Hindu worship communities, for example, divided when a large number of Gujaratis left to build a temple more reflective of that region's language and culture. Rangaswamy's study of Indians in Chicago (2000) noted a similar phenomenon. Similarly, pan-Nigerian worship communities have frequently given way to mainly Igbo and Yoruba churches as soon as the numbers of immigrants grew. In the last great wave of immigration, a similar process of forced deemphasis on regionalisms took place among earlier European immigrants to America, when, for example, Germans from Bavaria or the Rhineland felt pressure to see themselves as simply "Germans" and Italians from Piedmont or Tuscany feet pressure to become "Italians" (Herberg 1983); but in the later stages, individual churches often reflected local ethnic identities (Orsi 1985).

Not all the groups we studied had this sort of history. We did not find regional worship communities among the Koreans, and only limited evidence suggested such a direction among Chinese immigrants, where linguistic differences sometimes play a role in dividing communities. Among immigrants from Latin America and the Muslim world, specific national origin groups sometimes dominate particular worship communities, but, with a few exceptions, these specific groups have not formed exclusive enclave churches or mosques. (The Salvadoran evangelical churches with links to specifically Salvadoran denominations are a partial exception, as are mosques differentiated by national origin or language of worship, such as one Afghan mosque, where Farsi, rather than Arabic, is the language of worship.)

The religions brought to this country by immigrants carry the distinctive traits of the culture in which they were practiced. Even though universalistic world religions like Christianity and Islam dislike cultural barriers and teach endlessly that all humans are equal in God's eyes, both recognize that all religious expressions are local and enculturated. Traditional religious forms inevitably develop local identities, so that, for example, Nigerian Catholic communities feel distinct from Kenyan Catholic communities, and Pakistani Muslims feel that they are different from Arab Muslims. Questions about localisms become intense: for example, is the Korean Methodist from of worship of the immigrant's childhood the truest form and something that must be maintained at all costs, or should it be adapted to the needs of the second generation? Should the specifics of the Catholicism of the Guatemalan highlands be defended over against the variety of Catholicism promoted by official Catholic Hispanic ministries in the United States? For the new immigrants, there are pulls in both directions, in that the major religions preach goodwill and brotherhood across national lines, yet national or ethnic churches can feel more comfortable and spiritually empowering. Christian missionaries are acutely aware of ethnic and linguistic barriers that prevent formation of ethnically inclusive churches in mission countries. The widely read mission theorist Donald McGavran asserted that "people like to become Christians without crossing racial, linguistic, or class barriers" (McGavran 1970, 198), reiterating in a missionary context the old adage that Sunday morning is the most segregated time of the week. For some leaders, a true dilemma results. The core teachings of Christianity and Islam deemphasize ethnic identity and ethnic barriers, while the real-world experiences of ethnic, tribal, and national life build them up. For some who attend worship services, the dilemmas center around coping with the ethnic, national, and racial diversity that sometimes

characterizes worship in the new setting of the United States. In one way or another, however, worship communities tend to foster multiple identities among
those who participate in them.

The diversity of identities fostered in worship communities serving immigrants presents a conundrum for theories that suppose a simple binary op-
tion of "American" or something else. Clearly, many immigrants already enjoy
multiple identities; and most are rapidly adding "American" to the list. What
these phenomena mean for the incorporation of immigrants into American
society will occupy us throughout this chapter.

Immigration, Identity, and Civic Engagement

Most of the immigrant worship communities we surveyed are identified with a
specific national origin or ethnic group. Nevertheless, many of the churches
that serve Africans, virtually all of the mosques, and many of the worship
communities where Salvadorans are the majority include multiple ethnic
groups. And while Hindu temples attract mostly people of Indian origin,
devotees come from many ethnic and linguistic groups. Our survey sample
included worship communities that had at least 20 percent immigrants among
their members. In some cases, these members formed separate worship communities within the larger body that included significant numbers of white or
African American members—the Hispanic community at St. Francis is an
example. In others, they worship alongside nonimmigrants and immigrants
from a variety of countries in "multicultural" communities. In still others, they
were sufficiently numerous to constitute their own "ethnic" worship community. (See tables 2.7 and 2.8 for the breakdown by ethnic group and religious
tradition.)

Most of our cases fell into the last category. This was especially true for
Koreans, Chinese, and Salvadoran Protestants. Salvadoran Catholics tended to
find a place in an existing parish alongside other Catholics; with sufficient
numbers, and the pastor's permission, they form their own subcommunity
within the parish, with separate times of worship, events, and committee
structures. At the same time, membership in even the most stolidly Salvadoran
congregation, Protestant or Catholic, usually includes at least a scattering of
Hispanics from other countries of Latin America.

The West African Christians we encountered were much more likely to
worship in a multicultural setting. A fourth of the 39 African immigrant
communities we surveyed worshiped in churches where at least 50 percent of
the membership was white and/or African American. In most of these cases,

they worship together with the larger community rather than as a separate, African worship community. Even where Africans dominated, the congregation was likely to be of multiple national origins. In only 13 cases did a single national origin group make up more than 60 percent of a congregation; most of these were predominantly Nigerian churches, mainly Yoruba or Igbo in ethnic composition.

The diversity of ethnic and national origin groups is even more pronounced in the mosques. Two small mosques in the area are predominantly Afghan in membership, one is Turkish, and a fourth is Nigerian. The rest, mostly much larger, have a mix of national origin groups, with members of Arab ancestry predominant in one mosque, South Asians in another, Iranians in another. All of these multicultural mosques maintain inclusive policies, with English the favored language for sermons and everyday affairs (see table 2.10). Though ethnic distinctions persist, the leadership strives to present a portrait of a unified Islamic community, open to all, moderate in theology, and engaged in carving out a place for Muslims in American society.

Even among the most homogenous of the immigrant worship communities we studied—the Koreans and Chinese—linguistic differences could be important markers of diversity, and sometimes tension. Although virtually all of the 123 Korean churches initially surveyed are overwhelmingly Korean, almost 40 percent of these have at least one service in English, primarily for second-generation Korean Americans (see table 2.9). Sunday school classes are offered in both English and Korean in the bigger churches, but English has been accepted for youth programs and services for young adults of the second generation. In the Chinese worship communities, the major divides are between Mandarin and Cantonese speakers, and between Chinese-speaking immigrants and the primarily English-speaking second and third generations, but divisions between more recent immigrants from mainland China and an older generation of mostly Taiwanese Chinese can sometimes be significant. The apparent ethnic homogeneity of many immigrant worship communities thus belies significant divisions within them.

Immigrant worship communities also differ in the ties members maintain to the homeland. As we saw in chapter 2, most worship communities serving Koreans, Salvadorans, and Indians report high numbers of members (over 75 percent) born outside the United States. This is true for less than a third of the African worship communities and under half of the Chinese communities (see table 2.2). Yet the participants in these communities are not totally new to this country. With the exception of the Salvadoran communities, most say that only a small percentage of their number have come to the United States within the last five years.

There is little evidence of the sort of peripatetic transnationalism that the literature has led us to expect, but a modest number of immigrants do travel back and forth. Most worship communities report that fewer than 6 percent of their members have returned home for significant religious or life event ceremonies such as a baptism, marriage, or burial within the last year; most say that fewer than 10 percent of their members have traveled back to the home country for any reason during that period. And very few apparently send their children home to be raised in the home culture. There are some exceptions to these figures. Almost half the Catholic communities saw higher numbers of their members return home for religious events (over 10 percent did so in the previous year). The Muslim, Hindu, and Sikh communities were more likely to report significant numbers of members travelling home for other reasons. And a small percentage of the members of all the national origin groups did send their children home to be raised in an environment they considered more suitable.

These transnational behaviors, though confined to a small part of the immigrant population, attest continuing connection to the homeland. Do immigrants in these worship communities also pay attention to homeland affairs? The vast majority of religious leaders surveyed said that "some" or "most" of their members attended to national affairs in their homeland. Surprisingly, given the attention in the transnationalism literature on enduring ties with specific communities of origin, the numbers were significantly lower for community (as opposed to national) affairs in the homeland. Only the African and Indian worship communities reported higher levels of interest in community affairs back home.

With the high levels of interest in homeland affairs, we might expect that these immigrants would have little time, energy, or interest to invest in civic affairs in their new homes. In fact, the opposite appears to be the case.[1] The worship communities that reported high levels of interest in homeland affairs, whether at the national or community level, also reported high levels of interest in national and local affairs in the United States. As Peggy Levitt notes, "instead of loosening their connections and trading one membership for another, some individuals are keeping their feet in both worlds. They use political, religious, and civic arenas to forge social relations, earn their livelihoods, and exercise their rights across borders" (2001, 3).

The same is true for worship communities that pay special attention to ethnic identity. Those that sponsored events to celebrate their own ethnic or national heritage were more likely to participate in social service or community development projects in the United States. Similarly, those that held classes in the home language were more likely to be involved in local affairs in this

TABLE 6.1. Transnational Ties in Immigrant Worship Communities

	Catholic	Protestant	Muslim	Hindu	Sikh
Number of cases	22	150	14	9	4
Percent of members who have traveled back to the home country within the past 12 months. Mean:	24	13	24	29	a
Percent of members who have traveled back to the home country within the past 12 months for any religious ceremonies such as baptism or burial. Mean:	13	6	10	6	a
How many members keep up with *national* affairs in the United States? Percent answering "most"	27	37	39	100	50
How many keep up with *national* affairs in the home country? Percent answering "most"	46	45	62	100	50
How many keep up with *community* affairs in the United States? Percent answering "most"	9	23	15	44	25
How many keep up with *community* affairs in the home country? Percent answering "most"	23	19	31	0	0

[a]Too few cases to analyze.

country. In both cases, such worship communities were also more likely to have participated in joint worship services with communities outside their ethnic group or denomination. Heightened ethnic identity appears to be associated with higher levels of incorporation into American society, not the reverse. We have already seen evidence for this connection in chapter 5, where we noted that worship communities concerned with homeland affairs were also likely to be highly active in local and national affairs in the United States.

The one factor that seemed most to impede civic engagement among these worship communities was a high proportion of immigrants among the members. Worship communities with a higher proporation of immigrants were less likely to report high levels of interest in national and community affairs in the United States and less likely to have participated in social service or community development programs. Those with high proportions of recent immigrants (within the last five years) also reported lower levels of interest in civic affairs, though the effect is smaller. The relationship between high proportions of immigrants and lower levels of civic engagement holds up even when controlling for the effect of income. Thus, though strong transnational ties and ethnic identity are compatible with high levels of civic engagement, worship

TABLE 6.2. Transnational Ties and Civic Engagement

	Catholic	Protestant	Muslim	Hindu	Sikh
Number of cases	22	150	14	9	4
Programs to strengthen ethnic identity					
Percent of worship communities that had, in the past 12 months:					
Class for people to learn their parents' language	41	46	57	44	100
Event presenting the congregation's ethnic heritage	86	45	36	89	100
Institutional ties to the home country					
Worship community is linked to a specific congregation in the home country. Percent:	32	37	0	22	25
Percent of money for outreach, mission, and service that is sent to other nations. Mean:	8	16	13	24	5

communities that are more "mixed"—that is, include high proportions of American-born members alongside immigrants—are more likely to be civically engaged or promote civic engagement, just as more economically mixed congregations show higher levels of civic engagement (Foley et al. 2001).

Worship communities that are more ethnically mixed are also more likely to promote markers of ethnic identity and to be more deeply involved in civic affairs. Among the African churches, multiethnic churches and parishes sponsored more events celebrating the ethnic heritages of the members than predominantly immigrant churches. Multiethnic, mainline Protestant and Catholic worship communities, we found, were more likely than conservative Protestant churches to have such events. Explicit promotion of ethnic identity was evidently more important in such settings than in the more homogenous settings where ethnicity, while certainly strong, is largely taken for granted. Language classes promoting the native language of the members displayed a slightly different logic. They were most commonly offered in the Korean churches, but there, primarily in churches where a large proporation of the members were born in this country. As Waters and others have argued, ethnicity becomes a concern once it becomes optional (Alba and Nee 1997; Waters 1996). The worship communities that promoted ethnic awareness were also apt to be active in other aspects of civic life; and these were mainly communities with relatively high proportions of American-born members.

These findings are intriguing but incomplete. For one thing, our statistical analysis was not able to discern patterns among non-Christian worship communities, because the numbers were too small to yield statistically valid results. More important, they do not allow us to explore the dynamics of identity in these communities. To do that, we need to look more concretely at how individuals within these communities manage the question of identity and how the communities themselves choose, shape, and mobilize ethnic and religious identity.

Imagined Identities

Identity is often contested within immigrant worship communities. Here we ask what it means to ordinary participants in these communities. Our survey tapped the insights of religious leaders but cannot tell us much about the inner lives of their members. Lene Jensen's in-depth interviews with second-generation adolescents and their immigrant parents tells us more about how people think about themselves, their identities, and their relationships with American culture and politics. These interviews draw on samples from two communities (80 adolescents and parents from Salvadoran Catholic and Hindu Indian communities).

Immigration provokes often profound questions about identity. In some cases, this is a reaction to the stereotyping and prejudice that immigrants experience upon stepping into a new culture, as the theory of "reactive ethnicity" emphasizes. But the simple experience of difference may also provoke a new awareness and appreciation of one's own culture and heritage (Yang 1999). One Hindu parent, who initially described himself as an "international citizen," put it this way:

> Actually . . . when I was in India, I never really talked about what being an Indian or Hindu is about, because it was around. So we were surrounded by that, so it never—we never really gave much thought, even to learn our scriptures or anything of that sort, because we grew up with them hearing all the time . . . but only after we came here, especially after going to [temple]. I've learned a lot about Hinduism. I, I really learned . . .
>
> INTERVIEWER   So it's almost as though you're more Hindu now than [over there].
>
> RESPONDENT   Definitely, definitely.

Immigrant parents, moreover, are deeply concerned about the fate of their children, valuing the opportunities that immigration has opened up to them yet worried that their children will lose their cultural heritage. They face, as well, cultural clashes with their children, who are strongly influenced by American culture.

Young people in immigrant families face special challenges. Those who were born in the home country but raised and educated in the United States (the so-called 1.5 generation) may share some of their parents' memories and attachments to home, but they are generally immersed in whatever American subculture dominates their experience of school and neighborhood. They may well be fluent in their parents' language, but their everyday language is most likely to be English, which they manage with even greater fluency. They know intimately the cultural models that their parents and grandparents hold up, but they cannot help but be shaped by American culture, as conveyed by television, the movies, school, and friends.[2] The same is true with even more force for the second generation—those born of immigrant parents in the United States. Most immigrant worship communities are torn between inculcating in their children elements of the home culture and accommodating children's and teens' preferences for English-language services and activities and for American-inflected forms of worship and play. Many offer courses of instruction in the native language of the first generation; almost as many offer separate services in English to accommodate the 1.5, second, and third generations.

Young people and their parents thus struggle with questions of identity, because these are tied up with everyday comportment, parent–child relations, and children's future course. Few, if any, of Jensen's respondents evinced signs of the sorts of "politicized" identities that fueled civic engagement at St. Francis, among the Sikhs, or in many Muslim communities. For virtually all of the parents and young people, the question of identity was largely personal and often hard to articulate. When questioned about identity, in fact, many of them had to struggle to pin down their identities and to articulate just what made up the identities they ascribed to themselves.[3]

Most of the respondents, parents and adolescent children alike, saw themselves as bearers of multiple identities, American and something else. Even those adults who emphatically maintained their "Indian" or "Hispanic" or "Salvadoran" identities admitted that immigration had changed them in important ways. One Indian woman said she never calls herself Indian American: "Because my citizenship is still, you know, listed as Indian. I eat Indian food, I dress Indian, I speak Indian English [laughter]. Everything is Indian about me [laughter]." But she went on to say that there were many things about her now that were not "Indian." "Like letting my child leave the house before she's married. That is one. Then in India, it's terrible to talk about sex to your children, which I have spoken to her. I've described the bees—birds and the bees with her." On the other hand, many find that they are more appreciative of their religious heritage and more personally religious now than they were in their home country. As other analysts have observed, immigration may have a "theologizing effect" (Smith 1978; Yang 1999) that can be reflected in a renewal of religious identity; but it also provokes cultural assimilation to one degree or another (Alba and Nee 2003). For most people, these tensions produce multiple identities.

Much of the "material" of identity among these immigrants and children of immigrants has to do with cultural artifacts such as food and clothing. Embracing an American lifestyle made many feel "American" even if they were born in India or El Salvador and valued many deeper aspects of those cultures: "I don't know," one Indian father remarked, "like transportation-wise, like driving a car around going to work, it feels like American style. Like back in India . . . we didn't have that kind of luxuries. . . . Like all the TV . . . all that luxury . . . just utilizing them, and buying stuff from the stores"—this made him feel "American."

Language was also a crucial mark of identity for many respondents. Some explained their identity as stemming from their fluency in their mother tongue. For others, a passing acquaintance with the language of parents and grand-parents was enough to mark them as "Indian" or "Salvadoran" or "Spanish." And for still others, the fact that American English was their preferred way of expressing themselves made them first of all "American."

Cultural mores, and especially ways of raising children and relating to one's elders, were important markers for many respondents, especially Indian parents and children. One Indian woman put it this way:

> I mean the way I live everyday is the way I raise the children; the way
> I dedicate most of my energy to the family . . . the way my mother
> raised me . . . I guess that's sort of the Indian culture. I mean, our life
> is our children. That's our primary focus, and we don't tell them to
> leave the house at the age of eighteen. I mean, they are our children
> for as long as we are alive, and we support them in whatever they
> want to do. I mean we give them the education. We don't let them go
> on and work for the education. We don't let them go on and be
> independent in a sense. They're independent in their mind, but
> they're not independent of the family around them. We're always a
> presence around them.

But she added:

> I think in my outlook of giving the children the freedom to choose
> their spouses . . . I think that's not traditional Indian because we

believe in arranged marriages. . . . I think I'm different in that. I
think the fact that I give them the chances to argue their points
with me. They're very opinionated, and I think I, I give them
the freedom to do that, which is not the way my parents raised
me. What they [the parents] say is the final word and the only word
in some instances.

For these respondents, their ethnicity is scarcely of the "reactive" sort
postulated by some theorists. It is rooted, rather, in a sense of heritage directly
tied to family and, to a lesser extent, experience, including the experience of
immigration. One young woman admitted: "Well, I don't have experience in
Indian culture, so I—yes [laughter] . . . that's, that's who you are. That's—you
can't change . . . your Indian identity. That's who you are and that helps you.
That carries you throughout your life. And the only course is to learn more
about it and that will help you deal with situations here, I think." She feels she
has bonded more with her parents as a result of their immigration, "because if
we're not together then we'll be lost sort of here." The Indian community tends
to stick together, too, she thinks, "because people, if you don't stay together,
then we don't have any connection, any base." And she added, as an example,
"I think that some Indians in America are more religious than Indians in
India."

Another man emphasized cultural mores over religious requirements:

You know, you are molded by the value system when you're growing
up. . . . Even today I was talking to somebody else. Our culture teaches
four places are the respectable places in your life. The first one is
always your mother. Then the father. Then the teacher. And then the
God. So it's—contrary to popular belief . . . God is not in the first
place. Mother is in the first place. . . . I still remember the respect
and the awe I had for my teacher. Some of the teachers I still remember by their name because they made so much influence on me
in a very positive sense.

The theme of respect for elders pervaded the discourse of both teenagers and
parents among the Hindu respondents.

For many Salvadorans, family customs tie them to their heritage and
explain their identification with El Salvador. One teenager mentioned the
different dates for Mother's Day in the two countries and her family's adherence to a Salvadoran-style Christmas celebration: "They usually, like their
Christmas, they wait until midnight. They go to a mass before—on the twenty-

fourth. Then around midnight or an hour after midnight on Christmas Day, that's when they open their presents. And that's what we do. And for every holiday we always join in—everybody—we always join in as a family. So we have family reunions. So that's basically how it is in El Salvador." She planned to celebrate her *quinceaños*, the traditional fifteenth-birthday coming-of-age celebration for girls. Another boy noted that for Salvadorans, Christmas has nothing to do with Santa Claus, it's all about the baby Jesus. The traditional foods that accompany such celebrations were also mentioned as part of what makes one Salvadoran. Others noted that they also celebrate the Fourth of July or Thanksgiving as signs that, in these respects, they are "Americans."

These accounts emphasize an ethnicity rooted in family and an appreciation for one's heritage. Nevertheless, in keeping with the notion of reactive ethnicity, some ascribe a physiological dimension to their identity. One Salvadoran woman said emphatically that she is not American, though she has her citizenship and loves this country: "The fact that we live in the United States and have American citizenship doesn't make us Americans. I put it this way: I'm not white and I don't have blue eyes!"[4] An Indian parent said: "I am brown. I am Indian. No matter how much, how long—I, I tell the kids: [no matter] how long they live in this country...I don't think they'll ever be identified as an American. My son is born here, he has lived here all his life, but...I don't think he'll ever be an American. In the true sense. In the true sense." A young second-generation Salvadoran, asked why he claims that identity, replied, "Well, my name and my looks. I mean the way I look, I can't, I can't hide it, so it is." Several of the same respondents—but only a minority of the sample—said that prejudice was still a part of American life and that they had experienced discrimination.

Religion, whether in the form of traditional celebrations, the naming of a specific religious identity, or some broader moral and philosophical outlook, plays a role in many of these accounts of identity. One teenager noted: "my parents are not religious compared to a lot of people we know," and he added that he is even less religious than they: "And I don't like Sunday school. I don't like going Sunday morning, waking up early to go hear about God and stuff." But he declares that being Hindu is part of being Indian and he can't think of any way in which he's not Indian:

And I've always been taught that Hinduism is not a religion in
the sense that a lot of other religions, you know, have strict codes and,
and they have a set of, you know, guidelines and stuff. I've always
been taught that Hindus—there's nothing written that says you

can do this, you can't do this. That put limitations on your life.
It's just a set of values that you can, you know, customize for your
own life. And I guess that's what other religions are also, but I
never, you know, learned the nuances of Christianity or Judaism or
Islam.

Others would go further, however, insisting that they have become more
religious since immigrating, like the Indian father quoted earlier. Others
noted the difference between religious practice in the United States and those
practices they value. One Salvadoran woman ascribed her identity to her
"roots" and her "customs," including "religion, tradition and our foods." "For
example, the processions that we have in our countries when we celebrate
Easter time. We celebrate Holy Week like it should be. We don't go to work like
here, where you have to work on [Good] Friday and Holy Saturday." Religious
nostalgia of this sort finds much to be dissatisfied with here; and precisely this
sort of religious longing informs much of the practice of the immigrant worship communities we studied. Particularly when it comes to their children,
immigrant parents are apt to turn to worship communities as sources of cultural continuity and instruction for their young. Religious and ethnic identification simultaneously refer back to the homeland and provide motive and
template for action in the new home.

These interviews make little reference to civic roles or obligations in direct
discussions of identity, much less to a politically charged "ethnic identity" on
the American stage. Nevertheless, a sense of who they are does inform people's
reflections on what they owe their parents or children and the larger society.
This is an effect that ethnic and religious identity has on civic engagement that
is more subtle than the sorts of direct political appeals we will consider shortly,
but it is nonetheless real for all that—and perhaps ultimately more important.
One young man provides a good example. Drawing on a widely shared national
self-portrait of Salvadorans as at once deeply respectful and tireless workers, he
commented on what makes him identify as "Hispanic":

And also, also I think the way we respect each other, I guess. It's just
us Hispanics tend to, you know, stick together. I mean every culture,
I guess, sticks together. But we have this bond that, you know, we
have to work for what we want. And all my people, they, you know,
they don't give up. You know, and that's why, I guess, my generation
is probably going to end up, you know, in Congress and stuff and,
you know, we're going to rise. Because I know that, you know, my
generation, it's a new door to life here in America, I guess.

What Identity? Identity Politics in Immigrant
Worship Communities

Just as individuals struggle over their personal identities, immigrant worship
communities struggle over their communal identities. Conflicts over identity
have split some worship communities. Such conflicts can help us get a sense
for the sorts of issues that are at stake as immigrants forge communities in the
United States. In the next few pages, we look at cases where ethnic, national
origin, and even religious identity have been very much in question in immigrant worship communities.

The Battle over the Nigerian Catholic Community

The majority of Nigerian Catholics in the Washington area, as in Nigeria
itself, are of the Igbo ethnic group. Igbos began arriving in the area in some
numbers in the 1960s in the midst of the civil war that pitted the largely Igbo
region that took the name Biafra in a secessionist struggle against the rest of
the country. In the late 1970s, Igbo Catholics began meeting for masses in the
Igbo language; eventually, the group agreed to meet every third Sunday in a
chapel at Catholic University in northeast Washington, D.C. In the early
1980s, a dispute over the handling of funds by lay leaders led to an acrimonious split between the original group, the Igbo Catholic Community, under
Father Columba Aham, and a new group, which eventually called itself the
Igbo Catholic Association. Despite attempts to heal the division by the Washington area Nigerian Catholic priests' association and others, relations between the two festered until the Archdiocese of Washington intervened in
1992. The Archdiocese's solution, however, caused further rifts, as the Archbishop of Washington went to the Archbishop of Abuja, a non-Igbo city in
Nigeria, to seek a chaplain for the whole of what was now to be called the
Nigerian Catholic Community. Though the first chaplain was Igbo, the agreement reached between the two dioceses specified that regular masses were to
be conducted in English, with occasional celebrations in "tribal" languages.
The second chaplain appointed to the post was not Igbo and spoke no Igbo.

As a result of the hierarchy's intervention, the Nigerian Catholic Community now had a permanent home at Holy Names parish, in an African
American neighborhood not far from Howard and Catholic universities. The
community meets every Sunday, has its own recognized parish and financial
councils, and enjoys the official support of the Archdiocese of Washington,
as well as an official connection to a Nigerian archdiocese (Abuja). As the

community's worship service evolved, most of the hymns and prayers continued to be in the Igbo language, though sermons were necessarily in English. Roughly 200 people attend weekly masses. Yet the majority of Nigerians worship elsewhere. One group meets at the parish that housed the Igbo Catholic Association, though it now includes members of the rival Igbo Catholic Community. Another set up an independent Catholic community in a distant suburb of Washington under a priest not officially sanctioned by either archdiocese. Many Nigerian Catholics worship elsewhere, principally, it appears, in multicultural parishes throughout the diocese.

Some of those who are now dissidents had petitioned the archdiocese to officially recognize an Igbo Catholic worship community, with an appointed chaplain and permission to raise money for the purposes of building a church. Instead, the archdiocese turned to the archbishop of Abuja for support in creating and staffing an all-Nigerian worship community. Cardinal Hickey's letter to the community summarized the archbishop's rationale for this settlement:

> In the Archdiocese, we are well aware that Nigerian Catholics are not linguistically a monolithic group but number several language groups, all of the same Roman Catholic Faith. Because the differences in language created splits and disagreements in the past, I as Bishop, in dialogue with Cardinal Ekandem [archbishop of Abuja] and later on with Archbishop Joh Onaiyekem [his successor], appointed Father Aloysius to minister to all Nigerian Catholics as one group, the Nigerian Catholic Community. (James Cardinal Hickey, archbishop of Washington, D.C., unpublished letter to unspecified addressee, November 22, 1994)[5]

Cardinal Hickey's letter misstated the character of the controversy, prompting an appeal from one dissident leader that detailed the history of the Igbo community in the Washington area and made the case that Vatican II called upon bishops to recognize the rights of Catholics to worship in their own languages and according to their own indigenous customs.[6] Apparently the appeal, addressed to Cardinal Hickey and the Nigerian bishops, received no response. The result has been a continuing controversy, with dissidents periodically picketing services at Holy Names. The split comes up repeatedly in sermons in the official Nigerian Catholic Community and was the subject of open discussion at a ceremony welcoming the archbishop of Abuja in December 2001. In his opening remarks, the pastor, Father Pius Ajiki, addressed the archbishop: "We have seen an immigrant community striving to be one—what the Lord wishes. The division which you seem to be hearing will not overcome us." The chairman of the Pastoral Council, Chief Fred Olaoye, put the issue in more colorful terms: "With regards to the problem of divisions facing us, the Archdiocese of Washington have tried their best to assist us, and with your full cooperation, Bishop Onaiyekan, we are still existing. United we stand, divided we fall. We don't want our community to be divided. We are seven years old today, and it is our intent to be able to get our own place of worship with help of God and the help of the Bishop." He reminded the bishop that the contract with the Archdiocese of Washington says that Chaplain Ajiki was obligated to see to the pastoral needs of all Nigerian immigrants in Washington. "If there is a change, let us know. We understand that the Lord Jesus was humiliated and crucified, let alone us when we are persecuted [referring to the dissidents' campaign]." Bishop Onaiyekem replied:

> Our contract is clear, our intentions are clear. I know there are some people who are not satisfied with this arrangement—this is America. You choose your friends but God chooses your brothers and sisters. God also chooses your nationality. We have a Nigerian Catholic Community. Those who want to be a part of it are welcome. With regards to issues of placards and disturbance and constant harrassment of my priest and community, I hope that the Archdiocese of Washington can protect us. Those who want a different arrangement should go to the Archdiocese of Washington. I do not organize the Archdiocese of Washington but Abuja.

In the meantime, many Nigerian Catholics, including many Igbo, continue to worship in multicultural settings. Holy Names parish is one of those. Up until the 1980s, Holy Names was one of several African American Catholic parishes in Washington, D.C. Starting in the 1980s, however, the neighborhood began receiving an influx of immigrants from the Caribbean, Africa, and, eventually, Latin America and Asia. Besides the Nigerian Catholic Community, the parish now hosts a small Francophone African community (whose participants come mostly from Senegal and the Gambia) and is encouraging Hispanics to form their own subgroup within the parish. Most parishoners, however, including many Nigerians, worship at the distinctly multicultural masses that claim the main church at prime Sunday morning times (the subcommunities typically utilize the church basement). These masses may feature gospel singing by a Filipino choir and preaching by a visiting African American priest. They frequently incorporate songs and prayers in some of the languages spoken by members of the parish, and they emphasize the contribution of all cultures to the one faith. Bishop Onaiyekem's opening message to the Nigerian Catholic Community may have reflected the sentiments of these churchgoers more closely than those of his audience, when he said: "Help the parish host and contribute to the mosaic of American goodness. The Nigerian American has come to stay. Globalization facilitates your doing so and not forgetting your homeland at the same time. The whole world belongs to God and we are all brothers and sisters. The day when people can survive doing their own thing like in the village is gone" (December 2, 2001).

There are perhaps 10,000 Igbo in the Washington, D.C., area, according to Holy Names pastor Father Ray East (though the Census Bureau puts the total Nigerian population at a little over 5,000 persons). Although the vast majority undoubtedly continue to think of themselves as Igbo, most, if they worship at all, do not go to the trouble to locate a parish where they can worship in their own language. Yet the Nigerian Catholic worship communities in the area have become the arenas for intense struggle over how and to what degree ethnic identity is incorporated into the life of worship.

Divided We Stand

Both of the original Hindu worship communities in the Washington, D.C., area were founded on principles of inclusiveness, and both continue to practice them today. The All India Community Center has always emphasized the ecumenical character of Hinduism and has participated in a wide range of interfaith activities. Started in 1965, in its early years, the All India Center welcomed the Sikh and Jain communities into its midst, as well as representatives of a variety of Hindu religious movements. After two years of joint programs, the Jain community assumed an independent existence as the Jain Society of Metropolitan Washington. Later, many of the South Indian members left to create a new temple that gave greater scope to South Indian deities and incorporated South Indian languages into worship services. Both of these splits were amicable, but they left the All India Center smaller and weaker. They also left it more ethnically homogeneous, as most of the members were now from the Indian state of Gujarat. Plans to build a temple for the center were disrupted, however, when a segment of the Gujarati community seized the initiative and began working with a prominent Indian religious teacher to raise funds for their own temple. Tense negotiations yielded a partial settlement, with the All India Center reluctantly donating its small temple fund to the new group when the latter secured a parcel of land to build on. The board of trustees of the new organization asked the All India Center to continue to sponsor joint religious ceremonies while they focused their energies on building the new temple, but ended the joint venture abruptly a few months before the inauguration of the temple.

Behind these financial struggles lay profound theological differences, as well as personal and status struggles among the leadership. The new worship community, Temple Gujarat, was dominated by adherents of the militant "Hindutva" philosophy often referred to as "Hindu fundamentalism." Members of the D.C. chapter of the VHP, the central activist organization associated with the movement, play important roles in the new temple and have worked with the international wing of the RSS, their parent organization, to sponsor classes for young people in several area temples, as well as the summer school we encountered earlier.[7] Something of the flavor of the Hindu nationalism in these classes can be gathered from this excerpt from one of the textbooks:

> [The] task of Hindu reawakening has yet a long way to go. As long as even a single Indian remains bound by his or her parochial identity in terms of language, faith, sect, caste or province, this task will remain incomplete. It must continue until every Indian transcends all such divisions to grasp his or her true and larger identity as a Hindu. A day would come, not in too distant a future, when all Indians who practice Islamic or Christian faiths also view themselves as the children of "Bharat Mata," regard Ram and Krishna as their ancestors. (Singhal 1999)

The universalizing appeal subsumes regional linguistic and ethnic identities in a larger Hindu identity, but it also insists on transcending specifically religious ones, including those such as Christian and Muslim that themselves claim universal applicability. The tone often becomes much harsher when the specific case of India's Muslims is at issue, as we saw in chapter 5. At a major festival following the 2002 sectarian riots in Gujarat that left hundreds dead and thousands homeless (with most of the victims Muslim), speakers insisted on the injustice of media portrayals of the Hindu rioters and the culpability of the Muslims. One man put it succinctly: "I'm not saying revenge is good, but Muslims usually start the violence and we usually let it go.... This time was different. Because of this reaction by the Hindus, nothing else happened to Hindus anywhere else in the country. They [Muslims] will learn that if they do something wrong, there is this kind of reaction." He urged the audience to stand fast with the VHP volunteers whose murder by a Muslim crowd as they returned from building a temple at Ayodha sparked the riots. "Their humiliation is our humiliation." And he further urged the audience to have confidence that "we will prevail with honor."

Two weeks earlier, by contrast, the All India Center held a broadly ecumenical event lamenting the events in Gujarat and seeking common ground on which to address them. One of the first speakers said, "I am proud to be a Hindu, but what happened in Gujarat made me feel ashamed.... We must teach our children that we must respect all people and not to hate.... Our Hindu tradition teaches that every person is a part of God, and represents a piece of God. We should emphasize this teaching to children." An Indian Muslim from Andhrya Pradesh said, "India is my home. There are 140 million Muslims in India. I never thought I would see a mosque burnt down.... We have to be tolerant. We have no choice—it is our country, and we have nowhere else to go." Two young women came to the stage. The first, of Pakistani Muslim descent, insisted, "Worldwide, there is a recognition that India is a social experiment. A country made up of so many social, linguistic and religious groups. It will take time for them to coalesce, so patience is needed. I am Pakistani, so I recognize how unique and special and important the Indian experiment actually is." Her friend, an Indian Hindu, recounted remembering when the Babri Masjid (the mosque at Ayodha) was torn down, and thinking "Why? Why tear down a House of God?" And now she found herself thinking "Why? Why rebuild a temple on that same spot? Why? Why are they rioting in the street, and killing each other?" Later in the event, Dr. Rajwant Singh, a prominent Sikh leader, argued that in India there is always someone oppressing others:

> Sometimes it is the Muslims, sometimes the Christians, sometimes the Hindus (this has been clear especially since 1984). India must protest this. Also, the increasing insecurity of the Christian community since the BJP government has taken power. Priests are being killed. And in 1984 the riots in Delhi claimed over 1,800 lives, with 2,000 more over the rest of India. There must be more political power given to the states. A more decentralized state will help stabilization. Religious leaders must take on a new role. Real leaders must stand together.[8]

The notions of Hindu and Indian identity in these two settings could not be more different, though most of the leadership of the two organization shares not only a common Indian nationality but a common ethnic origin in the culture of Gujarat. The distance of the All India Center from Temple Gujarat is clearly religious and ideological. Similar differences have riven the Sikh community in Washington, but here the issue of caste is an added complication.

Caste, Religious Fidelity, and Fissure in the Sikh community

The Sikh religion was founded as much on the notion of human equality and a rejection of India's caste system as on an assertion of monotheism against

polytheistic Hinduism. Nevertheless, since the religious wars of the seven-
teenth century, when Sikhs faced forced conversion by the Mughal rulers of
India, the Jat caste of rural Punjab has tended to dominate the Sikh community. Though many Jats have become professionals in the modern era, their
origins in the farmers who provided much of the resistance to their Muslim
rulers gives them a sense of being the natural inheritors of the authority of the
nine founding Gurus. The first Sikh foundation in the Washington area was
broadly inclusive and liberal in its outlook. Personality conflicts, magnified by
caste and religious differences, led to splits in the community and the formation of new congregations. Both of the first two breakaway congregations
were led by more conservative Jats.

The Siri Guru Singh Sabha has grown into one of the most prosperous
congregations in the area since its founding in the early 1970s, but it, too, was
rent by conflict in the early 1980s, when another conservative, mostly Jat group
left in protest at what they saw as a failure to instill strong Sikh cultural, religious, and political values in youth and an unwillingness to support Sikhs in India
during a time of persecution. The new group picketed the Indian Embassy and
carried out an aggressive campaign to correct what it saw as U.S. media distor-
tions of the struggle, which tended to portray militant Sikhs as "terrorists" and
downplay the human rights abuses perpetrated by Indira Gandhi's government.

At the time of our research visits, the Siri Guru Singh Sabha was again
rent by strife, as the faction that had controlled the board of trustees up until
the 2001 election protested the policies of the new board. The new board is
generally more conservative, more Jat, and more working-class in origin. It is
favored by people who feel that only Amritdharis (those who have undergone
Sikh baptism and who adopt the strict rules of dress associated with being a
"religious Sikh") should sit on the board. The former board included so-called
cut-hair Sikhs, those who have cut their hair Western-style and do not wear
the ritual turban. Its supporters insist that the congregation should be open to
Sikhs of all sorts and that having cut-hair Sikhs on the board symbolizes such
openness. These ideological differences, reinforced by the caste divide, un-
derlie the dispute. But the specific issues involved include the new board's
widening membership, to the extent that a constitutional quorum cannot be
reached for elections, allowing the board to appoint new directors to fill vacant
seats and perpetuate their control of the congregation. The struggle has thus
raised legal issues, with each side filing briefs in civil court and the current
leadership at one point bringing in the police to bar the opposition from holding a meeting in the building.

By contrast, the third-generation breakaway, the Guru Granth Sahib
congregation, remains relatively united and very active in area community

affairs, as we saw in chapter 4. Though dominated by Jats and committed to a religiously conservative doctrine, it is open to cut-hair Sikhs and commited to building ties with other religious communities and secular nonprofits in the Washington area. It also has a strong youth program which, like that of the VHP Hindus in area temples, inculcates Sikh nationalism in young people as part of its religious indoctrination. Sikh Punjabi culture, not Punjabi culture alone, shapes the identity of the congregation. A distinctive immigrant identity, honed and enforced in struggles with sometimes more assimilationist fellow immigrants, informs civic activism on the American stage, a combination that has been a common immigrant formula since at least the nineteenth century.

Identity and Politics

Struggles over identity, both ethnic and religious, have troubled the worship communities we have just looked at. In other cases, religious and cultural identities are widely agreed upon and constantly reinforced in the sermons of leaders and the practices of the community. Those identities help orient members in their relations with the larger society, their commitments and concerns, and their own daily lives. Most of the parents and young people with whom Lene Jensen spoke had little involvement in the political life of American society, but most were civically engaged in other ways. Many were cynical about their ability to influence political decisions; but as many, if not more, thought it important for people to be politically involved precisely to let politicians hear people's voices. Such arguments draw on common American notions of the importance of popular participation in a democracy. While identity politics didn't enter into these discussions, most of these respondents felt that, indeed, they could make a difference through community service and volunteering, and they had a responsibility to try to do so. This sense of responsibility, coupled with causes and concerns that members of a worship community have in common, can provide the basis for civic engagement and political mobilization in immigrant worship communities.

Though personal identity among immigrants and their children may be largely cultural and nostalgic, it can clearly contribute to civic engagement and political self-consciousness, particularly where it helps leaders crystallize a sense of common concern. We have already seen this process at work in parts of the Hindu and Sikh communities. In the following pages, we explore the role of religious and ethnic identity in the activities of the Potomac Islamic Center, Father Mesa's St. Francis, and the Korean Protestant churches.

Religious Identity and Political Incorporation: Muslims

In chapter 4, we explored the political activism of the Potomac Islamic Center and other mosques and their responses to the events of September 11, 2001. The Washington area mosques, particularly the larger, more multicultural ones, have been quite active for years in promoting a positive image of Islam in the United States and in their local communities, encouraging members to become more active socially and politically, and mobilizing Muslims to support causes important to the community. Some of their prominent members have played important roles in local civic and political affairs, and they have been instrumental in the creation of national-level organizations representing Muslim interests. If there was any change in behavior after September 11, it was in the direction of deepening and broadening these activities and in delivering a more forceful message to their own community that Muslims are not sojourners in a foreign land in the United States, but Americans like any others.[9]

Religious identity is the prevailing force in these efforts. The larger mosques are all multicultural in nature, reflecting the dispersed character of the Muslim population, the lack of large concentrations of Muslims from any one national background, and a theological conviction that Islam is a universal religion whose tenets permit people of all backgrounds to come together under one roof. Liturgical practice, including the widespread use of classical Arabic as the language of worship and almost universal adherence to a simple ritual formula for the conduct of Friday prayers, make such multiculturalism possible. Nevertheless, the centrality of the Arab world to Islam historically means that the political preoccupations of the Muslim community tend to center on events and causes there. The same sort of fervor that unites many immigrant Catholics around the abortion issue characterizes Muslim responses to Israeli–Arab relations and to U.S. policy in the Arab world. Since the 1989 Gulf War and Israel's withdrawal from Lebanon, these concerns have focused on Israeli policy toward the Palestinians (and U.S. involvement in the issue) and U.S. policy toward Iraq.

These foreign policy preoccupations show how religious identity can widen the constituency for issues that might otherwise be the concern of just one ethnic or national group. Muslims of all nationalities joined in protesting the Sharon government's response to the second *intifada* and U.S. hostility toward Iraq, in a massive Washington demonstration in early 2002. On this occasion, Muslims were mobilized through mosques in many communities across the country, and Washington area mosques served as hosts and staging areas for contingents from other parts of the country. This was a time of continued vulnerability for Muslims in the United States following the events of September 11, 2001. The centrality of these issues to Muslim self-consciousness and the participation of well-established and well-connected mosques helped overcome the fears that might have inhibited participation in this demonstration. The demonstration, moreover, was coordinated with a large mobilization by the national peace movement, which brought thousands of non-Muslims to the scene. In contrast, the small Afghan community was mostly silent in response to the bombing and invasion of Afghanistan in the fall of 2001, largely because most members were refugees from the Taliban regime. At the same time, there was little hope of solidarity on the part of the larger society or even the larger Muslim community. And these mosques were themselves vulnerable—small, financially weak, and consisting mainly of recent immigrants.

The other major cause around which Washington area Muslims have united is civil rights. While the post–September 11 assault on Muslims and some of their charitable organizations galvanized new responses from the Muslim community, concerns about the treatment of Muslims in the community and efforts to build a political voice for Muslims in the United States long antedated the events of September 11, 2001, particularly in the Washington, D.C., area. As we saw in chapter 4, many of the founding members of the national Muslim organizations have also been active in area mosques. The mosques regularly publicize events such as the October 2000 Annual Conference of the American Muslim Social Scientists Association, with panels on youth and education, Islamic philosophy, Muslim minorities around the world, Islamic economics, civil society in the Muslim world, and Islam in America. Members of one mosque were encouraged to attend round tables on emerging legal issues for Muslims in America, institution building for Muslim Americans, Islamic identity in America, and educating the Muslim community for skilled leadership. Other national organizations encouraged the members of area mosques to participate in workshops on building a Muslim political voice in the United States and training American Muslims for civic participation. Participation varies a great deal, but, as we might expect, second-generation youth and adults appear to be much more likely to take part in these activities than recent immigrants. And despite a heavy focus on the Middle East, the politically salient identity for this community is mainly religious, not ethnic.

National Origins and Immigration Politics: Salvadorans

The case is quite different for the Hispanic community at St. Francis Catholic Church. Here, the appeal is mainly to members' ethnic identity, though this might be conceived as broadly "Hispanic" or more narrowly Salvadoran, according to need. Father Mesa shows no hesitation in moving from one to another, or in singling out the community's Salvadoran majority as particularly worthy of attention. Though St. Francis's pastor speaks of the parish as "multicultural," it in fact consists of two congregations, one largely white, English-speaking, and native-born, the other Spanish-speaking and led by Puerto Rican Americans and immigrants from a number of countries in Latin America, principally El Salvador. Ignoring the distinction between the two sides of the parish, Father Mesa often refers to the parish as a whole as Hispanic: "it has been you, through your generosity and work, who have made Saint Francis a Hispanic parish," he tells his congregation. Though the parish is still 25–35 percent "Anglo," the vitality of the Spanish-speaking congregation encourages this sort of identification. According to Father Mesa,

> some of the Hispanic members, they are definitely those who feel the parish belongs to them and they take care of it in all ways. You don't see the Anglo members of the community cleaning the church or picking up the leaves. The Anglo community is not as active as the Latino parishioners because of the age composition of this community, you know, because the Anglos are much older than the Latinos. There is a lot of energy within the Latino community given they are younger people with more needs. That's why there are more programs for Hispanics, because there are more needs within this community. The Anglo group has long-established programs that are self-sustaining but which haven't grown at the same speed and rate as the programs for the Hispanics.

The "Anglos" express some anxiety about what they define as "the need for better integration of the English and Spanish speaking congregations." For example, Anglo members at one small group meeting agreed on the imperative of becoming a "multicultural" parish, and of moving beyond the image of Saint Francis as "Hispanic" alone.

These disputes aside, Father Mesa does not hesitate to celebrate the specific national identities of members of the Hispanic congregation or to emphasize the important role played by the Salvadorans, who make up roughly 85 percent of the Hispanics. In an earlier study of Washington area churches, Cecilia Menjívar found that Catholic pastors hesitated to use national labels to differentiate among Hispanics for fear of antagonizing minority groups (Menjívar 1999, 2003). Father Mesa's apparent solution is to make free acknowledgement of the contributions of each. Mexicans in the congregation are invited to celebrate the feast of the Virgin of Guadalupe with an early morning procession featuring a rendition of "Las Mañanitas" played by a mariachi band. But Salvadorans came in for special attention because of their numbers and needs. The devastation of Hurricane Mitch was answered by parish fundraising efforts that yielded some $350,000 in donations for the victims. After the January 2001 earthquake in El Salvador, Father Mesa traveled to that country, bringing donated goods and a check in the amount of $88,000 for the Archdiocese of San Salvador to use in the relief effort.

Fr. Mesa is particularly appreciative of his Salvadoran members:

> When I arrived to Saint Francis seven years ago, most of my Salva-
> doran parishioners had come from the eastern provinces of La
> Union, San Miguel, and Usulutan and from towns such as China-
> meca, Chirilagua, and Intipuca. During and in the aftermath of the
> civil war in El Salvador, immigrants from this area came to settle to
> the northern Virginia area. Thus, St. Francis began a postwar sce-
> nario where the parish was deeply involved in instituting a campaign
> of forgiveness, conflict resolution, and national reconciliation. This
> group had a slightly better level of education, it has better absorbed
> the American system, it sends the largest remittances back home,
> and is the most religious group. In short, they are the most thriving
> of the Salvadoran communities. I call them the Phoenicians of
> Central America. They are the ones with the most solidarity, most
> spirituality, most talent, and most cohesiveness. Look, with the whole
> issue of Hurricane Mitch, this parish alone collected $350,000 for the
> victims of this natural disaster. This was the case because our pa-
> rishioners are one of the most united and cohesive groups because
> they have known the meaning of pain for a long time.

The size and energy of the Salvadoran community are not the only factors that make it stand out. Most of its members came as undocumented immigrants. Those who arrived before 1991 are eligible to regularize their standing through TPS; but this is a temporary measure, periodically renewed, which requires that Salvadoran immigrants living in the country since that date register at each renewal. Many others remain undocumented. These realities, like the disasters that have stricken their homeland over the last several years, have provided impetus to mobilizing the community. As we have already seen, Father Mesa urged his parishioners to vote in the November 2000, elections, insisting that they could contribute that way to changing government policy toward undocumented immigrants.

Ethnic identity thus shifts in Father Mesa's usage according to context. The pan-ethnic "Hispanic" is useful in differentiating the Spanish-speaking congregation from the older Anglo group that still considers the parish their

own. Specific country-of-origin labels may celebrate particular elements of
national heritage, especially those that have religious significance, like the
figure of the Virgin of Guadalupe. Or they may be deployed in response to
specific events or causes that mobilize the community on behalf of compatriots
at home or in this country. And unlike the evangelical pastors we encountered,
Father Mesa was ready to mobilize ethnic identity not just in solidarity with the
victims of natural disaster but politically as well. His parishoners responded
with enthusiasm, contributing to the sense that this was a parish that served
the immigrant community particularly well.

Ethnic Identity, Religion, and Homeland Politics: Korean Protestant Churches

Overt political mobilization along ethnic lines was much less apparent among
the largely evangelical Korean and Chinese Christian churches we studied.
Yet a few political concerns emerged as we looked at these churches—all of
them tied to the ethnic and national origins of their members.

A veteran Korean Protestant pastor offered a rather sophisticated account
of ethnic identity formation among Koreans:

> The first generation Koreans live in this country as ethnic Koreans,
> neither Americans nor Korean Americans. It does not take them
> long to realize that they are literally not able to get over the linguis-
> tic and social status barriers. Even worse, because the majority of
> them are self-employed in business, they look at both Caucasians and
> African Americans as nothing but their customers. They simply do
> not have time and opportunity to learn about American society.
> If anything, they learn about it through their ethnic mass media, not
> through American mass media. . . . [For some] their acceptance of
> difference from others becomes their ethnic identity, and their ac-
> ceptance of their new societal membership becomes a new collec-
> tive identity. Their hyphenated American identity becomes an
> important asset for incorporation into the larger society. It seems to
> me that only a few first-generation Koreans reach this stage, re-
> gardless of the length of their stay in the United States.

Korean churches in the Washington, D.C., area today are still dominated by
first-generation immigrants. For these people, church involvement clearly
helps reinforce Korean identity. Regular worship services are a shared emotional space through which the members reinforce their identity as Koreans
and as Christians. Sermons stress the primacy of their Christian faith but do

not neglect to give an ethnic character to their identity. Some pastors argue that Koreans are a special people chosen by God to bring Christ to Asia. One invited speaker at a Korean Protestant church balanced the tension between religious and ethnic identity this way: "Regardless of race and ethnicity, whoever holds Christian faith is a person selected by God. They are sons of God. We are not just Koreans, but we are selected Korean Christians."

Nevertheless, attention to Korean-specific issues, both abroad and in this country, occupies much of the sermonizing and prayer in Korean churches. Pastors spoke about the 2002 Winter Olympics held in Korea, the World Cup soccer tournament the same year, the conflict between the two Koreas, racial tensions between Koreans and African Americans, and U.S. immigration policies. Pastors prayed on a regular basis for the well-being of their immigrant community and of the home country. As in other immigrant worship communities, only the most noticeable of domestic U.S. issues gained attention from the pulpit—presidential elections, the severe flooding of the Mississippi River basin in 2000, and the terrorist attack of September 11, 2001.

Much of the charitable and missionary outreach of these churches was directed toward Korean causes. Funds were raised to support clandestine efforts to aid North Korean refugees in northern China and victims of famine within North Korea. One important umbrella for these sorts of activities is the Korean Church Council of the Greater Washington Area, to which close to half the Korean Protestant churches in the area contribute financially. But the churches and their umbrella organizations do little to try to influence U.S. policy on these issues. This stands in stark contrast to the situation in the 1980s, when the Korean community in the United States worked with the National Council of Churches and other organizations in solidarity with the prodemocracy movement in Korea. Some pastors expressed disillusionment with the outcome of the movement and had undertaken a "return to the sanctuary" and a renewed emphasis on religious values. One sign of the relative political quiescence of the churches is that, while many Korean church leaders encourage members to become citizens of the United States, few churches offer citizenship classes or participate in get-out-the-vote efforts (see table 4.1). It falls to secular Korean and Asian American organizations to try to incorporate these immigrants politically.

Conclusions

Both ethnic and religious identities may have political salience, but, as we have seen, "identity politics" does not always flow from an assertion of a group's distinctiveness. Nor does a claim to one identity preclude claims to other identities. People's senses of themselves can include a variety of group allegiances, each with implications for their relations to the larger society. The worship communities we have surveyed clearly play a role in shaping members' identities and directing their energies. But what sort of identity a worship community emphasizes and how that identity is mobilized varies enormously from worship community to worship community. How can we explain this variation?

Individuals often choose to participate in an immigrant or ethnic worship community because they enjoy the company of those like themselves and are proud of their ethnic heritage. But individuals may also be driven to an ethnic community because of their perception of being outsiders in the larger society. A member of the Korean Christian Center who is a news reporter commented:

> As a newspaper correspondent, I have lived in various European countries. The longer I live in foreign countries and the more countries I live in, the stronger feeling I have for Korean culture. I personally do not appreciate many components of the Korean culture, and I don't know what makes me feel so close to it. It may be because of many Europeans' perception of non-Europeans. I have seen Europeans look down on other races and ethnic peoples. I sometimes think that they do not think we are the same human beings as they are. What can I do, with my appearance and my culture, when I feel that way? I think it is reasonable for us to protect our own.

Other first-generation Korean church members echoed these sentiments. They found it difficult to have good relationships with members of other ethnic groups because of cultural and linguistic differences. One veteran Presbyterian pastor noted: "I have long observed that many members of our church were afraid of meeting other ethnic or racial group members. It is largely because of their limited linguistic ability. But even quite a few members who speak English fluently still express their feeling of uncomfortableness when they have a chance to worship together with other racial or ethnic groups."

Whether out of pride, in reaction to prejudice, or from such feelings of discomfort, people's association in ethnic worship communities implies a certain choice of identity and reinforces that choice. For an Indian of Hindu background, attending temple is an assertion of identity as an Indian and a Hindu; and attending a primarily South Indian or Gujarati or Tamil temple is an assertion of a still more particular identity. But such assertions of identity are not necessarily exclusive of other identities. Some of those Lene Jensen spoke with noted that they had become more Hindu as well as American as a result of immigration. But participating in a worship community that is defined around a particular immigrant community establishes common referents among members.

As a basis for common action, and for civic engagement in particular, identity must be shaped and mobilized. This is where the circumstances of immigration come into play, the organizational culture of the worship community, its theological traditions, and the uses to which these are put by leaders. Circumstances of immigration, as we have already noted, explain more the causes around which ethnically or religious defined groups come together than whether or not they are mobilized. Salvadoran Catholics at St. Francis have mobilized in response to natural disasters and around immigration issues affecting Salvadorans; their pastor urges them to seek citizenship and vote on behalf of causes dear to the community. Most Salvadoran Protestants, by contrast, confined their efforts to disaster relief. Some mosques participate in both local and national civic affairs on behalf of Muslims causes; others are much less involved. Some Sikh congregations have been active defenders of Sikhs in India and in the United States; others have abstained from public protest and coalition building. Neither the causes themselves nor religious tradition alone explain all the differences. We have to look elsewhere for explanations.

The organizational culture of the worship community plays an important part in whether the community's identity will be mobilized for political or civic causes. In the smaller, family-style communities, ethnic identity is one of the elements that bind the community together, but it is rarely mobilized for political purposes. In the smaller Korean, Chinese, and Salvadoran Protestant churches, membership is overwhelmingly of one ethnic group; but such groups take up ethnic causes mainly in emergency situations and mainly "at arm's length," through assistance to other groups representing the ethnic community. At the same time, these are the groups that are most concerned to communicate their ethnic heritage to the young. Family-style congregations are more preoccupied with religious, cultural, and educational goals than with civic engagement.

Larger, community-style churches and temples also sponsored events celebrating members' ethnic heritage, particularly in the African and Indian Hindu communities. In the African case, such events occurred mainly in multicultural, mainline Protestant and Catholic churches, where pastors were concerned to promote understanding among the various groups in the community. Among Hindus, such celebrations were part of a larger effort to preserve the distinctiveness of Hindu culture in the American setting. Whereas Korean and Chinese Protestants have embraced a largely Western cultural template for religious observance, for Hindus, religious observance *is* cultural as well as theological. Salvadoran Catholics similarly conflate cultural form and religious practice. Muslims were the least likely to emphasize ethnic or national origin—a fact that is explained by the multicultural reality of most mosques more than by the universal claims of Islam.

Religious tradition obviously plays a role in the degree to which a community melds cultural and religious identities. More ritualistic traditions, like Hinduism and Catholicism, foster an identification of religious observance and culture. Traditions that center on the revealed word of God, such as conservative Protestantism and Islam, tend to subordinate ethnic to religious identities. A sacred language closely tied to the vernacular may serve to bind together even those who do not share the vernacular, thus superseding ethnic ties, as in the case of Islam. But it may also reinforce attachment to a particularistic culture, as in the case of the Sikhs. In either case, though, the second generation will bring pressures for accommodation, Anglicizing and eventually Westernizing worship services on behalf of the youth and young adults. Ethnic or panethnic identities may well persist in such communities, especially where racial stereotyping continues to set apart members of the second and third generation, as the Chinese experience suggests, but the aspects of ethnicity that these postimmigrant generations maintain will be increasingly selective.

Both ethnic and religious identity are more likely to be mobilized for political or civic engagement in the community-style and civic leader worship communities. Religious leadership plays a big role in shaping the organizational culture of a community and mobilizing it. Leaders may choose to build community around an activist ethnic or religious identity, focused on causes close to the members, as we saw Father Mesa doing. They may claim a single national or ethnic identity, or they may embrace pan-ethnic categories like "Hispanic" or "Asian." Or they may choose to avoid ethnic labels altogether, especially where worship communities are ethnically divided, and to insist on the primacy of religious identity.

Ethnic and religious identity are thus both foundations for worship communities and their product. Communities sometimes struggle over which identity should prevail, and religious leaders are often influential in shaping the character, content, and implications of the community's identity. In some worship communities, leaders appeal to ethnic or religious identity (or both) to promote action on behalf of the larger community of coethnics or coreligionists, engaging members civically and politically around homeland causes or in defense of immigrant rights in this country. Such appeals have been common in immigrant communities throughout our history. Paradoxically, they integrate immigrants more deeply into American civic and political life even as they preserve and reinforce their sense of difference. Immigrants and their children are rapidly assimilating, our evidence suggests, but selectively, and in ways that are shaped powerfully by the worship communities in which they participate.

7

Conclusion

Immigration challenges the resources of both the immigrants themselves and the society in which they settle. It calls up remarkable strengths as it makes remarkable demands. Immigrants must struggle with a new language, a new culture, new ways of doing things, and new ways of living. As they struggle, they adapt, learning new skills and habits and discarding older ones. At the same time, they cling to their identities as people shaped by particular cultures and experiences. And they seek out others like themselves—family members, members of the same neighborhood or community "back home," those who share the same language and religion, compatriots, sojourners from the same region of the world. As they come and settle in their new home, they affect the lives and perceptions of those around them; and the more massive their presence, the more profound the effect. Ethnic foods and tastes spill over from immigrant groceries and restaurants and shops to supermarkets and eating places and department stores serving the larger society. Terms and phrases from their languages become common currency in the English spoken in some quarters, and bosses and managers and social service providers pick up enough of the language of their workers and clients to get their job done. Politicians come to court a new constituency and recruit rising leaders from emerging ethnic groups to political office, and pundits and political scientists speculate about the impact of this or that "ethnic vote" on the next, or last, election.

It is natural to wonder about the character and pace of "assimilation" of the new immigrants. But whatever the answer to such questions, it is apparent that the new immigrants, like the old, are rapidly incorporating themselves into American society in multiple ways. This book has explored the role of churches, mosques, temples, and other worship communities in that process, and in particular in the incorporation of the new immigrants and their offspring into civic life. We have encountered extraordinary diversity and extraordinary vitality, for these are communities created out of the process of adaptation we have just sketched.

Immigrant worship communities, we have argued, provide important resources for adaptation to the difficult circumstances of immigration. They are not only psychological, moral, and cultural refuges but also important sources of social capital for many immigrants. Depending on circumstances, such social capital may entail richer or poorer resources for their encounter with the larger society. Worship communities are also an important manifestation of the immigrant presence in American civil society. To one degree or another, all of them must interact with government agencies, neighbors, and other civil society organizations. They may maintain themselves in relative isolation, of course, but they nevertheless symbolize the pluralism Americans continue to value and cultivate. Many are well connected to other worship communities and beyond. A few are actively involved in American civic and political life.

Whether isolated or deeply involved, moreover, most worship communities contribute to some degree to the development of skills that are relevant to civic life. Many encourage volunteer service to the larger community. A few avidly promote active citizenship. Finally, the efforts of worship communities to shape the identities and moral outlooks of their members inevitably have implications for the incorporation of recent immigrants and their offspring into American life. An enhanced sense of identity, even where it portends an assertion of difference from other Americans, as it invariably does, does not detract from civic incorporation but shapes the terms on which immigrants and their children work out their engagement with American society. In short, churches, mosques, temples, and other sorts of worship communities are schools for living, where immigrants and their children address some of the issues of living in a strange new land and acquire tools and resources, moral and spiritual, social and economic, for making their way in our society.

The diversity we have found warns us against making broad claims about the role of religion in the lives of the new immigrants. That role varies from worship community to worship community, just as it varies from person to person. Religious institutions certainly have much to contribute to the lives of immigrants as they struggle to adapt, but they do so in diverse ways and with diverse results. A small Protestant congregation may provide a great deal of moral and even economic support in times of need; but in a poor congregation, that social capital may do little to advance one's connections to the larger society. Richer and more diverse worship communities may fail the social capital test in other ways, providing few opportunities for members to interact and forge the connections that would make the success of one family an opportunity for the advancement of others. Worship communities that actively try to connect with the larger society and provide their members with opportunities for learning, training, and becoming involved in American life enhance the social capital of their members while building up human capital among them and promoting civic engagement.

Such variation demands explanation. The differences we have found among worship communities are less the product of the unique cultural heritage of the different immigrant groups they serve than the result of the concatenation of the concrete circumstances of immigration and settlement in the United States, organizational culture, religious tradition, and local leadership. Local leadership may be the most important of these, for it can shape and reshape organizational culture and adapt religious tradition to the challenge of helping a community adapt.

The task of this concluding chapter is twofold. First and foremost, we attempt to unravel some of the complexity of the analysis already presented. Second, we want to delve into the question of the degree to which immigrant worship communities are themselves becoming "Americanized" and the impact of this process on the ways they address their members' needs. We start with this second question, because it may be crucial to understanding just how and why some worship communities contribute more than others to immigrant incorporation into American civic and political life. Perhaps it is the case, for example, that immigrant worship communities that are more advanced on some spectrum of approximation to an "American" template of religious organization are precisely those that contribute more richly to immigrant incorporation. The assumption of a predominant "congregational" template is widespread in American sociology of religion. And some scholars have made a powerful case that even amid the religious diversity of the new immigration, there is inexorable movement toward assimilation to the prevailing forms of organization of American religious life. We take up these arguments in the following section, finding a good deal of reason to reject them in the particular but also important insights. On this basis, we will return in the next section to delineating the features among immigrant worship communities that most contribute to the civic and political incorporation of the new immigrants.

Congregationalism or Multiple Adaptation?

Stephen Warner has long argued that the American Protestant congregational form is the dominant pattern for religious organization in this country and that the new immigrants, like the old, are adopting this form as they adapt to life in the United States (Warner 1994, 1998, 2000). Fenggang Yang and Helen Rose Ebaugh, drawing on research on immigrants in Houston, Texas, agreed with Warner and extended his argument (Yang and Ebaugh 2001). Warner defines the "congregational form" as

> (1) a voluntary membership association, whose identity is (2) defined
> more by the people who form it than by the territory they inhabit (cf.
> the "parish" form of organization). A congregation typically features
> (3) lay leadership and (4) systematic fund-raising and a system of
> trustees. Because of its lay leadership and voluntary funding, there is
> (5) a tendency for clergy to be professionals hired as employees. The
> congregation also has (6) a tendency to ethnic exclusiveness. Be-
> cause the people who establish the congregation have multiple needs,
> there is (7) a tendency for it to be multi-functional, offering religious
> worship but also educational, cultural, social, and social service ac-
> tivities. (2000, 277)

Warner also notes that most immigrant religious groups meet on Sundays, no matter what their traditional sacred day of worship was (277). Yang and Ebaugh add to this list of characteristics a tendency to adopt communal forms of worship, to expand the role of the clergy to include counseling and informal social services, and to adopt English as the language of worship. They also note a frequent return to theological fundamentals, often spurred by the ethnic diversity within the congregation. An emphasis on theological revival, in turn, often prompts efforts to include people from diverse ethnic backgrounds, contrary to the expectation of ethnic exclusivity in Warner's model.

These generalizations obscure the diversity among immigrant religious groups in the United States. The use of the term "congregation" is itself questionable, as members of some religious groups do not recognize their worship community as an American-style congregation. Even in the study of American religion, using the congregational template obscures important differences. Nancy Ammerman's description of the "typical" American congregation in her book *Congregation and Community*, for example, reflects the dominant Protestant experience. Ammerman writes that "congregations are social collectivities no less than—indeed perhaps more than—places where ideological work is done. They are gatherings of people who form a network of primary (face-to-face, family-like) relationships" (1997, 57). But this characterization hardly describes most Catholic parishes, where the majority of participants come and go to mass once a week with barely a pause to greet a neighbor at the ceremony's close, however much parish activists may occasionally aspire to a richer community life.

If the "congregational" template mischaracterizes American Catholic parishes, it can hardly be expected to describe non-Christian immigrant communities. Warner and Yang and Ebaugh, nevertheless, correctly point to important tendencies among some of the worship communities serving immigrants. Our evidence helps assess the degree to which the template fits. The "congregational" argument can be divided into the components of polity and governance, lay participation in worship, degree of multifunctionality, and ethnic exclusiveness. We will treat each briefly.

Governance

"Congregationalism" is, first of all, a particular form of religious polity, characterized by lay leadership and ownership. It is distinguished from the hierarchical arrangement of the "episcopal" (governance by bishops) and the "presbyterian" (governance by a permanent and self-perpetuating board of "elders") polities. Our research indeed found several striking instances of the adoption of congregational governance, in this sense, by non-Christians. This should not be surprising, but the reasons may lie less with self-conscious adoption of the congregational template than with the legal requirements for setting up a local worship community. As Warner notes, in the legal environment of the United States, lay people have both the motivation and the legal capability to set up worship communities under their own management. The mosques in our sample were all established by lay people and continue to be governed by them. The Hindu temples were likewise created by groups of lay people. They have had to recruit priests from India and persuade them to adapt to subordination to lay employers, a situation that is foreign to Indian tradition. The two ashrams represented here, however, which in form of worship more closely resemble the Protestant "congregation," have governing committees appointed by their religious leaders, who maintain firm control over the governance of the worship community, subordinate to the larger movement of which they are representatives. When we look at the details of local governance in the remaining worship communities, moreover, we find much variation.

When we asked Muslim respondents whether the governing body of the mosque was appointed by the religious leader, elected by the congregation, or elected by some special body, all but one reported that the governing bodies were elected by the larger worship community. This reflects the democratic ethos of Islam. In all but two cases, moreover, this body had responsibility not only for finances but for appointing the religious leader. The situation among Hindus was more diverse, with two communities (the ashrams) reporting that their governing body was appointed by the religious leader, two reporting election by the larger community, and four election by a special body. The three Sikh communities that answered this question were similarly diverse. The Christian ones show similar variation. In 17 percent of the Protestant communities, the pastor appointed the leadership body, probably reflecting the power of the pastor in the smaller congregations. In another 10 percent, a special body appointed the leadership group, representing a more presbyterian form of polity than we encountered among Muslims. Overall, 52 percent of Protestant congregations, but just 32 percent of Catholic parishes, reported that their leadership body was elected by the congregation. The Catholic leadership groups had no power over the appointment of religious leaders and, in 61 percent of cases, no power over finances, a limitation found in less than one-fourth of all the other groups. Thus, while the congregational form of governance has a clear plurality (with 43 percent of our cases having a lay board with the authority to appoint religious leaders), it is not the only form of polity we found, and the situation varies even within religious traditions.

Lay Participation in Worship

The congregational model rests on an image of voluntary membership that includes the expectation that members will recognize one another as part of a distinct "community," even "family." A "congregation" in this sense is scarcely to be found in Hindu or Buddhist temples or in Muslim mosques in their home countries. To what extent, then, have non-Christian religious traditions adopted "congregational" forms of membership—from membership rolls, to the social hour or meal after services, to regular social gatherings for members? The answers vary widely.

It was notable, first of all, that most of the Muslim and Hindu respondents to our survey rejected the notion of "membership" (along with the term "congregation") in describing their institution. Few kept records of those who participated in services, and those who did viewed the records more as mailing lists than membership rolls. Muslims and Hindus go to one place of worship or another depending on specific events scheduled in different places, or according to convenience. Among Hindus in particular, lay people were much more likely to regard themselves simply as worshipers at this or that temple than as "members" in the Protestant sense. Muslims, too, regard devotion as a personal matter, for which the place of prayer was optional. Some sense of this came across in our questions about participation. When asked about "the number of people associated *in any way* with the religious life of this group," respondents from Muslim and Hindu worship communities cited very large numbers, in the thousands and even tens of thousands. The average number in both groups was over 4,000. When asked how many persons *"regularly participate* in the religious life of your congregation," many of the same respondents balked, saying that people come and go or, in the case of the Hindu temples, that there is no set time of worship that would draw "regular participants." For the majority of worshipers at these institutions, the "congregational" or community dimension remains an accidental part of their relationship to the institution, which is more a "house of worship" than a "community" or "family."

Yang and Ebaugh report tendencies among immigrant worship communities to adopt Christian forms of worship, from adoption of Sunday as the prime gathering day to lay participation in religious rituals and the introduction of preaching in the service. They also argue that immigrant congregations are adopting English as a language of worship or teaching and are translating sacred texts into English (Yang et al. 2001, 276–78). We found evidence for these adaptations, but we also found much diversity. On the one hand, we were surprised to find religiously oriented summer camps for young people as an important part of Hindu and Sikh cultures. And in virtually all of the Korean Protestant congregations, we found that Western music and Protestant hymns (in Korean translations) play central roles in the worship services—though this can be largely attributed to the work of Protestant missionaries in Korea. On the other hand, we found a great deal of variation in the degree to which lay people participated in religious services and used English.

Among Muslims, Friday prayers are traditionally led by a single speaker, the imam, and the only other public role is that of the lay person who issues the call to prayer. This remains true among the mosques in our study. None reported more than one or two speakers at Friday prayers. Among Hindus, similarly, religious services are dominated by the priest, who alone says certain prayers and leads chants. Only in the two cases of the Hindu ashrams— which are teaching centers promoting greater lay devotion and the training of monks—did lay people participate actively in religious services. Among Sikhs, priests or professional singers conduct much of the service, but lay people are encouraged to come forward to lead one or another chant. And the principal weekly service is followed by a ritual meal prepared and served by members of the community. These practices are core to Sikh worship in India as well as the

United States, but they give Sikh services much more of the feel of an American congregation.

We found variation in lay participation among Christians as well. Somewhat surprisingly, Catholics are more likely than Protestants to have multiple lay participants during services. The larger size of Catholic services may explain this and the fact that in many of the smaller Protestant congregations, worship is dominated by the pastor.

As for the use of English in services, we found great diversity, with the most ethnically homogenous groups, no matter what the religious tradition or style of worship, using a single non-English language throughout the service. Moreover, as we noted earlier, the multiethnic worship communities first organized in immigrant communities tend to splinter when one or another ethnic group becomes strong enough to launch its own monoethnic worship community. Whereas the earlier multicultural communities used English as a bridge uniting different groups, the specialized groups commonly use their own languages. This tendency is thus precisely the opposite of that postulated by Yang and Ebaugh. The difference might simply be one of timing. Older communities might be expected to follow the trajectory Yang and Ebaugh describe. As immigrant communities age and are forced to confront the demands of the second and third generation for services in English, the use of English increases. Most Korean and Chinese Protestant communities, for example, offer a service in English. Their solution is not to abandon Korean or Chinese language services but to add an English service. The double dynamic of new immigrants continuing to arrive while a second generation grows up will produce a complicated set of solutions regarding use of English. We doubt if any uniform transition to English will go on in the near future in these communities.

Multifunctionality

Immigrant worship communities, according to both Warner and Yang and Ebaugh, often set aside home country patterns that made a temple, church, or mosque mainly a "house of worship," adopting instead an organizational form that includes broader functions—religious, social, and political. This multifunctionality is normal in American congregations, whether Protestant, Catholic, or Jewish. Indeed, the pioneering study of American congregations, H. Paul Douglass's *One Thousand City Churches* (1926), takes as its major task the categorizing of urban churches according to the number and range of activities they undertake. Douglass's work underlined the diversity of adaptations in this respect, and our own data confirm that worship communities serving immigrants vary a great deal in the sorts of functions they have taken on. As he argued, "there is a complete set of options before any group of religious people who want to perform any function or group of functions or services in the name of their faith; namely, to do them through a church or through a non-church organization; for virtually all functions performed by either class are performed now by the one, now by the other" (49).

Some of our cases confirm the transformation that advocates of the congregational template point to. For example, while in much of the Islamic world the mosque is solely a house of worship, in the United States, Muslims have often organized to create multipurpose mosques with numerous educational and social programs. Yet most mosques claim fewer services and activities than the average Catholic parish. Hindu temples remain largely houses of worship, as we saw, and some Catholic parishes are more like the Hindu temples in their overwhelming emphasis on worship and religious education. Thus, there remains considerable diversity among immigrant worship communities in their adoption of the multifunctional model.[1]

Both the extent to which immigrant worship communities follow the pattern of transformation suggested by Warner and Yang and Ebaugh and the degree of multifunctionality among their religious institutions vary considerably, as we saw in chapter 4. Thus, a majority of worship communities participated in or sponsored social service, community development, or neighborhood organizing projects. Even here there was considerable variation in the number of programs sponsored and the level of resources that communities devoted to them. The size of the worship community, not surprisingly, has much to do with its ability to mount multiple programs. Thus, larger worship communities are more likely to sponsor or support social service, community development, or neighborhood organizing projects and much more likely to spend over $10,000 on such projects. Catholic parishes, as we saw, are often much larger than Protestant churches. Thus, size can account for relatively high rates of Catholic participation in a variety of programs and services. But religious tradition also plays a role. Hindu temples and Muslim communities claim large numbers of regular attenders, but their rate of offering the sorts of programs mentioned earlier is considerably lower, in most cases, than that of Catholic parishes and is more in line with that of the smaller Protestant congregations. Hindu and Muslim places of worship thus tend not to have diversified as widely as their Catholic (and Sikh) counterparts. Indeed, many worship communities in both traditions have taken on no or few nonreligious functions.

Ethnic Exclusiveness

Warner and Yang and Ebaugh differ in their expectations about inclusiveness and exclusiveness. Warner sees a tendency to ethnic exclusiveness, following the classic Protestant pattern of homogeneous churches (2000, 277). "Like tends to worship with like" is a constant finding in American sociology of religion. Yang and Ebaugh, on the other hand, argue that "adopting congregational forms and theological changes toward emphasizing the original grand tradition over more recent subtraditions is accompanied by increasing inclusiveness in membership" (Yang et al. 2001, 281). Our data, once again, present a much more mixed story, though we find some evidence of a shift over time toward increasing ethnic exclusiveness.

First, ethnic exclusiveness or multiculturalism prevailed in the worship communities we studied to different degrees, varying across distinct immigrant communities and religious traditions. Korean and Chinese churches, whether Catholic or Protestant, tend to be ethnically exclusive. Salvadorans overwhelmingly worship in "Hispanic" worship communities. Immigrants from other countries of Latin American make up a sizable portion of most of these communities, and we found little evidence of efforts to found exclusively "national" congregations. Most Muslims, similarly, worship in multicultural settings, though one or another national group might dominate the leadership of a given mosque. The major exceptions were Turkish and Afghani mosques, where the language of worship impeded access for most Muslims of other backgrounds. We also found among Muslims the tendencies noted by Yang and Ebaugh toward a broader interpretation of Islam, rejecting "cultural accretions" in favor of a grand tradition accessible to more people. Despite the conservative influence of the Saudi Embassy, none of the mosques in the area represented the sort of fundamentalist Islam common in Saudi Arabia. Nor did Shi'ites among the Iranian founders of a prominent Washington area mosque emphasize differences between the Shi'ite and Sunni versions of the faith.

We encountered different tendencies, nevertheless, among African Christians and Hindus. Among Africans, as we have seen, the largest ethnic groups have tended to form their own congregations, whether self-standing or under the umbrella of a larger church or parish. This was particularly true among Nigerians, who split into Yoruba and Igbo congregations. Though the Washington archdiocese attempted to channel Nigerian Catholics into a single "Nigerian Catholic Community," as we saw in chapter 6, many Igbo, committed to an Igbo Catholic community, left the fledgling congregation to worship elsewhere, and some established a renegade Catholic community in a distant suburb. Among Hindus, the tendency has been for the multiethnic temples of the early years of settlement in the area to be superseded by temples with more regional and even single-ethnic characteristics. Thus, increasing ethnic exclusiveness seems to be the rule among African Christians and Hindus, in contrast to the Muslim cases.

Thus, the reality of immigrant adaptation turns out to be messier and less certain than the portrait of increasing Americanization drawn by Stephen Warner and by Yang and Ebaugh. While they are correct in pointing to specific adaptations apparent among immigrant worship communities, such as the prevalence of lay leadership or a turn to more multifunctional forms of worship community, it would be premature to claim these tendencies as evidence for the inevitable spread of a congregational template among the new immigrant worship communities. While some of the adaptations postulated by that argument are visible in our study, others are unclear or are missing entirely. Hindus and Muslims continue to worship in much the style they were accustomed to in their countries of origin. Or, as in the case of some of the more inclusive Hindu temples, they have adopted new forms, such as the enshrinement of diverse deities under one roof, that are strange to both Indian and American religious experience.

In some quarters, indeed, immigrant religious practices are actively reshaping existing American religious institutions. Among Catholics, for example, an earlier study by Foley (1998) found widespread adoption of the icons and practices of immigrant Catholics in the larger American church. The figure of the Virgin of Guadalupe is by now common in Catholic churches in the United States. And accommodation to the religious devotions of the new immigrants has brought other new images of the Virgin to Catholic America, such as Our Lady of Lavang, honored by Vietnamese Catholics and patroness of one of the most rapidly growing religious orders in the United States. Several dioceses have adopted the Philippine pre-Christmas procession, the Simbang Gabi, while parishes around the country sponsor re-creations of the Mexican *posada*. Mainstream Protestant denominations, meanwhile, have largely accepted Spanish and other languages as languages of worship in immigrant communities, sometimes even finding ways to honor such figures as the Virgin of Guadalupe. At the same time, Presbyterians, Methodists, and Baptists have experienced divisions as Korean congregations change affiliations to the corresponding Korean denominational body and Chinese worship communities increasingly take on a nondenominational identity.

Such crosscurrents suggest neither a straight-line assimilationist nor a melting pot model. Rather, immigrant worship communities are engaged in a complex give and take as they adapt to the new setting and assume a place in

American religion and civil society. In this respect, as in all the others we have taken up in this study, immigrant worship communities are varied. The task of the next and final section will be to attempt to wrest some pattern from this diversity and assess the contribution of different adaptations to the civic incorporation of the new immigrants.

Religion and Civic Incorporation

Our study has found great diversity among the worship communities serving new immigrants. Generalizations about religion and the new immigrants are not easy to come by. Nevertheless, we have found distinctive patterns, grounded less in the national origins or even the religious traditions of the new immigrants than in distinctive ways of organizing the local worship community. Lay and religious leadership are key ingredients in how a community interprets its religious tradition and organizes its practices. The most active communities were not just the products of strong religious leadership; they also reflected a heightened sense of identity, of religious and ethnic *difference*, that leaders mobilized on behalf of causes dear to members. Meanwhile, those communities that were most effective in providing formal social services and, often, in engaging their members with the larger society were those that were most embedded in larger networks, often thanks to the denominational structure of their religious tradition. Finally, the contribution of worship communities to the development of civic skills that could be applied to civic engagement depended on the commitment of the community itself to civic life. Where communities were focused on worship or the building up of a "blessed community," even widespread lay participation would not translate readily into practiced civic skills. Active, engaged communities encouraged active, engaged members. In the following section, we take up each of these conclusions in turn.

Leadership and Organizational Culture

One of the most stiking findings of our look at immigrant worship communities was the degree to which religious and lay leadership shaped the organizational culture of the most civically active communities. Regardless of national origin or religious tradition, certain worship communities were especially active and engaged in the wider society. Often, the same communities also stood out for the range of services and activities they provided their members. All involved lay people in the decision-making process and direction of the worship community. In one case, an interdenominational Chinese church, a long-standing pattern of service to the Chinese community had evolved into a separate community service arm, serving local residents of all racial and ethnic backgrounds. Pastors came and went, but the lay leadership saw to it that the community's commitment to social service and civic involvement continued to be a priority. In all the other cases, a single figure could be identified who had shaped the community's commitment to civic engagement or community service; and the organizational culture of the community reflected this commitment.

Given the importance of pastors in the Christian tradition, this should come as no surprise. Pastors generally have the authority and longevity to decisively shape a community's culture and expectations of what church is all about. In the more hierarchical traditions, ecclesiastical authorities may limit the activities of pastors, removing them at their discretion. At the same time, however, pastors have considerable authority among the laity and can use that authority to reshape pastoral life. Catholic parishes present a telling example, since the central emphasis on the ritual life of the community would seem to ordain a "house of worship" organizational culture. Yet individual clergymen frequently create communities based on lay participation and communal solidarity. Unless such efforts enjoy the support of the diocese, however, they are likely to founder when the priest responsible for them moves on.[2]

The smaller, evangelical churches typically depend on their pastors for another reason: the pastor as founder is the only effective authority in the congregation. This is particularly the case where the pastor retains control of church finances, something that may be impossible once fundraising for a building becomes a priority. Prickly relations between pastor and the laity may ensue in these circumstances, and this may hinder church growth or lead to rancorous splits. Only with difficulty could such a community take time from managing the tensions to devote to social services or civic activism, and pastors are unlikely to be able to lead such a community in that direction. The larger, more successful churches will have the resources and leisure to expand the range of their activities; it will be up to the pastor or groups of lay people whether to move beyond religious functions to civic and social engagement.

Only under forms of presbyterian or congregational governance could we expect the laity to have a large degree of control over the direction of church life and the sorts of activities that will occupy the members' time, because then the congregation plays a decisive role in choosing their minister. The situation is similar in most of the non-Christian worship communities we encountered, but not because a long history favors lay control. In these cases, lay people have been decisive in founding the community and remain in effective control of governance. Lay leaders and boards thus play the decisive role in shaping the community's engagement with the larger society. Lay boards in most Hindu, Sikh, and Muslim communities hire and fire religious personnel. Lay boards determine general policy, and lay leaders take the initiative in the activities and services that the community offers; they shape the agenda, and thus the organizational culture, of the temple, gurdwara, or mosque. And lay leaders break away to found new communities in response to personal and political disputes within these communities.

Among Hindu worship communities, the two that stood out for their civic activism were led by strong-minded lay leaders. In one instance, a single figure had shaped the community through efforts that included a regular newsletter, emphasizing a pan-Indian approach to creating a worship community and a broadly tolerant vision of Hinduism's mission to the world. In the other case, lay people associated with the VHP broke away from an existing worship community to found their own as a vehicle for furthering their program of building Hindu pride and militancy. The most civically engaged of the mosques was founded and is currently led by prominent Muslims, many of whom have also been founders or supporters of leading national and local Muslim organizations. Among the Sikh gurdwaras, the most visible and civically active congregation was created when a charismatic lay leader led protests in front of the Indian Embassy over the Indian government's assault on the Golden Temple in Amritsar and the subsequent massacre of Sikhs.

Religious Outsiders and Civic Engagement

In his *Religious Outsiders and the Making of Americans* (1986), R. Laurence Moore defends Irish American archbishop John Hughes in his 1830s dispute with the convert Orestes Brownson, who wanted to "Americanize" the mainly immigrant church of the time. Hughes's "clannish appeals to Irish Catholics," Moore writes, "encouraged a minority consciousness and discouraged mingling with Protestants" and even "helped perpetuate a belief among American Catholics that Protestants held the upper hand" (56). But these appeals were part of a strategy whose fundamental premise was that "Catholics did not have to become American. They already were." Moore insists that Hughes "convincingly argued to Irish American Catholics that the essence of Americanness did not reside in accepting norms created for them by native-born Protestants. Further, he demonstrated that American institutions could be made to work to their advantage." And Hughes "waged his fight in the most familiar cadences of American political patriotic rhetoric" (56).

Today's religious outsiders differ as widely as yesterday's Catholics, Jews, and Mormons in their approaches to integration into American society. Some take the position of the German immigrant leaders mentioned in the introduction who insisted that pluralism *was* Americanism and that German immigrants could make their greatest contribution to American society by nourishing their own cultural heritage. Many of the first-generation Korean lay people and pastors we spoke with echoed this contention. The same contention takes a religious form whenever religious leaders insist that religious difference is the "leaven" of society—a frequent, biblically sanctioned trope. Few of the religious leaders who share a focus on religious or cultural integrity face the public battles that Archbishop Hughes fought. Most, however, must help their people cope with the difficulties of immigration. They have to address the divide between young and old that the American experience widens. They have to speak to the experience of difference that immigration imposes upon people.

The efforts of religious leaders to address the dilemma of difference and the difficulties of immigration, however, do not contribute in any uniform way to civic engagement. Only where religious and lay leaders actively promote engagement, we have found, do worship communities become involved and help their members develop civic skills that are likely to be employed beyond the community itself, in the larger civic arena. One circumstance that produces these results is where the leadership sees itself and its community not just as religious outsiders but also as political outsiders. Leaders who, like Hughes, see their people as part of a beleaguered minority are more likely to engage the larger society and promote such engagement among their members. This was the case with Father Mesa in our study, whose charitable work with disabled children from El Salvador led to relief efforts on behalf of hurricane victims there and advocacy on immigrant rights issues here. Rallying the Hispanic community of St. Francis around the beleaguered Salvadoran people was one means of building Hispanic pride, promoting a wide range of parish and social services, and educating the membership about their rights and duties as citizens.

The Sikh advocates for a separate "Khalistan" state in the Punjab were political outsiders in relation to both their fellow Sikhs in this country and to public opinion in Washington following the assassination of Indira Gandhi by her Sikh bodyguards. They could mobilize members of the community to defend the reputation of Sikhs in the American press and in Congress, and they were among the leadership in the mobilization of a defensive Sikh response to the events of September 11, 2001. Similarly, the young people in several gurdwaras who participated in the emergency meetings in late September and October 2001 were motivated by a real sense of danger, as well as by their

genuine concern for others. The language of defensive mobilization even per-
meates the Hindu fundamentalist movement, whose members portray their
fellow Hindus in India as victimized by Muslims, and who cite the American
press's "bias" against Hindus in the Gujarat riots as evidence that Hindus in
this country have to be more active in defense of their religious tradition.

In each of these cases, leaders strive to emphasize a distinctive identity
that entails solidarity with a larger class of disadvantaged brothers and sisters.
A heightened sense of group identity—religious, ethnic, or ethnoreligious—
goes hand in hand with increased civic activism. In these cases, group identity
is utilized for an activist agenda. More important, though, an activist agenda
on behalf of "outsider" causes promotes deeper involvement in American
society, from naturalization and get-out-the-vote campaigns to active lobbying
and demonstrations, to participation in ecumenical and civic associations. In
our cases, the worship communities with such an agenda were precisely those
that were the most active politically and most likely to involve their members
broadly in civic affairs of all sorts.

One result is that throughout the region, civic leaders and politicians have
been courting immgrants with increasing fervor, and they have turned especially to the more activist worship communities for help. Growing numbers
of Hispanics occupy seats in the Maryland legislature and in city and county
councils, most often as partners on local Democratic Party tickets. Asian Americans have enjoyed special access to the mayor's office in Washington, D.C.,
for some time in the person of a special representative who is also an active
member of the city's oldest Chinese Protestant church. The Muslim community in the area was courted by the Bush campaign in 2000, and many
prominent Muslims were able to call upon the administration in the wake
of September 11, 2001, to try to stem a national backlash against Muslims.
Churches, mosques, and other worship communities generally play a minor
role in civic engagement at this level (we found few immigrant worship communities that invited politicians to the pulpit, for example), but they remain a
base of support of ethnic politicians and a recognized constituency for other
civic and political leaders who have a message to communicate.

Resources, Social Capital, and Civic Engagement

Not all worship communities were as intensely civically engaged as those mentioned here. Indeed, the vast majority in our study were not. But the majority
made efforts to provide their members and others with social services, education and training, and opportunities for service. What factors shaped these
efforts?

One of the most striking differences we found in our survey was between the relatively well-off worship communities and those that served a mostly poor population. Among the former, we found few social services directed to the members. Nor did many of these communities sponsor social services for the surrounding neighborhood. This is not surprising, since most are located in affluent suburbs. Many of them, nevertheless, took part in social service programs directed toward the needy elsewhere. Many Korean congregations gave regularly to support aid to North Korean refugees in China. Many of the Hindu, Sikh, and Muslim communities raised money to support the victims of the terrorist attacks of September 11, 2001. Many participated in Red Cross blood drives. Korean congregations gave to Korean social service agencies, and the more affluent mosques helped support a variety of social service agencies in the region. Many Korean, Chinese, and Muslim worship communities sent food, and sometimes volunteers, to soup kitchens in the inner city. A key factor in the type of social engagement a worship community undertakes is thus the level of resources available to the immigrant population itself. To the degree that the majority are well off, social welfare needs within the worship community will be relatively small. Surplus resources will go to causes beyond the worship community. As we saw, in this respect immigrant worship communities are "good citizens," sometimes better citizens than their native-born counterparts.

The poorer immigrant worship communities present a different story. These communities took one of two distinct paths. Among the smaller ones, we found informal social services aimed at members and their immediate families and friends. Small size and a small resource base account for much of these congregations' preference for this approach, but organizational culture and theological orientation also play a role. Most of these smaller communities see themselves as families, with familial obligations to one another. For such communities, "family comes first," including close relatives of members who are not members of the community. Theologically, too, these are communities that are generally oriented toward building up the "blessed community" of the saved rather than toward service to the world.

Some Catholic parishes and mainline Protestant congregations took a different path. Drawing on denominational resources and traditions, these worship communities worked with other organizations to provide formal services to their members and neighbors, in some cases engaging actively in civic affairs and encouraging their members to do the same. Despite the general poverty of their membership, they were able to mobilize sizeable funds, both from among their own members and from a larger support community, to aid others. Both theological tradition and the organizational culture of these communities contributed to these efforts; but the leadership of individual pastors was crucial to the interpretation of the tradition and its implementation in an organizational culture oriented toward building community and serving the needy. This was as true of the smaller Methodist missions to the Hispanic community we looked at as of the larger Catholic, Lutheran, and Episcopalian churches serving Hispanic or African immigrants.

Leadership is thus important in enabling poorer worship communities to provide formal social services, play a role in the larger civic arena, and promote civic engagement by members. But the extensive social capital that pastors enjoy who are embedded in the hierarchical churches also helps. Such pastors draw not just on theological traditions that are supportive of service to the poor and of civic activism but also on the contacts and material resources their denominations provide. They have access to established, denomination-ally based social service agencies. They have credibility with secular agencies. They can draw on volunteers and material resources from a large circle of de-nominationally related institutions as they build their programs and mount campaigns of aid or action.

Social capital of this sort is not entirely absent among other groups, but it may be thinner. Among Hindus, each temple founding has been a project of a distinctive group of lay people, only rarely drawing support from coreligionists already committed to another temple community. Personal, ethnic, and busi-ness ties have contributed to new foundings. Similar patterns seem to have been at work in the founding of the area's mosques. But mutual aid and con-tinuing support for poorer worship communities seem most developed within the Christian community. Among Koreans, the resources that denominations represent are replaced by ethnic ties. One Korean church with roots in the Men-nonite tradition has devoted itself to serving a poor African American clientele and working with Korean shopkeepers in African American neighborhoods of Washington, D.C. Its work is widely supported by Korean Protestant churches, thanks to Korean contacts across denominations. Similarly, one or two orga-nizations, who enjoy contacts across denominations, coordinate many of the overseas charitable projects to which Korean worship communities contribute.

The social capital that some pastors and lay leaders enjoy is crucial to poorer worship communities' ability to provide social services. It also contrib-utes to the level of civic engagement of the community as a whole. The social capital that ordinary members share as a result of their integration into the community is much more ambiguous in its import. In more diverse com-munities, we found, membership implies access to resources in the form of material aid, contacts, and opportunities of all sorts. In poor communities, strong ties among members might be important psychic resources but are much less powerful in helping immigrants advance in American society. In both cases, social capital is valuable for individual adaptation in the difficult circumstances of immigration; but it does not necessarily lead to greater integration into the larger society or to civic engagement. Indeed, whether the community enjoys significant resources or is poor, membership might have few implications for civic engagement; and in some cases, like that of Nuestro Señor, dense networks seemed to contribute to continuing social isolation. "Bridging social capital," as Robert Putnam (2000) and others have argued, is often far more effective than "bonding social capital" in advancing individual fortunes. Whether it also promotes civic engagement depends very much on where the bridges are being built and to what ends.

Civic Skills, Identity, and Civic Action

Churches, particularly Protestant churches, are important equalizers in American society, according to the authors of *Voice and Equality*, thanks to their contributions to equipping ordinary citizens with the civic skills necessary for democratic participation (Verba et al. 1995). Our study has confirmed this view, but with some important qualifications. First, we have found support for this conclusion in a broader array of cases, including several non-Christian religious traditions. Second, however, we find that worship communities vary both in the civic skills cultivated and in the degree to which these might transfer to actual participation in the political system, making generalizations about specific religious traditions tenuous.

The Protestant evangelical churches we observed, for example, certainly promoted the development of a range of skills among their members (though with a clear male bias); but they rarely encouraged their members to exercise these skills outside the worship community. In some instances, a jealous theology of devotion to the worship community itself discouraged civic engagement. Some Catholic parishes, by contrast, despite the nearly absolute authority of bishops and pastors over pastoral life, promoted widespread participation among parishioners, volunteering outside the community, and civic activism. In the larger mosques, though lay participation in worship services was extremely limited, lay people found extensive opportunities for participation in a rich community life, and they exercised dominant influence in governance. The Sikh and Hindu communities were much more limited in the scope of activities they sponsored, but lay people managed most of the life of these communities.

The characteristic differences in this regard among worship communities were not primarily ethnic or religious in origin but arose from the organizational culture and theological orientation of particular communities. Those in which a primarily "house of worship" or "family" style of organization prevailed were much less likely to provide wide opportunities for civic skills to be developed and applied to civic engagement outside the community. In many of the family-style communities, a conservative theology counseled separation from the world rather than active service in it. Community- and civic leader–style worship communities, by contrast, provided a wide range of activities that could cultivate civic skills. Some of them also provided opportunities to apply these skills in the civic arena, and in some cases, leaders encouraged or mobilized members to do so. The cultivation of civic skills with real impact on civic engagement was most pronounced where lay and religious leaders espoused religious and ethnic identities that underlined the community's responsibilities to others—coethnics and coreligionists first of all but the larger society, too, as a target and potential partner in social justice.

There is no one pattern that would capture in a few words the impact of religion on civic engagement and social incorporation among recent immigrants. Instead, we have encountered diverse patterns, divided less according to immigrants' countries of origin or even religious tradition than diverse styles of worship and community life. These styles draw on practices and ideas that are rooted in the distinctive religious traditions of each community, but their application depends on the interpretation each community and its leadership makes of the tradition. Religion for the new immigrants—just as for the rest of the population—may mean little more than a passing encounter with ritual practices and religious teaching. But it may also entail an all-encompassing immersion in a self-styled community of the blessed. It will have the most impact where it is most seriously practiced. Survey evidence suggests that religion plays a larger role in the lives of recent immigrants than in the lives of the wider population. Whether or not religion encourages greater civic engagement and promotes the incorporation of immigrants into American civic life, however, depends on the character of the individual worship community in which immigrants participate.

Far from alienating immigrants from American life, we have found, worship communities that attempt to preserve elements of the culture the immigrants have come from may actually promote integration—through the contacts and opportunities, civic skills, and active engagement they provide. The communities that do this best are those that build on immigrant identities to promote ethnic and religious agendas that are sometimes at odds with prevailing sentiment in the larger society. Immigrants, of course, may incorporate themselves into American society through individual and familial strategies of assimilation. They may enjoy psychological and financial resources that enable them to ignore racial and cultural stereotypes and assume a place in a presumptively merit-based system of rewards. But for many immigrants, probably the majority, worship communities provide not just a haven in a heartless world but also an opportunity to engage with American society on their own terms, grounded in their own culture and the convictions that come with it, joining with others of their own kind in civic action on behalf of causes close to their hearts. Insisting on their own identities and making claims on the larger society, as religious and ethnic "outsiders" always have, they are quickly becoming insiders, sought-after interlocutors, constituents, and political allies in a society that has long since found ample ways to make way for newcomers.

Notes

INTRODUCTION

1. Tamar Jacoby's not unsympathetic *Washington Post* review ends with a well-placed jibe at Huntington's insistence that American identity is founded on a "creed" derived from the Anglo-Protestant culture of its founders: "In the end, what's most disturbing about Who Are We? is its lack of confidence in the power of American identity. It's as if Huntington can't believe that our tolerant, universalist spirit could possibly stand up to an old-fashioned, ethnic nationalism of the kind that, say, today's Mexican immigrants arrive with. And, as a result, he needs to define our diffuse, big-tent essence down to the narrow orthodoxies of a more easily grasped culture, like Anglo-Protestantism. Of course, he's entitled to his fears and his pessimism, but it's a sorry approach for a self-styled 'patriot' proposing to chart America's way into the global future" (Jacoby 2004).

2. Numerous studies underline effects of assimilation on adolescent behavior: "First-generation (foreign-born) and second-generation (American-born with immigrant parents) adolescents are less likely to engage in delinquent and violent acts, to use drugs and alcohol, and to have had sex [than their peers from American-born families]. [They are] less likely to be in poor health, to be obese, to have asthma, and to have missed school because of a health or emotional problem ... first-generation youths tend to be healthier and less likely to engage in risky behavior than their second-generation counterparts." As Andrew Fuligni puts it, "Rather than asking whether these unique children will adjust to American society, the question now seems to be, how can they be doing so well?" (Fuligni 1998, 99). On the other side of the ledger, Ruben Rumbaut has reviewed the large number of studies that show the superior health characteristics of

first-generation immigrants, even given higher rates of poverty among them. Birth outcomes among even poor first-generation immigrants, for example, are significantly better than for native-born Americans, white and black. By the second generation, the advantages that the first generation bring with them have begun to disappear, and by the third generation, infant mortality rates, levels of obesity, heart disease, and diabetes match national levels, as do tobacco and alcohol consumption and other risky behaviors. Second- and third-generation members of all immigrant groups (except the Japanese) have worse health, and make worse lifestyle choices, than the first generation, resembling in all major respects the native-born American population by the third generation. Rumbaut concludes, with ample justification, that "assimilation may be bad for your health" (Rumbaut 1997).

3. The notion of "organizational culture" and the categories utilized here are drawn from the work of Penny Becker on conflict in worship communities. See Becker 1998, 1999.

4. The last year the U.S. census gathered religious data was 1910. Recently the General Social Survey (GSS), conducted every year since 1972, has included some questions on religious preferences and practices of random samples of Americans. Because it is administered in English only, and because many immigrants are likely to be missed in a telephone survey, the GSS cannot answer many questions about immigrants today. This situation will be remedied to some extent with the launch of the New Immigrant Survey, which will poll a large sample of immigrants who have recently received authorization for long-term residency in the United States from the Immigration and Naturalization Service. For a brief overview of recent research on the role of religion in the lives of the new immigrants, see Ebaugh and Chafetz 2000, 14–20. Tom Smith, of the National Opinion Research Center, which administers the GSS and a variety of other surveys, has recently summarized what we know about the extent of participation in non-Christian religions in the United States. See Smith 2002.

5. Thus, Robert P. Swierenga could write: "Economics explains the 'why' of immigration but religion largely determines the 'how' of immigration and its effects. Although most immigrants left their homelands in the hope of economic betterment, religious institutions facilitated the move, guided the newcomers to specific destinations, and shaped their adjustment in the new land. Religion was the very 'bone and sinew' of immigrant group consciousness and the 'focal point' of their life" (1994, 119, citing Randall Miller and John Bodnar).

6. The New Immigrant Survey Pilot sampling frame includes all persons admitted to legal permanent residence during the months of July and August 1996. While many of these are newly arrived immigrants, others are previously undocumented immigrants who have succeeded in adjusting their status. Nevertheless, the sampling frame results in undersampling undocumented immigrants, including many of the poorest migrants to the United States.

7. Roger Waldinger and his associates have shown that these generalizations are well grounded in the distribution of immigrant groups in distinct job and industry-specific economic "niches." See Waldinger 2001; Waldinger and Der-Martirosian 2001.

8. In the end, there were too few Buddhist temples to make for meaningful comparison. In the interests of time and ethnographic depth, moreover, our Korean and Chinese researchers chose to focus on the Protestant congregations.

9. Because most of the mosques in the area are multiethnic in character, and none features a predominantly Indian population, it was impossible to study Indian Muslim worship communities as separate entities. We looked instead at mosques in which Indian Muslims were members but as coparticipants with members from Pakistan, Afghanistan, the Middle East, and elsewhere.

10. Though many mosques include significant numbers of African American and Euro-American converts to Islam, they rely heavily upon an immigrant population predominantly from the Middle East and South Asia. Most mosques are multiethnic, though a few are identified with Iranian, Afghan, or Turkish communities.

11. The National Congregations Study (NCS) yields data on congregations as the unit of analysis. The sampling frame for the NCS survey starts with the 1998 GSS. If respondents indicated attendance at religious services, they were asked to provide a link to their congregation. Telephone or face-to-face interviews were then conducted with key informants from each designated congregation, in most cases the pastor. This "hypernetwork sample" of congregations makes this survey of congregations the most comprehensive, and accurate, one to date. Where earlier congregational surveys depended upon telephone books to locate congregations and thereby missed many small congregations, the NCS sample is able to include just such groups. Greater detail about the sampling method and the data set can be found in Chaves et al. (1999).

12. The response rate for the NCS was 80 percent, and the total number of congregations was 1,236. Because of the relatively small sample size of the NCS, we are unable to compare NCS results on congregations serving specific immigrant groups with our own results.

CHAPTER I. BECOMING AMERICAN

1. For an overview of the development of the notion of civil society and its uses in recent debates in the United States, see Foley and Hodgkinson 2003.

2. Mark R. Warren, for example, found that among African American Protestant participants in Industrial Areas Foundation organizing in Texas, pastors often dominated their own worship communities' involvement, with little participation among ordinary lay people. Hispanic Catholic congregations, on the other hand, were likely to produce a larger supply of lay leaders to participate in coalition activities and interact with local officials (Warren 2001). Note that Warren's findings tend to contradict Verba and colleagues' observation that Catholic parishes are less likely to promote civic skills than Protestant churches because of the hierarchical character of Catholic parish organization. Warren cautions that some Protestant churches center leadership on one charismatic figure, whereas priest-short Catholic parishes have increasingly turned to lay people to assume leadership roles, particularly in nonsacramental ministries.

3. Recently Mark R. Warren and Richard Wood have demonstrated the potential for civic engagement in faith-based community organizing efforts that cross religious, ethnic and racial lines. See Warren 2001; Wood 2002, as well as Anner 1996; Hart 2001.

CHAPTER 2. PROFILES IN DIVERSITY

1. Mid-Atlantic region estimates based on the 1997 Current Population Survey of the U.S. Census Bureau for the following countries: Afghanistan, Bangladesh, Indonesia, Iran, Iraq, Jordan, Lebanon, Malaysia, Pakistan, Saudi Arabia, Syria, Turkey, and "other Middle East," without country specification (United States Census Bureau 1999).

2. These figures are based on an analysis of 1997 census data by Che-Fu Lee and Xiaoyan Wang (Lee and Wang 2000).

3. See, for example, Robert Orsi's fine account of the tensions between "lax" recent Italian immigrants and the largely Irish hierarchy who ruled New York City's Catholic community at the end of the nineteenth century and the beginning of the twentieth (Orsi 1985). Ana María Díaz-Stevens and Anthony Stevens-Arroyo (1998) have argued that religiosity among Hispanics is rarely contained by official worship and institutions.

4. Note that these figures are only for those who claim a religious preference.

5. Another 19 percent declared themselves without religious preference, and 18 percent refused to answer the question, the largest percentage among those polled (Lien and Carnes 2004, 39–42). Note that these figures are for a sample of all persons of Chinese descent, not just immigrants. For more details on the survey, see Lien 2004.

6. As mentioned in the introduction, the NCS is the most sophisticated attempt to date to generate data on a wide variety of questions concerning local worship communities (Chaves et al. 1999). In contrast to older studies, however, the National Congregations Study may overestimate the number of smaller worship communities (Wuthnow 2004, 39). This should be taken into account in the comparisons that follow. Finally, the NCS data include only a small number of non-Christian worship communities. We have restricted our comparisons, accordingly, to the Catholic and Protestant churches in our study.

7. Sikh discontent with the Gandhi government in the 1970s spilled over into a vigorous prodemocracy movement when Gandhi declared a state of emergency in 1977 and suspended parliament. Thousands were jailed in protests against the Emergency. When Gandhi was forced to renew democratic processes in the country in 1979, she attempted to build a broader base of support by appeals to Hindu nationalism. In 1984, elite government forces invaded the Sikh's most sacred gurdwara, the Golden Temple, on the pretext that they were rooting out armed Sikh militants. Somewhere between 500 and 5,000 civilians were killed, and five months later Gandhi was assassinated by two of her Sikh bodyguards in retaliation. Hindus in Delhi killed as many as 3,800 Sikhs in response, and the Indian government laun-

ched an international campaign to portray Sikh militants as "terrorists" (Singh 1999, 213–16).

CHAPTER 3. SOURCES OF SOCIAL CAPITAL

1. For a fuller account see Foley, McCarthy, and Chaves 2001.

2. The Catholic Church insists that only baptized Catholics "free from stain of mortal sin" are entitled to take Communion; but there are no mechanisms in the ordinary parish for monitoring compliance with these conditions even among regular participants, much less in the case of the occasional visitor.

3. And Sikhs refused to join in the one early effort to build an all-India worship center.

4. As in other religious traditions, the education of children often brings adults back into regular participation in a worship community. Temple- or home-based education programs for children can provide a principal source of interaction among parents. See Kurien 1998.

CHAPTER 4. IMMIGRANT WORSHIP COMMUNITIES IN THE PUBLIC SQUARE

1. It is important to note that the Chaves et al. and Wuthnow findings quoted earlier refer to social programs alone, not "civic activism." In regard to social programs, historically black churches are less likely to provide most such services than mainline Protestant or Catholic churches (Wuthnow 2004, 54–55). Probably more important than denominational differences, as Wuthnow notes, are size and class composition: "the large downtown congregation composed of middle-class people but located near or in low-income neighborhoods is the church in which service activities are most likely to be found" (Wuthnow 2004, 52; Foley, McCarthy, and Chaves 2001).

2. For numerous examples, see the case studies reported in Ebaugh and Saltzman Chafetz 2002.

3. Robert Wuthnow has also looked in some depth at the meaning of professionalization in such agencies; see Wuthnow 2004, chap. 5.

4. One complication is that some of the "stand-alone" worship communities are actually parts of larger parishes or congregations but have separate worship services. In these cases, the social service and community involvement data generally reflects the whole congregation, not just the immigrant worship community. This affects the data on Salvadoran Catholic worship communities as well as a few of the African congregations.

5. For our purposes, "mainline Protestants" include Episcopalian, Methodist, Lutheran, and Presbyterian churches. Our sample included none of the other denominations usually included under this label. Baptist, Pentecostal, evangelical, and independent Protestant churches are treated here as "other Protestant."

6. "Arlandria" is the colloquial name for a densely populated area on the border between the City of Alexandria and Arlington County, where many Salvadorans

have settled. The nickname "Chirilagua" refers to a Salvadoran town from which many of the residents have come.

7. The term "megachurch" refers to a recent tendency within the evangelical movement to establish large-scale, independent churches that employ lively presentations, popular music, and a "cell-group" structure to attract middle-class churchgoers. See Miller 1997; Sargeant 2000.

8. The latter maintains a dual mission: on the one hand, it ministers to African Americans in its neighborhood through a number of outreach activities; on the other, it trains Korean store owners and members of other congregations in interracial relations.

CHAPTER 5. BUILDING CIVIC SKILLS

1. In these respects, the comparison with the average Catholic and Protestant worship community as represented in the NCS produces strikingly different results from our earlier comparison on lay leadership in worship services. The average Catholic parish reports almost three times the percentage of lay participation in leadership (30 percent of members) that immigrant parishes have; the average Protestant congregation claims a leadership participation rate of (a scarcely credible) 53 percent, according to NCS, versus 28 percent for immigrant congregations.

CHAPTER 6. WHO WE ARE

1. Since we are not measuring individual immigrant behaviors directly but only reported levels of interest and activity across worship communities, we cannot assume that correlations between one indicator and another in our survey reflect individual-level correlations. All we can legitimately argue is that worship communities that have certain characteristics also share others, that is, worship communities that are settings for one sort of interest or activity, in this case transnational attachments, may also be settings for civic engagement in U.S. society.

2. As we noted in the introduction, there is considerable evidence that second-generation immigrant children today, even those who live in largely immigrant enclaves, are adopting English, and the American customs and tastes that go with it, much faster than was the case a century ago. See especially Portes and Schauffler 1996.

3. Communal identities, as we shall see, are often profoundly important in immigrant worship communities, but they are scarcely visible in these interviews, which tell us more about how the personal dimensions of identity are negotiated among immigrant families who participate in some of our worship communities.

4. "El hecho de que vivamos en Estados Unidos y que adoptemos la ciudadanía americana no quiere decir que somos americanos. Yo digo: yo no soy blanca ni tengo los ojos azules!"

5. The Father Aloysius is Aloysius Achonwa, the first Igbo pastor to the Igbo Catholic Community, originally appointed by Cardinal Ekandem to serve that community as associate pastor in a parish in Washington, D.C.

6. In fact, under Pope John Paul II, the Catholic Church has become ever more emphatic in asserting this right. See, for example, the recent statement of the U.S. Catholic bishops (U.S. Catholic Conference 2000). The U.S. bishops, nevertheless, have been reluctant to establish separate parishes for distinct ethnic groups, and somewhat blind to ethnic differences within national origin groups, in part because of their bitter experience of closing down the diverse "national parishes" that were left over from the last great wave of immigration. Though demographic changes in their neighborhoods, as the first generation has passed on, have largely rendered these churches irrelevant, the remaining parishoners, who continue to value the ethnic distinctiveness they represent, have often vigorously defended them. Bishops have also been increasingly careful to establish relations with foreign bishops to ensure that priests staffing immigrant worship communities will be reliable and will abide by diocesan rules and regulations, especially in financial matters. See Foley 1998.

7. The RSS was associated with the assassination of Mohandas Gandhi by an adherent who was enraged by Gandhi's accommodation to Indian Muslims. In 1964, the RSS spun off the VHP to develop a clear (some say simplified) version of Hinduism and to spearhead an effort to subordinate all of India's religions to the Hindu faith. The VHP organized the infamous destruction of the ancient mosque at Ayodha in 1984, claiming that it was built on the site of a shrine to the Hindu god Ram.

8. Singh's remarks on decentralization reflect his view that only an autonomous Punjab state could protect the region's Sikhs from religious violence stirred up by ambitious national politicians.

9. Before September 11, 2001, there was still lively debate over whether Muslims should participate politically in the United States. Since then that debate has largely disappeared, with attention turned much more to questions about mobilizing the Muslim vote. For a thoughtful survey of the options by an advocate, see Khan 2004.

CONCLUSION

1. Again, it is important to note the considerable diversity in this regard within American Protestantism. See the recent reports from the National Congregations Study (Chaves, Giesel, and Tsitsos 2002) and Ammerman's fieldwork (2002).

2. In the case of St. Francis, for example, many members of the Hispanic community talked of moving to another parish when Father Mesa was reassigned, depending on who came to replace him.

References

Alba, Richard D. *Ethnic Identity: The Transformation of White America*. New Haven: Yale University Press, 1990.

Alba, Richard, and Victor Nee. *Remaking the American Mainstream: Assimilation and Contemporary Immigration*. Cambridge, Mass.: Harvard University Press, 2003.

———. "Rethinking Assimilation Theory for a New Era of Immigration." *International Migration Review* 31, no. 4 (winter 1997): 826–74.

Alumkal, Antony W. *Asian American Evangelical Churches: Race, Ethnicity, and Assimilation in the Second Generation*. New York: LFB Scholarly Publishing, 2003.

Ammerman, Nancy K. "Connecting Mainline Protestant Churches with Public Life." In *The Quiet Hand of God: Faith-Based Activism and the Public Role of Mainline Protestantism*, edited by Robert Wuthow and John H. Evans, 129–58. Berkeley: University of California Press, 2002.

Ammerman, Nancy Tatom. *Congregation and Community*. New Brunswick, N.J.: Rutgers University Press, 1997.

Anner, John, ed. *Beyond Identity Politics*. Boston: South End Press, 1996.

Arthur, John. *Invisible Sojourners: African Immigrant Diaspora in the United States*. Westport, Conn.: Praeger, 2000.

Bagby, Ihsan, Paul M. Perl, and Brian T. Froehle. *The Mosque in America: A National Portrait*. Council on American-Islamic Relations, 2001.

Barkan, Elliott R. "Race, Religion and Nationality in American Society: A Model of Ethnicity—From Contact to Assimilation." *Journal of American Ethnic History* 14, no. 2 (winter 1995): 38–75.

Basch, Linda, Nina Glick Schiller, and Cristina Szanton Blanc, eds. *Nations Unbound: Transnational Projects, Postcolonial Predicaments, and Deterritorialized Nation-States*. Amsterdam: Gordon and Breach, 1994.

Becker, Penny Edgell. "Congregational Models and Conflict: A Study of How Institutions Shape Organizational Process." In *Sacred Companies: Organizational Aspects of Religion and Religious Aspects of Organizations*, edited by N. J. Demerath, Peter Dobkin Hall, Terry Schmitt, and Rhys H. Williams, 231–55. New York: Oxford University Press, 1998.

———. *Congregations in Conflict: Cultural Models of Local Religious Life*. New York: Cambridge University Press, 1999.

Bennett, William J. *The De-valuing of America: The Fight for Our Culture and Our Children*. New York: Summit Books, 1992.

Berger, Peter L., and Richard John Neuhaus. *To Empower People: From State to Civil Society*. Washington, D.C.: American Enterprise Institute, 1996. Originally published 1977.

Bourdieu, Pierre. "The Forms of Capital." In *Handbook of Theory and Research for the Sociology of Education*, edited by John Richardson, 241–58. New York: Greenwood Press, 1986.

Burt, Ronald S. *Structural Holes: The Social Structure of Competition*. Cambridge, Mass.: Harvard University Press, 1992.

Cavendish, James C. "Church-Based Community Activism: A Comparison of Black and White Catholic Congregations." *Journal for the Scientific Study of Religion* 39 (September 2000): 371–84.

Chai, Young Chang, ed. *Washington Korean History: 1883–1993*. Seoul: Baek-San, 1993.

Chaves, Mark, Helen M. Giesel, and William Tsitsos. "Religious Variations in Public Presence: Evidence from the National Congregations Study." In *The Quiet Hand of God: Faith-Based Activism and the Public Role of Mainline Protestantism*, edited by Robert Wuthnow and John H. Evans, 108–28. Berkeley: University of California Press, 2002.

Chaves, Mark, Mary Ellen Konieczny, Kraig Beyerlein, and Emily Barman. "The National Congregations Study: Background, Methods, and Selected Results." *Journal for the Scientific Study of Religion* 38, no. 4 (1999): 458–576.

Chaves, Mark, and William Tsitsos. "Congregations and Social Services: What They Do, How They Do It, and with Whom." *Nonprofit and Voluntary Sector Quarterly* 30, no. 4 (December 2001): 660–83.

Coleman, James. "Social Capital in the Creation of Human Capital." *American Journal of Sociology* 94 (1988): 95–120.

Conzen, Kathleen Neils, David A. Gerber, Ewa Morawska, George E. Pozzetta, and Rudolph J. Vecoli. "The Invention of Ethnicity: A Perspective from the U.S.A." *Journal of American Ethnic History* 12, no. 1 (fall 1992): 3–41.

DeSipio, Louis. *Counting on the Latino Vote: Latinos as a New Electorate*. Charlottesville, Va.: University of Virginia Press, 1996.

———. "Making Citizens or Good Citizens? Naturalization as a Predictor of Organizational and Electoral Behaviour among Latino Immigrants." *Hispanic Journal of Behavioural Sciences* 8, no. 2 (May 1996): 194–213.

Díaz-Stevens, Ana María, and Anthony M. Stevens-Arroyo. *Recognizing the Latino Resurgence in U.S. Religion: The Emmaus Paradigm.* Boulder, Colo.: Westview Press, 1998.

Dolan, Jay P. *The Immigrant Church: New York's Irish and German Catholics, 1815–1865.* Baltimore: Johns Hopkins University Press, 1975.

Douglass, H. Paul. *One Thousand City Churches.* New York: Doran, 1926.

Eastes, Carla M. "Organizational Diversity and the Production of Social Capital: One of These Groups Is Not Like the Other." In *Beyond Tocqueville: Civil Society and the Social Capital Debate in Comparative Perspective,* edited by Bob Edwards, Michael W. Foley, and Mario Diani, 157–68. Hanover, N.H.: University Press of New England, 2001.

Ebaugh, Helen Rose, and Janet Saltzman Chafetz. *Religion and the New Immigrants: Continuities and Adaptations in Immigrant Congregations.* New York: Altamira Press, 2000.

———, eds. *Religion across Borders: Transnational Immigrant Networks.* Walnut Creek, Calif.: AltaMira Press, 2002.

Eck, Diana L. "Religious America: Perspectives on Pluralism." In *The Papers of the Henry Luce III Fellows in Theology,* vol. 1, edited by Gary Gilbert, 69–105. Atlanta: Scholars Press, 1996.

Evans, Sara M., and Harry C. Boyte. *Free Spaces: The Sources of Democratic Change in America.* New York: Harper and Row, 1986.

Fenton, John Y. *Transplanting Religious Traditions: Asian Indians in America.* New York: Praeger, 1988.

Foley, Michael W. *Welcoming the Stranger: The Catholic Church and the New Immigrants.* Working Paper no. 1. Working Papers on Religion and the New Immigrants. Washington, D.C.: Life Cycle Institute, 1998.

Foley, Michael W., and Bob Edwards. "Escape from Politics? Social Theory and the Social Capital Debate." *American Behavioral Scientist* 40, no. 5 (1997): 550–61.

Foley, Michael W., Bob Edwards, and Mario Diani. "Social Capital Reconsidered." In *Beyond Tocqueville: Civil Society and the Social Capital Debate in Comparative Perspective,* edited by Bob Edwards, Michael W. Foley, and Mario Diani, 266–79. Hanover, N.H.: University Press of New England, 2001.

Foley, Michael W., and Virginia A. Hodgkinson. Introduction to *The Civil Society Reader,* edited by Virginia A. Hodgkinson and Michael W. Foley. Hanover, N.H.: University Press of New England, 2003.

Foley, Michael W., John D. McCarthy, and Mark Chaves. "Social Capital, Religious Institutions, and Poor Communities." In *Social Capital and Poor Communities,* edited by Mark R. Warren, Susan Saegert, and Philip Thompson. New York: Russell Sage Foundation, 2001.

Fuligni, Andrew J. "The Adjustment of Children from Immigrant Families." *Current Directions in Psychological Science* 7, no. 4 (1998): 99–103.

Gans, Herbert. "Comment: Ethnic Invention and Acculturation: A Bumpy-Line Approach." *Journal of American Ethnic History* 11, no. 1 (1992): 42–52.

————. "Symbolic Ethnicity: The Future of Ethnic Groups and Cultures in America." *Ethnic and Racial Studies* 2 (1979): 1–20.

Gerber, David A., Ewa Morawska, and George E. Pozzetta. "Response." *Journal of American Ethnic History* 12, no. 1 (fall 1992): 59–63.

Glazer, Nathan, and Daniel P. Moynihan. *Beyond the Melting Pot: The Negroes, Puerto Ricans, Jews, Italians, and Irish of New York City.* 2nd ed. Cambridge, Mass.: MIT Press, 1970.

Gleason, Philip. "'Americanism' in Catholic Discourse." In *Speaking of Diversity: Language and Ethnicity in Twentieth-Century America,* 272–300. Baltimore: Johns Hopkins University Press, 1992.

————. *Speaking of Diversity: Language and Ethnicity in Twentieth-Century America.* Baltimore: Johns Hopkins University Press, 1992.

Gordon, Milton. *Assimilation in American Life.* New York: Oxford University Press, 1964.

Granovetter, Mark S. *Getting a Job: A Study of Contacts and Careers.* Cambridge, Mass.: Harvard University Press, 1974.

Greeley, Andrew. *The American Catholic: A Social Portrait.* New York: Basic Books, 1977.

————. *Why Can't They Be Like Us? America's White Ethnic Groups.* New York: Dutton, 1971.

Green, John C., Mark J. Rozell, and Clyde Wilcox, eds. *The Christian Right in American Politics: Marching to the Millennium.* Washington, D.C.: Georgetown University Press, 2003.

Greenhouse, Carol. *Praying for Justice.* Ithaca, N.Y.: Cornell University Press, 1986.

Hammond, Phillip E., and Kee Warner. "Religion and Ethnicity in Late Twentieth Century America." *Annals of the American Academy of Political and Social Science* 527 (May 1993): 55–66.

Harris, Frederick C. *Something Within: Religion in African-American Political Activism.* New York: Oxford University Press, 1999.

Hart, Stephen. *Cultural Dilemmas of Progressive Politics: Styles of Engagement among Grassroots Activists.* Chicago: University of Chicago Press, 2001.

Herberg, Will. *Protestant, Catholic, Jew: An Essay in American Religious Sociology.* Chicago: University of Chicago Press, 1983.

Huntington, Samuel P. *Who Are We? The Challenges to America's National Identity.* New York: Simon and Schuster, 2004.

Hurh, Won Moo, and Kwang Chung Kim. "Beyond Assimilation and Pluralism: Syncretic Sociocultural Adaptation of Korean Immigrants in the U.S." *Ethnic and Racial Studies* 16, no. 4 (1993): 696–713.

————. "Religious Participation of Korean Immigrants in the United States." *Journal for the Scientific Study of Religion* 29 (1990): 19–34.

Jacoby, Tamar, ed. *Reinventing the Melting Pot: The New Immigrants and What It Means to be American.* New York: Basic Books, 2004.

————. "Rainbow's End: A Renowned Student of America's Maladies Detects a New Threat to Our Identity." *Washington Post Book World,* May 16, 2004.

Jasso, Guillermina, Douglas S. Massey, Mark R. Rosenzweig, and James P. Smith. "Family, Schooling, Religiosity, and Mobility among New Legal Immigrants to the United States: Evidence from the New Immigrant Survey Pilot." In *Immigration Today: Pastoral and Research Challenges*, edited by Lydio F. Tomasi and Mary G. Powers, 52–81. New York: Center for Migration Studies, 2000.

Khan, M. A. Muqtedar. "Presidential Elections 2004: What Should American Muslims Do?" *Ijtihad*, July 2004. Available at the website of Muqtedar Khan www.ijtihad.org/American-Muslim-Votes.htm#_edn2.

Kosmin, Barry A., and Seymour P. Lachman. *One Nation under God and Religion in Contemporary American Society*. New York: Harmony, 1993.

Kurien, Prema. "Becoming American by Becoming Hindu: Indian Americans Take Their Place at the Multicultural Table." In *Gatherings in Diaspora: Religious Communities and the New Immigration*, edited by R. Stephen Warner and Judith G. Wittner, 37–70. Philadelphia: Temple University Press, 1998.

Kwon, O'Kyun. "The Role of Religious Congregations in Formation of the Korean Community in the Washington, D.C. Area." In *Korean Americans: Past, Present, Future*, edited by Ilpyong Kim, 239–71. Hollym International, 2004.

Lee, Che-Fu, and Xiaoyan Wang. *Socio-Demographic Profiles of Six Immigrant Groups*. Unpublished research report. Washington, D.C.: Life Cycle Institute, 2000.

Leighley, Jan E. *Strength in Numbers? The Political Mobilization of Racial and Ethnic Minorities*. Princeton, N.J.: Princeton University Press, 2001.

Levitt, Peggy. *The Transnational Villagers*. Berkeley: University of California Press, 2001.

Lien, Pei-te. "Religion and Political Adaptation among Asian Americans: An Empirical Assessment from the Pilot National Asian American Political Survey." In *Asian American Religions: The Making and Remaking of Borders and Boundaries*, edited by Tony Carnes and Fenggang Yang, 263–85. New York: New York University Press, 2004.

Lien, Pei-te, and Tony Carnes. "The Religious Demography of Asian American Boundary Crossing." In *Asian American Religions: The Making and Remaking of Borders and Boundaries*, edited by Tony Carnes and Fenggang Yang, 38–54. New York: New York University Press, 2004.

Light, Ivan, and Steven J. Gold. *Ethnic Economies*. San Diego: Academic Press, 2000.

Lin, Nan. *Social Capital: A Theory of Social Structure and Action*. New York: Cambridge University Press, 2001.

Lollock, Lisa. *The Foreign Born Population of the United States: March 2000*. Current Population Reports. Washington, D.C.: U.S. Census Bureau, 2001.

López, David E., and Ricardo D. Stanton-Salazar. "Mexican Americans: A Second Generation at Risk." In *Ethnicities: Children of Immigrants in America*, edited by Rubén G. Rumbaut and Alejandro Portes, 57–90. Berkeley: University of California Press, 2001.

Marty, Martin E. "Ethnicity: The Skeleton of Religion in America." *Church History* 41, no. 1 (1972): 5–21.

Massey, Douglas, Rafael Alarcón, Jorge Durand, and Humberto González. *Return to Aztlan: The Social Process of International Migration from Western Mexico.* Berkeley: University of California Press, 1987.

McGavran, Donald. *Understanding Church Growth.* Grand Rapids, Mich.: Eerdmans, 1970.

Menjívar, Cecilia. *Fragmented Ties: Salvadoran Immigrant Networks in America.* Berkeley: University of California Press, 2000.

———. "Religion and Immigration in Comparative Perspective: Catholic and Evangelical Salvadorans in San Francisco, Washington, D.C., and Phoenix." *Sociology of Religion* 64, no. 1 (2003): 21–45.

———. "Religious Institutions and Transnationalism: A Case Study of Catholic and Evangelical Protestant Salvadoran Immigrants." *International Journal of Politics, Culture, and Society* 12, no. 4 (summer 1999): 589–612.

Menzel, Peter. *Material World: A Global Family Portrait.* San Francisco: Sierra Club Books, 1994.

Miller, Donald. *Reinventing American Protestantism.* Berkeley: University of California Press, 1997.

Min, Pyong Gap. "The Structure and Social Functions of Korean Immigrant Churches in the United States." *International Migration Review* 26, no. 4 (1992): 1370–94.

Moore, R. Laurence. *Religious Outsiders and the Making of Americans.* New York: Oxford University Press, 1986.

Morawska, Ewa. "In Defense of the Assimilation Model." *Journal of American Ethnic History* 13, no. 2 (winter 1994): 76–87.

Newton, Kenneth. "Social and Political Trust in Established Democracies." In *Critical Citizens: Global Support for Democratic Governance,* edited by Pippa Norris, 169–87. New York: Oxford University Press, 1999.

National Center for Education Statistics. *National Household Education Survey of 1996.* Washington, D.C.: U.S. Department of Education, 1996.

Olson, Daniel V. A. "Church Friendships: Boon or Barrier to Church Growth?" *Journal for the Scientific Study of Religion* 28 (1989): 432–47.

Orsi, Robert A. *The Madonna of 115th Street: Faith and Community in Italian Harlem, 1880–1950.* New Haven, Conn.: Yale University Press, 1985.

Park, Robert E., and Ernest W. Burgess. *Introduction to the Science of Sociology.* Reprint, 1969; Chicago: University of Chicago Press, 1924.

Pattillo-McCoy, Mary. "Church Culture as a Strategy of Action in the Black Community." *American Sociological Review* 63 (1998): 767–84.

Portes, Alejandro. "Children of Immigrants: Segmented Assimilation and Its Determinants." In *The Economic Sociology of Immigration,* edited by Alejandro Portes, 248–79. New York: Russell Sage Foundation, 1995.

———. "Economic Sociology and the Sociology of Immigration: A Conceptual Overview." In *The Economic Sociology of Immigration,* edited by Alejandro Portes, 1–41. New York: Russell Sage Foundation, 1995.

Portes, Alejandro, and Patricia Landolt. "The Downside of Social Capital." *American Prospect* 26 (May 1996): 18–22.

Portes, Alejandro, and Ruben G. Rumbaut. *Immigrant America: A Portrait.* 2nd ed. Berkeley: University of California Press, 1996.

Portes, Alejandro, and Richard Schauffler. "Language and the Second Generation: Bilingualism Yesterday and Today." In *The New Second Generation,* edited by Alejandro Portes, 8–29. New York: Russell Sage Foundation, 1996.

Portes, Alejandro, and Min Zhou. "The New Second Generation: Segmented Assimilation and Its Variants." *Annals of the American Academy of Political and Social Science* 530 (November 1993): 74–96.

Putnam, Robert D. *Bowling Alone: The Collapse and Revival of American Community.* New York: Simon and Schuster, 2000.

————. *Making Democracy Work: Civic Traditions in Modern Italy.* Princeton, N.J.: Princeton University Press, 1993.

Rangaswamy, Padma. *Namaste American: Indian Immigrants in an American Metropolis.* University Park: Pennsylvania State University Press, 2000.

Rosenblum, Nancy L. *Membership and Morals: The Personal Uses of Pluralism in America.* Princeton, N.J.: Princeton University Press, 1998.

Rosenstone, Steven J., and John Mark Hansen. *Mobilization, Participation, and Democracy in America.* New York: Macmillan, 1993.

Rumbaut, Rubén G. "Assimilation and Its Discontents: Between Rhetoric and Reality." *International Migration Review* 31, no. 4 (winter 1997): 923–60.

Rumbaut, Rubén G., and Alejandro Portes, eds. *Ethnicities: Children of Immigrants in America.* Berkeley: University of California Press, 2001.

Saegert, Susan, J. Phillip Thompson, and Mark R. Warren. *Social Capital and Poor Communities.* New York: Russell Sage Foundation, 2001.

Sargeant, Kimon Howland. *Seeker Churches: Promoting Traditional Religion in a Nontraditional Way.* New Brunswick, N.J.: Rutgers University Press, 2000.

Sassen, Saskia. *The Global City: New York, London, Tokyo.* Princeton, N.J.: Princeton University Press, 2001.

Schlesinger, Arthur M., Jr. *The Disuniting of America.* New York: Norton, 1993.

Schneider, Jo Anne. "Newcomers Serving the City: Immigrant Church and Non-profit Connections in Washington, DC, and Kenosha, WI." Cleveland: Urban Affairs Association, 2003.

Schneider, Jo Anne, and Michael W. Foley. "Immigrant Churches and Immigrant Social Services: Nonprofit and Congregation Connections in Washington, D.C." *The Role of Faith-Based Organizations in the Social Welfare System,* 2003 Spring Research Forum Working Papers, pp. 261–281. Washington, D.C.: Independent Sector, 2003.

Shor, Juliet. *Born to Buy: The Commercialized Child and the New Consumer Culture.* New York: Scribner, 2004.

Singer, Audrey. *At Home in the Nation's Capital: Immigrant Trends in Metropolitan Washington.* Washington, D.C.: Brookings Institution, 2003.

Singer, Audrey, Samantha Friedman, Ivan Cheung, and Marie Price. *The World in a Zip Code: Greater Washington, DC, as New Region of Immigration*. Washington, D.C.: Brookings Institution, 2001.

Singh, Patwant. *The Sikhs*. New York: Doubleday, 1999.

Singh, Santokh. *Fundamentals of Sikhism*. Princeton, Ontario, Canada: Institute for Spiritual Studies, 1994.

Singhal, Ashok. "Vishwa Hindu Parishad and Hindu Awakening." In *Chaitanya Bharati: Hindu Parivar in America*, edited by Ashok Singhal, Washington, D.C.: VHP of America, Metropolitan Washington, D.C., Chapter, 1999.

Smith, Jane I. *Islam in America*. New York: Columbia University Press, 1999.

Smith, Timothy L. "Religion and Ethnicity in America." *American Historical Review* 83 (1978): 1155–85.

Smith, Tom W. "The Muslim Population in the United States: The Methodology of Estimates." *Public Opinion Quarterly* 66, no. 3 (fall 2002): 404–18.

———. "Religious Diversity in America: The Emergence of Muslims, Buddhists, Hindus, and Others." *Journal for the Scientific Study of Religion* 41, no. 3 (September 2002): 577–86.

Sollors, Werner, ed. *The Invention of Ethnicity*. New York: Oxford University Press, 1989.

Stark, Rodney. "German and German American Religiousness: Approximating a Crucial Experiment." *Journal for the Scientific Study of Religion* 36, no. 2 (June 1997): 182–93.

Stolle, Dietlind, and Thomas R. Rochon. "Are All Associations Alike? Member Diversity, Associational Type, and the Creation of Social Capital." In *Beyond Tocqueville: Civil Society and the Social Capital Debate in Comparative Perspective*, edited by Bob Edwards, Michael W. Foley, and Mario Diani, 143–56. Hanover, N.H.: University Press of New England, 2001.

Swierenga, Robert P. "The Religious Factor in Immigration: The Dutch Experience." In *Immigrant America: European Ethnicity in the United States*, edited by Timothy Walch, 119–39. New York: Garland 1994.

Takaki, Ronald. *Strangers from a Different Shore: A History of Asian Americans*. Boston: Little, Brown, 1989.

Tomasi, Lydio F. *The Italian American Family: The Southern Italian Family's Process of Adjustment to an Urban America*. Staten Island, N.Y.: Center for Migration Studies, 1972.

United States Census Bureau. *Census of Population and Housing (2000)*. Washington, D.C.: U.S. Government Printing Office, 2000.

———. *Profile of the Foreign-Born Population in the United States: 1997*. Current Population Reports Special Studies. Washington, D.C.: United States Census Bureau, 1999.

United States Conference of Catholic Bishops. *Welcoming the Stranger among Us: Unity in Diversity*. A Statement of the U.S. Catholic Bishops. Washington, D.C.: United States Catholic Conference, 2000.

Verba, Sidney, Kay Lehman Schlozman, and Henry E. Brady. *Voice and Equality: Civic Voluntarism in American Politics*. Cambridge, Mass.: Harvard University Press, 1995.

Waldinger, Roger, ed. *Strangers at the Gates: New Immigrants in Urban America*. Berkeley: University of California Press, 2001.

Waldinger, Roger, Howard Aldrich, and Robin Ward. "Opportunities, Group Chracteristics, and Strategies." In *Ethnic Entrepreneurs: Immigrant Business in Industrial Societies*, edited by Roger Waldinger and Robin Ward, 13–48. Newbury Park, Calif.: Sage, 1990.

Waldinger, Roger, and Claudia Der-Martirosian. "The Immigrant Niche: Pervasive, Persistent, Diverse." In *Strangers at the Gates: New Immigrants in Urban America*, edited by Roger Waldinger, 228–71. Berkeley: University of California Press, 2001.

Warner, R. Stephen. "Immigration and Religious Communities in the United States." In *Gatherings in Diaspora: Religious Communities and the New Immigration*, edited by R. Stephen Warner and Judith G. Wittner, 3–36. Philadelphia: Temple University Press, 1998.

———. "The Korean Immigrant Church as Case and Model." In *Korean Americans and Their Religions: Pilgrims and Missionaries from a Different Shore*, edited by Ho-Youn Kwon, Kwang Chung Kim, and R. Stephen Warner, 25–51. University Park: Pennsylvania State University Press, 2001.

———. "The Place of the Congregation in the American Religious Configuration." In *American Congregations*, edited by James P. Wind and James W. Lewis, 54–99. New Perspectives in the Study of Congregations. Chicago: University of Chicago Press, 1994.

———. "Religion and New (Post-1965) Immigrants: Some Principles Drawn from Field Research." *American Studies* 41, nos. 2/3 (summer/fall 2000): 267–86.

Warner, R. Stephen, and Judith G. Wittner, eds. *Gatherings in Diaspora: Religious Communities and the New Immigration*. Philadelphia: Temple University Press, 1998.

Warren, Kay B. *Indigenous Movements and Their Critics: Pan-Maya Activism in Guatemala*. Princeton, N.J.: Princeton University Press, 1998.

Warren, Mark E. *Democracy and Association*. Princeton, N.J.: Princeton University Press, 2001.

Warren, Mark R. *Dry Bones Rattling: Community Building to Revitalize American Democracy*. Princeton, N.J.: Princeton University Press, 2001.

Waters, Mary C. *Ethnic Options: Choosing Identities in America*. Berkeley: University of California Press, 1990.

———. "Optional Ethnicities: For Whites Only?" In *Origins and Destinies: Immigration, Race, and Ethnicity in America*, edited by Silvia Pedraza and Rubén G. Rumbaut, 444–54. Belmont, Calif.: Wadsworth, 1996.

Wellmeier, Nancy. "Santa Eulalia's People in Exile: Maya Religion, Culture, and Identity in Los Angeles." In *Gatherings in Diaspora: Religious Communities and the*

New Immigration, edited by R. Stephen Warner and Judith G. Wittner, 97–122. Philadelphia: Temple University Press, 1998.

Williams, Raymond Brady. *Religions of Immigrants from India and Pakistan: New Threads in the American Tapestry*. New York: Cambridge University Press, 1988.

Wood, Richard L. *Faith in Action: Religion, Race, and Democratic Organizing in America*. Chicago: University of Chicago Press, 2002.

Synod of Bishops. *Justice in the World*. Vatican City: Portified Commission for Justice and Peace, 1971.

Wuthnow, Robert. "Mobilizing Civic Engagement: The Changing Impact of Religious Involvement." In *Civic Engagement in American Democracy*, edited by Theda Skocpol and Morris P. Fiorina, 331–65. New York: Russell Sage Foundation, 1999.

———. "Presidential Address 2003: The Challenge of Diversity." *Journal for the Scientific Study of Religion* 43, no. 2 (2004): 159–70.

———. *Saving America? Faith-Based Services and the Future of Civil Society*. Princeton, N.J.: Princeton University Press, 2004.

Yang, Fenggang. *Chinese Christians in America: Conversion, Assimilation, and Adhesive Identities*. University Park: Pennsylvania State University Press, 1999.

Yang, Fenggang, and Helen Rose Ebaugh. "Transformations in New Immigrant Religions and Their Global Implications." *American Sociological Review* 66, no. 2 (April 2001): 269–88.

Zhou, Min, and Carl L. Bankston III. *Growing up American: How Vietnamese Children Adapt to Life in the United States*. New York: Russell Sage Foundation, 1998.

Index